Global Perspectives on Digital Literature

Global Perspectives on Digital Literature: A Critical Introduction for the Twenty-First Century explores how digital literary forms shape and are shaped by aesthetic and political exchanges happening across languages and nations. The book understands "global" as a mode of comparative thinking and argues for considering various forms of digital literature—the popular, the avant-garde, and the participatory—as realizing and producing global thought in the twenty-first century. Attending to issues of both political and aesthetic representation, the book includes a diverse group of contributors and a wide-ranging corpus of texts, composed in a variety of languages and regions, including East and South Asia, parts of Europe, Latin America, North America, Australia, and Western Africa. The book's contributors adopt an array of interpretive approaches to make visible new connections and possibilities engendered by cross-cultural encounters. Among other topics, they reflect on the shifting conditions for production and distribution of literature, participatory cultures and technological affordances of Web 2.0, the ever-changing dynamics of global and local forces, and fundamental questions, such as, "What do we mean when we talk about literature today?" and "What is the future of literature?"

Torsa Ghosal is the author of a book of literary criticism, *Out of Mind: Mode, Mediation, and Cognition in Twenty-First-Century Narrative*, and an experimental novella, *Open Couplets*, and is the co-editor of *Fictionality and Multimodal Narratives*. She has a PhD in English from the Ohio State University, where she was awarded a Presidential Fellowship as well as a John Muste Award for best dissertation. Currently, she is Assistant Professor of English at California State University, Sacramento.

Global Perspectives on Digital Literature
A Critical Introduction for the Twenty-First Century

Edited by Torsa Ghosal

NEW YORK AND LONDON

Designed cover image: Mamoona Riaz, *Like Clockwork IV*, 21 inches in diameter, Ink on paper, 2022

First published 2023
by Routledge
605 Third Avenue, New York, NY 10158

and by Routledge
4 Park Square, Milton Park, Abingdon, Oxon, OX14 4RN

Routledge is an imprint of the Taylor & Francis Group, an informa business

© 2023 selection and editorial matter, Torsa Ghosal; individual chapters, the contributors

The right of Torsa Ghosal to be identified as the author of the editorial material, and of the authors for their individual chapters, has been asserted in accordance with sections 77 and 78 of the Copyright, Designs and Patents Act 1988.

All rights reserved. No part of this book may be reprinted or reproduced or utilised in any form or by any electronic, mechanical, or other means, now known or hereafter invented, including photocopying and recording, or in any information storage or retrieval system, without permission in writing from the publishers.

Trademark notice: Product or corporate names may be trademarks or registered trademarks, and are used only for identification and explanation without intent to infringe.

ISBN: 978-1-032-10351-8 (hbk)
ISBN: 978-1-032-10349-5 (pbk)
ISBN: 978-1-003-21491-5 (ebk)

DOI: 10.4324/9781003214915

Typeset in Bembo
by Newgen Publishing UK

Contents

List of Figures   viii
Notes on Contributors   x
Acknowledgements   xv

Introduction: Global Literary Studies and Digital Literature   1
TORSA GHOSAL

PART I
Reimagining Digital Literary Studies   17

1 Textual Instability: Paradoxes of Literary Remix   21
SIMONE MURRAY

2 Diverse Mappings of Electronic Literature: Expanding the Canon(s)   34
MARIUSZ PISARSKI

3 Ludonarrative Postcolonialism: Re-Playing the Colonial Discourse   49
SOUVIK MUKHERJEE

PART II
Digital Embodiments and Disabilities   63

4 Games as Critical Literature: Playing with Transhumanism, Embodied Cognition, and Narrative Difference in *SOMA*   67
CODY MEJEUR

5 The Horror of Networked Existence: Affect, Connection, and Anxiety in Classic Creepypasta Narratives   81
SARA BIMO

6 Networked Chronic Pain Narratives: Locating Disability through Fibromyalgia Facebook Community   93
RIMI NANDY

PART III
Forms of Resistance   105

7 The Erasing Impulse: Veiling and Unveiling the Poetic and the Political   109
ÁLVARO SEIÇA

8 Digital Cartoons: Collaborative Activism in Hong Kong   124
KIN WAI CHU

9 Between Two Screens: The January 25th Revolution in Egypt   146
REHAM HOSNY

10 "If this document is authentic": On Bill Bly's Archival Fiction   161
BRIAN DAVIS

PART IV
Medial and Cultural Crossings   177

11 From Oral to Digital and Back: Adinkra Symbols and Kweku Ananse on YouTube   181
J.B. AMISSAH-ARTHUR AND KWABENA OPOKU-AGYEMANG

12 Bending Voices, Opening Ears: Voice, Music, Sound, and Affect in Digital Literature   196
HAZEL SMITH

13 Intermedial Experience and Discursive Voice in Printed Text, Audiobook, and Podcast: H. P. Lovecraft's "The Statement of Randolph Carter" 210
JARKKO TOIKKANEN AND MARI HATAVARA

Notes on Potentials and Limitations 224
Index 228

Figures

4.1 The Construct, a Mockingbird enemy encountered several times throughout the game. This Mockingbird is slow and makes loud, disturbing noises as it moves that are similar to garbled radio, static, sharp cracks, and screaming — 71
4.2 Simon Jarrett's robot body, visible in a mirror in a later area of PATHOS-II — 73
4.3 An underwater scene on the ocean floor outside of Site Delta and the Zeppelin Transport Theta locations in *SOMA*. The lighting is dim and tinted green, and there are numerous objects, tools, and plant life strewn around the ground — 75
6.1 Women with Fibromyalgia community page "About" ("(5) Women with Fibromyalgia | Facebook" n.d.) — 98
6.2 Women with Fibromyalgia post ("(5) Women with Fibromyalgia | Facebook" n.d.) — 100
6.3 My post on the community page of Women with Fibromyalgia — 101
8.1 Chao Yat. "Meow Meow Mi Mi Mo". *Ming Pao*, 19 February 2019 and *Facebook*, 20 February 2019. © 2019 Chao Yat. Used with permission from Chao Yat and Ming Pao (Hong Kong) — 131
8.2 Chao Yat. (No title). *Facebook*, 9 April 2019. © Chao Yat. Used with permission — 134
8.3 Lo, Cuson. (No title). *Facebook*, 9 April 2019. © 2019 Cuson Lo. Used with permission — 135
8.4 Mandycat. (No title). *Facebook*, 10 April 2019. © 2019 Mandycat. Used with permission — 136
8.5 Ah To. (No title). *Facebook*, 10 April 2019. © 2019 Ah To. Used with permission — 137
8.6 Lo, Cuson. (No title). *Facebook*, 10 April 2019. © 2019 Cuson Lo. Used with permission — 138
9.1 Screenshot of the Arabic version's main page of *A Dictionary of the Revolution* by Amira Hanafi — 152

9.2	Screenshot of the thread "Rab'a" of the English version of *A Dictionary of the Revolution* by Amira Hanafi	155
10.1	Screen Grab of "this work" from *WDv3*	163
10.2	Narrative layers and historical periods, including readerly figured layer	167
11.1	Screenshot from an Ananse Tale	182
11.2	Examples of Adinkra symbols	184
11.3	Sankofa as an Adinkra Symbol	187
11.4	The Sankofa Bird	187
11.5	Ananse Ntontan Adinkra Symbol	188
11.6	Screenshot of "Ananse and the sticky gum (grave mischief) pt_1"	190
11.7	Screenshot of "Ananse and the Sticky Gum/ The Grave Mischief pt_2"	191
11.8	Screenshot of "Ananse and the Sticky Gum/ The Grave Mischief pt_3"	192
11.9	Cover of *The Economist*	193
12.1	Video frame from "In the Middle of the Room" for audiovisual fixed media	198
12.2	Screenshot of "The Rubayaat" (Naji 2014) running in the test mode of Brown University's Department of Literary Arts cave writing software	201

Contributors

J.B. Amissah-Arthur is a lecturer of Literature at the Department of English in the University of Ghana. He holds a PhD in English from the University of Ghana and is a Carnegie scholar and Fellow of the American Council of Learned Societies and the African Humanities Program. His research interests straddle the structural poetics of African cultural phenomena, grammar of erotica, colonial discourse, interrelations of folklore and literature, and digital poetics.

Sara Bimo is a PhD student in the Joint Program for Communication & Culture at York University and Toronto Metropolitan University. Working from a perspective informed by phenomenology, her research examines the ways humans perceive, sense, and imagine underlying digital architectures and the influence such processes have on individual- and community-level identity formation.

Kin Wai Chu is an independent researcher who has recently got her PhD at KU Leuven. She was research fellow of the Research Foundation of Flanders (FWO) and her PhD thesis is on the post-2000 Hong Kong Comics from transmedial and nostalgic approaches. She has published articles on cultural studies, comics, and postcolonial studies. She obtained her bachelor's degree at City University of Hong Kong and master's degrees at The Chinese University of Hong Kong and King's College London.

Brian Davis currently holds the position of Lecturer at University of Maryland, where he teaches courses in literature, writing, film, and digital studies. His research and writing on digital and multimodal literature has been published at *Electronic Book Review*, *Orbit: A Journal of American Literature*, and *Frontiers of Narrative Studies*. He is currently working on a monograph called *Archiving the Future: Science Fiction and the Archive*, which examines the history of science fiction's engagement with and invention of technologies and methods used for documentation and preservation.

Torsa Ghosal is Assistant Professor of English at California State University, Sacramento. Her research focuses on the formal strategies used to represent cognition in twenty-first century literature and the nature of aesthetic experiences offered by multimodal narratives across media. She is the author of the monograph *Out of Mind: Mode, Mediation, and Cognition in Twenty-First-Century Narrative* (The Ohio State University Press, 2021), an experimental novella, *Open Couplets* (Yoda Press, 2017), and co-editor (with Alison Gibbons) of *Fictionality and Multimodal Narratives* (University of Nebraska Press, 2023). Her critical essays have been published in journals such as *Studies in the Novel*, *Poetics Today*, *Storyworlds*, and *Media-N: Journal of the New Media Caucus*. She has also published on films and comics in *Latinos and Narrative Media* (Palgrave MacMillan, 2013) and *Comics Studies Here and Now* (Routledge, 2018).

Mari Hatavara is Professor of Finnish Literature and Director of *Narrare – Centre for Interdisciplinary Narrative Studies* at Tampere University, Finland. Her research interests include interdisciplinary narrative theory and analysis, fictionality studies, intermediality and the poetics of historical fiction and metafiction. She specializes in the analysis of narrative voices across fictional and non-fictional narrative environments and in intermedial settings. During her professorship at Tampere University (since 2009), Hatavara has worked at Ohio State University Project Narrative (2019), York University Interdisciplinary Centre for Narrative Studies (2017), Aarhus Institute of Advanced Studies (2016), and The Swedish Collegium for Advanced Studies (2011). Hatavara is co-editor of *The Travelling Concepts of Narrative* (2013), *Narrative Theory, Literature, and New Media* (2015), and special issues on *Narrating Selves in Everyday Contexts* (Style 2017), *Narrating Selves from the Bible to Social Media* (Partial Answers 2019), and *Real Fictions. Fictionality, Factuality and Narrative Strategies in Contemporary Storytelling* (Narrative Inquiry 2019).

Reham Hosny is an award-winning digital creative writer and a British Academy Visiting Fellow at the University of Cambridge. She is an Assistant Professor of digital literary studies and critical theory at Minia University and previously, she was a Lecturer at the University of Leeds, UK. Her interdisciplinary research focuses on investigating the cultural, social, and political contexts of Arabic and Anglo-American electronic literature and digital culture. Her forthcoming book *@ArabicELit: Electronic Literature in the Arab World* (Bloomsbury) highlights new aesthetics and perspectives of electronic literature. Her co-authored novel, *Al-Barrah* [The Announcer] (2019, 2021), the first Arabic artificial intelligence novel, won the 2022 Robert Coover Award's Honorable Mention, and her short story collection Amma Baʿd [and thereafter] (2012) won the Ihsan Abdel Quddous Literary Prize for short story writing. She is the first Arab and African to be elected as a director at the international Electronic Literature Organization (ELO). She is directing *arabicelit*, the first initiative focusing on globalizing Arabic electronic literature in English.

xii *Notes on Contributors*

Cody Mejeur is Assistant Professor of Game Studies at University at Buffalo, SUNY. They have published on games pedagogy, gender and queerness in games, and video game narratives and player experiences, and they are currently the game director for Trans Folks Walking, a narrative game about trans experiences. They are Director of the Amatryx Gaming Lab & Studio at UB and work with the LGBTQ Video Game Archive on preserving and visualizing LGBTQ representation. They are editor at *One Shot: A Journal of Critical Games & Play* and served as Diversity Officer for the Digital Games Research Association.

Souvik Mukherjee is Assistant Professor in cultural studies at Centre for Studies in Social Sciences, Kolkata. Mukherjee has been researching video games as an emerging storytelling medium since 2002, examining their relationship to canonical ideas of narrative and also how these games inform and challenge current conceptions of technicity, identity, culture, and postcolonialism. He is the author of two monographs *Videogames and Storytelling: Reading Games and Playing Books* (Palgrave Macmillan, 2015) and *Videogames and Postcolonialism: Empire Plays Back* (Springer UK, 2017). Besides maintaining an active interest in issues related to portrayals of empire and postcolonialism in video games, he is involved in researching ancient Indian boardgames. Mukherjee has been named a "DiGRA Distinguished Scholar" by the Digital Games Research Association. In addition to a range of topics in Game Studies, he researches and teaches Early Modern English Literature and Digital Humanities in Kolkata, India.

Simone Murray is Associate Professor in Literary Studies at Monash University, Melbourne, where her research centres upon sociologies of literature. Her book *Mixed Media: Feminist Presses and Publishing Politics* (Pluto Press UK, 2004) was awarded the 2005 DeLong Book Prize by the Society for the History of Authorship, Reading and Publishing (SHARP). Her second monograph, *The Adaptation Industry: The Cultural Economy of Contemporary Literary Adaptation* (Routledge US, 2012) has been widely reviewed in English-, French-, German- and Swedish-language publications and was reissued in paperback in 2013. Her third monograph, *The Digital Literary Sphere: Reading, Writing, and Selling Books in the Internet Era* (Johns Hopkins University Press, 2018) examines how the internet has transformed literary culture. Most recently, she has published a textbook titled *Introduction to Contemporary Print Culture: Books as Media* (2021) with Routledge UK. She is an elected member of the Australian Academy of the Humanities, the Board of SHARP, and an Advisory Editor of its journal *Book History*.

Rimi Nandy is pursuing PhD from the School of Media, Communication and Culture, Jadavpur University, India. She has a master's degree in English and a PG Diploma in Digital Humanities and Culture Studies. Her research areas include Digital Humanities, Narratology, Social Media

Studies, Posthumanism, and Japanese Studies. She has recently published a book chapter in *Storytelling in Luxury Fashion* (Routledge, 2021).

Kwabena Opoku-Agyemang is a senior lecturer at the English Department of the University of Ghana, where he earned his undergraduate degree and a master's degree. He is also Academic Director for SIT Ghana, a study abroad program. He completed his masters and PhD degrees in English Literature at West Virginia University, and his scholarly interests revolve around African digital literature. His work has appeared in *Research in African Literatures*, and he has guest edited journals such as *Journal of Gaming and Virtual Worlds* and *Hyperrhiz*.

Mariusz Pisarski is an assistant professor at the Department of Journalism and Media, University of Technology and Communication in Rzeszów, Poland. He has been a translator, editor, and director of several digital literature projects in Poland, as well as translations of Michael Joyce's hypertexts *afternoon. a story* and *Twilight a Symphony*, Stephanie Strickland and Nick Montfort's poetry generator *Sea and Spar Between*. His recent publication activities include "Two Ends and One Beginning: Notes on the Future of Writing in the Post-Medial Context" in *On the Fringes of Literature and Digital Media Culture* (Brill, Amsterdam, 2018), and the co-editing of collective monography *Remediation: Crossing Discursive Boundaries. Central European Perspective* (Peter Lang, 2019).

Álvaro Seiça is a Portuguese writer and researcher based in Bergen, Norway. He is currently an Associate Professor in Digital Culture at University of Bergen (UiB). Before, he was a Marie Skłodowska-Curie Global Fellow, a visiting researcher in Information Studies at the University of California, Los Angeles, and a postdoctoral fellow in Materialities of Literature at the University of Coimbra, where he investigated the poetics and politics of erasure within the EU-funded project "The Art of Deleting." Seiça holds a PhD in Digital Culture from UiB, with the thesis "setInterval(): Time-Based Readings of Kinetic Poetry" (2018). His publications include the poetry books *Supressão* (2019), *upoesia* (2019), *Previsão para 365 poemas* (2018), *Ensinando o espaço* (2017), *Ö* (2014), *Permafrost* (2012), and the scholarly book *Transdução* (2017). Website: alvaroseica.net.

Hazel Smith is Emeritus Professor in the Writing and Society Research Centre, Western Sydney University. From 2007 to 2017 she was Research Professor in the Centre. She is author of *The Contemporary Literature-Music Relationship: Intermedia, Voice, Technology, Cross-cultural Exchange* (Routledge, 2016); *The Writing Experiment: Strategies for Innovative Creative Writing* (Allen and Unwin, 2005); and *Hyperscapes in the Poetry of Frank O'Hara: Difference, Homosexuality, Topography* (Liverpool University Press, 2000). She is co-author with Roger Dean of *Improvisation, Hypermedia and the Arts Since 1945* (Harwood Academic/

Routledge, 1997), and co-editor with Roger Dean of *Practice-led Research, Research-led Practice in the Creative Arts* (Edinburgh University Press, 2009). Hazel is also an experimental poet, performer, and new media artist. She has published five volumes of poetry, most recently, *Ecliptical* (ES-Press, Spineless Wonders, 2022), and numerous performance and multimedia works. In 2018, *novelling*, her collaboration with Roger Dean and Will Luers, was awarded first place in the Electronic Literature Organisation's international Robert Coover Award.

Jarkko Toikkanen is senior lecturer in English at the University of Oulu, Finland, and Adjunct Professor at Tampere University, Finland. His research is focused on the concept of intermedial experience, or how experiencing literature and other media produces sensory perceptions, both imagined and non-imagined, through medium-specific ways of presenting that mediate the conceptual abstractions of language and culture.

Acknowledgements

The idea of this book developed through my discussions about digital literature with teachers, peers, and students over the last several years. At the onset of my graduate career, I was deeply interested in the representations of characters and scenes from Indian epics and myths in digital fictions and games. I found a few instances of such representation in mobile games of the early 2000s, such as, *Bheema: The Asura Temple* (2009), developed by the Mumbai-based Synqua Games. However, these kinds of digital texts were few and far between a decade ago. Moreover, the examples I did find seemed to be deficient in the aesthetic features examined at length in digital literary criticism. My research took different turns, and it would be years before I started questioning the role of geopolitical relations and hierarchies in defining literariness within a digital media ecology.

On the non-linear, protracted path this book took, I have benefitted from the guidance of many mentors: Jared Gardner's graduate seminars still remain instrumental in my thinking about media history and popular culture. Frederick Luis Aldama has been influential in my thinking about ethnic and racial coordinates of narratives across media as well as the significance of scholarly anthologies in advancing a field of study.

The three reviewers who commented on the proposal of this book helped refine my project—I am thankful for their encouraging evaluation. When I was working on this book, I was supported by the Invigorating Scholarly and Creative Activities Program of the California State University, Sacramento, which proved invaluable for the project's completion. Routledge editor Michelle Salyga has been a champion of this project from the outset, and I have also appreciated the experience of working with Bryony Reece.

Islamabad-based interdisciplinary artist Mamoona Riaz, who I have had the pleasure of collaborating with in the past, contributes the book's cover image. Her artwork—"Like Clockwork IV" (2022)—imagines the intersections and connections generated through spatial and temporal encounters. Riaz uses and layers maps to capture sociopolitical and cultural quandaries of the present. In her statement of work, she says that in "Like Clockwork IV" she transformed "the pattern of Shamsa, a traditional motif from Indo-Persian illumination art," into "a pattern made from cogs and gears, which in all their delicacy and glory are depicting the forever ongoing machine, which a city is." I am grateful to her for granting us the permission to use her intricate artwork.

The strength of an anthology of critical essays depends to a great extent on the scholars contributing to the volume, and thus, I am thankful to the contributors who joined the project and collectively helped shape it.

My family continues to be a source of support and strength—above all else, I appreciate the patience of my parents as I complete work on this book.

Torsa Ghosal
October 2022

Introduction

Global Literary Studies and Digital Literature

Torsa Ghosal

In 2014, Nigerian American author Teju Cole sidestepped more traditional methods of publishing a short story and asked some of his followers and friends to serialize its segments on Twitter. The users tweeting parts of Cole's story mark themselves on the platform as based out of various places, including New Delhi, East Anglia, and New York. Cole retweeted the segments, arranging them in a particular sequence. The resulting sequence was titled "Hafiz" (Cole 2014). The narrator of "Hafiz" finds a man sitting on the sidewalk surrounded by strangers. When one of the strangers informs the narrator that the seated man is suffering from chest pain, the narrator calls 911 for help. All the characters in the story are without names with the exception of an EMT, who we are told "had a beautiful name…Ahmed, or Hamid, or Aziz, or Hafiz" (n.pag.). "Hafiz" is thus a story about a group of strangers helping a man, published and distributed by a group of friends and followers selected by the author. Just as the characters of "Hafiz" could be anyone, the tweets could be retweeted by anybody, based anywhere in the world, with access to the social media platform and the Internet.

Even though Cole's story was first drafted outside the social media platform, the social media milieu and the platform's affordances impact its progression and segmentation. For instance, none of the segments are longer than 140 characters given Twitter's character limit back in 2014. Thus, "Hafiz" is an instance of digital fiction which is "written for and read on a computer screen" (Bell et al. 2010, n.pag.). As Alice Bell, Astrid Ensslin, and Hans Rustad (2014) observe, digital fiction "is fiction whose structure, form and meaning are dictated by, and in dialogue with, the digital context in which [they are] produced and received" (4). The origins of digital fiction can be traced to 1980s' Interactive Fictions (IF), even though a digital fiction like "Hafiz" does not involve the same level of interactivity as IF or possess the ludic qualities associated with IF. The elegant and precise sentences constituting "Hafiz" also lack the spontaneity of ordinary

DOI: 10.4324/9781003214915-1

tweets. However, the story's thematic focus on kindness of strangers turns the narrative into what Tess McNulty has called an "uplifting anecdote," a genre of writing designed for sharing on social media (2019, n.pag.). And Cole himself has commented on the generosity of his followers who agreed to participate in his literary experiment.

Cole is neither the first nor the only author primarily associated with print literature who has attempted to utilize Twitter for storytelling. Back in 2011, Manoj Pandey, an illustrator in Delhi, started tweeting epigrammatic stories from his handle @talesontweet. Pandey tagged authors across the globe and these authors responded to his tweets with stories of their own. The authors included Margaret Atwood, Shashi Tharoor, Salman Rushdie, Nilanjana S. Roy, and Cole, among others. Pandey's literary experiment generated popular and critical attention, resulting in a book that compiled micro-narratives tweeted in response to Pandey's posts. The book *Tales on Tweet* (2016) was published by Harper Collins India and to market the book as an artifact distinguished from the tweets, the book description stressed how the Japanese illustrator Yuko Shimizu's images added to the text allowed the collection to transition from "the scrollable vortex of a webpage and into the tactile intimacy of the reading experience" (Book description; also see Press Trust of India 2016).

Pandey's and Cole's projects are examples of cross-border and cross-media collaborations informing literary activities in today's web culture. And though both my examples are Anglophone, digital literary activities are by no means confined to the English-speaking world. Yet, few scholarly works address the cultural and political import of such worldwide activities through a comparative lens. *Global Perspectives on Digital Literature* fills a critical gap in digital literary criticism by investigating how digital literary forms shape and are shaped by aesthetic and political exchanges happening across languages, nations, and cultures. Adopting a wide array of interpretive approaches, the chapters in this volume make visible new literary connections and possibilities engendered by the twenty-first century media ecology.

The scholars contributing to *Global Perspectives on Digital Literature* focus their attention on a range of artists and authors, including the Egyptian-American poet Amira Hanafi, the Hong Kong comic artist Chao Yat, the Irish writer-musician Claire Fitch, among others. They analyze texts like the YouTube series *Ananse and the Sticky Gum/Grave Mischief*, based on Akan oral culture, and Swedish developer Frictional Games's survival horror game, *SOMA* as well as participatory literary projects and phenomena like the Brisbane-based Remix My Lit project and "creepypasta narratives." However, discussions in the chapters are not centered solely around social and national identities of the authors and artists. Instead, chapters in *Global Perspectives* concentrate on issues related to cross-cultural and cross-medial encounters, regulation and control, resistance and transgression. The book as a whole intends to rethink dominant frameworks of categorizing and studying digital literature. To this end, artists and texts are placed outside neat social and national identity containers and drawn into conversations with one another. While finding common ground for such conversation to happen, the book is also careful about not devaluing the specific social conditions from which digital literature emerge in different parts of the world. In the following sections of this chapter, I offer the theoretical framework for the volume by tracing its connections with global literary studies and influential scholarship on digital literary and cultural expressions.

Global Literary Studies

Within the broader field of comparative literature, global literary studies can be understood as one of many approaches locating and studying aesthetic practices outside the narrow framework of national traditions. Global literary studies is at once an emerging field across disciplines as well as an exhausted one. At the turn of the millennium, *PMLA* published a special issue focused on the topic: "Globalizing Literary Study." In an essay published in the special issue, Ian Baucom (2001) notes that due to a "prevalent" call in the academy for "globalization of literary study" a couple of different modes of scholarship have gained prominence—"global literary study as project and as method" (162). As project, global literary study encompasses "the study of something called global literature" while as method it seeks to account for "the global spread of particular ways of studying something called literature" (162). As both project and method, Baucom argues, the call for globalization attempts to grapple with the increased corporatization of academic institutions, among other crises, but he observes that the "challenge of the global is that of rethinking the form of the globe" (170). Perhaps because of this challenge, global literary studies remains a contentious territory. While tracing the history of the 'global turn' in the humanities and social sciences, Neus Rotger, Diana Roig-Sanz, and Marta Puxan-Oliva (2019) observe that particularly in disciplines like literary and cultural studies and art history, there are heated controversies "around the terms 'world,' 'global,' and 'planetary,' in which users of the words 'world' and 'planet' try to distance themselves from the critique levelled at the 'global,' emphasizing a cosmopolitan and ecocritical view" (329; also see Roig-Sanz and Rotger 2022). Literary scholar Christian Moraru (2014) represents the skeptical stance on 'global' as a concept when he says, "The world and the globe are both immensities; both boggle the mind quantitatively. But, unlike the world and insofar as it results from relationally totalizing reinscriptions of the world, the globe is no longer a worldly *opera aperta*, an open-ended boundlessness, a *project*" (n.pag.).

Despite such critiques, 'global' as a descriptor for approaches to literary studies continues to gain traction. Reflecting on the uptake of the term 'global' in literary studies (particularly in the context of the disciplinary expertise labelled "Global Anglophone"), Nasia Anam (2019) asks "is there a burgeoning corpus of literature exhibiting distinct characteristics from what we consider to be postcolonial and/or World Literature?" (n.pag.). World literature, as conceptualized by David Damrosch (2006), refers to "works that are read and discussed beyond home-country and area-specialist audiences" (48). Damrosch's chief concern is canon formation, and to constitute the canon of world literature, he suggests we draw "[n]ot one line, but many: lines of connection across the conflicted boundaries of nations and of cultures, and new lines of comparison across the persisting divisions" (53). Analytic frames decentering single nations in literary studies also include the transnational, the hemispheric, the oceanic, and the postcolonial. Given these alternatives, Anam probes whether 'global' is an aesthetic imperative, denoting a generic shift within literature, or an economic-political one, given that the term conjures debates about globalization, neoliberalism, and technocracy.

This volume understands 'global' as a mode of comparative thinking in which digital literature plays an integral role. In other words, the term 'global' in *Global Perspectives on Digital Literature* not only attests to digital literature's worldwide reach but also calls attention to how digital literary texts and practices arise from the interconnectedness of regions and cultures. However, I do not use 'global' to signal an encyclopedic ambition. Rather I follow Heather H. Yeung (2019) who observes that 'global' thinking "is a question of scale and of possibility; of evidence and of speculation; of maintenance and of disruption all predicated on the formal, geometrical, material reality of this planet" (1). Without undermining the particularities of authors and texts, regions and histories, this book argues for considering the proliferation of digital literature—the popular, the avant-garde, and the participatory—across distinct social contexts as realizing possibilities of global thought and opening new cultural imaginaries in the twenty-first century.

As the plural term 'perspectives' in the title suggests, this book does not attempt to offer a homogenizing overview of a vast and diverse range of cultural expressions. Indeed, the book seizes on the term 'global' to track conversations and tensions in between sites and cultures, recognizing and addressing the impact of global capitalism, political and economic inequalities, among other urgent concerns. Using the suspect term 'global,' the book engages with the long-term consequences and multiple temporalities of globalization. Besides, conceptual alternatives to 'global,' including 'world' and 'planetary,' are not radically dissimilar: as Jacob Edmond (2021) notes,

> literary studies in its new or renewed "world" or "planetary" formulations emanating from North America and Europe over the past few decades often looks suspiciously like another version of Anglo-European colonialism and imperialism, another extractive industry in which the West (now, often, "the North") exploits the resources of the rest. In this respect, the new global studies would be nothing new

to this (or any other) part of the world but merely an extension of the old story of the exploitation of Indigenous and other non-European peoples by settler colonials like myself and my ancestors.

(194)

Yet, as Edmond observes, "global comparison" remains a critical method for grappling with "the politics of unequal encounters between languages, cultures, and intersectional identities, and with the insidious histories and ongoing power of racialized and gendered ideologies and prejudices" (195). What is required therefore is a probing into the methods and modes of comparison. Edmond argues,

> in the case of institutionalized modes of global literary studies – including comparative literature, global modernism, global romanticism, global anglophone, global settler studies, and the like – what is needed is not discipline but indiscipline, not a universalizing global perspective but a recognition of the limits of dominant disciplinary objects, frameworks, and perspectives and an openness to being surprised into new ways of seeing the world.
>
> (221)

This book attempts to practice such indiscipline by displacing "dominant disciplinary objects" of digital literary criticism—avant-garde electronic literature primarily produced in Anglo-America—and reimagines the notion of digital literature comparatively across regional and ethnolinguistic contexts.

Digital Literature

The framework of global literary studies prompts us to rethink the category of the literary in the digital sphere. Digital literature has always had a complex relationship with national literary traditions and contexts. Whereas traditional publishing trained us to think in terms of nations—the printing press has been associated with the rise of nation-states (Anderson 2006 [1983], 39–48)—digital technologies seemed to encapsulate possibilities of international collaboration and dialogue from the outset (Poster 2001; Landow 2006). Yet, in practice, corporate origins of digital technology and other structural inequities constrained these possibilities. Moreover, the scope of the literary—what literature is and can be—in a digital media ecology continued to be defined from within the Anglo-American cultural and academic spheres. For example, George P. Landow and Paul Delany's *Hypermedia and Literary Studies* (1991), representative of the first wave of criticism about born-digital literary texts, foregrounded literature composed using proprietary software developed in the United States, like Storyspace and HyperCard. Theodor Holm Nelson's *Literary Machines* (1982), Landow's *Hypertext 2.0: The Convergence of Contemporary Critical*

Theory and Technology (1992), Terry Harpold's *Ex-Foliations* (2009), Astrid Ensslin's *Canonizing Hypertext: Explorations and Constructions* (2007) are other foundational works of digital literary criticism that privilege a particular type of literary production, identify hypertextual and other experimental electronic productions as digital texts meriting the attention of literary scholars.

By the late 1990s, text-based, single-authored hypertexts were becoming outmoded. Literature with multimodal, networked, and ludic elements was beginning to be generated worldwide, and the next wave of digital literary criticism acknowledged these aesthetic shifts (see Coover 1999; Montfort 2000; Ciccoricco 2007). Nick Montfort's *Twisty Little Passages: An Approach to Interactive Fiction* (2003), David Ciccoricco's *Reading Network Fiction* (2007) and Alice Bell, Astrid Ensslin, and Hans Kristian Rustad's *Analyzing Digital Fiction* (2014) attend to combinatorial and networking strategies used in digital literature, mainly focusing on fictions and text-based adventure games. N. Katherine Hayles continued to consistently study the relationship between print texts and digital media in books such as *Electronic Literature: New Horizons for the Literary* (2008). Ruth Page and Bronwen Thomas's edited collection *New Narratives: Stories and Storytelling in the Digital Age* (2011) explored hypertext, video games, and fan fiction through the lens of a digital narratology whilst Roger Dean and Hazel Smith's *Improvisation Hypermedia and the Arts since 1945* (2013) charted how hypermedia and electronic technologies challenged composer/performer/audience relationships. Jessica Pressman's *Digital Modernism* (2014) considered the resurgence of modernist aesthetic principles in the first wave of electronic texts.

And yet, as Scott Kushner (2015) observes, the kind of experimental literature categorized and studied in most of the prominent instances of digital literary scholarship, "does not offer the only or most direct access to the poetics, ethics, politics, and technics of digital culture" (n.pag.). In the aftermath of the rise of social media, "[a]n unprecedented flood of textuality means that everyday writing, preserved with varying levels of care, offers a window into the ethics and cultural practices of an era" (2015, n.pag.). While it is possible to think of social media posts as generating 'non-literary textual artifacts,' the writings that are produced and circulated on these platforms are not always clearly distinguished from the category of the literary on aesthetic or any other grounds. In fact, today numerous professional artists as well as amateurs across the world access a variety of popular (Twitter, Instagram) and niche platforms (such as Bitsy) to generate interactive and associative literary experiences. As Aarthi Vadde and Jessica Pressman (2019) succinctly put it, the Web 2.0 participatory culture is "changing the literary" (n.pag.). Pressman's *Bookishness* (2020) and Simone Murray's *The Digital Literary Sphere* (2018) thus take a more expansive view of literature and the literary culture as they consider amateur and kitsch texts produced in the digital media ecology, survey new kinds of book-related communities and new modes of cultural criticism, alongside more traditional literary productions.

Even as the participatory web culture and social media, among other factors, are transforming what is considered "literature" these transformations are not happening everywhere at the same time. Technological transformations and adoptions of particular platforms and styles of expressions happen across multiple temporalities. Bearing in mind the shifting conditions for the production and distribution of literature across different temporal and spatial coordinates, the ever-changing dynamics of global and local forces, the present volume explores new ways of understanding digital literary works. The book's contributors think about the participatory culture and technological affordances of Web 2.0. Concerned with the possibilities of global thinking indexed in digital literature, they take up fundamental questions such as, what do we mean when we talk about literature today? What is the future of literature? While the essays use heterogeneous approaches and offer eclectic responses to the questions, their methods are always "comparative and media focused" (Pressman and Hayles 2013).

Among recent scholarly works advancing critical approaches to digital literature, such as Scott Rettberg's *Electronic Literature* (2018) and *The Bloomsbury Handbook of Electronic Literature* (2017) edited by Joseph Tabbi, *Global Perspectives on Digital Literature* is unique for explicitly attending to the uneven global spread of digital literary productions and scholarship. Tabbi's volume anthologizes essays that chart the implications of "universalization and *normalization* of affordances and potentials" of digital media whereas chapters of this book (take Chapter 8 by Kin Wai Chu, for example) show how both access to and use of digital media's affordances are not easily universalized. This is not only because of global inequities marking the adoption of technologies but also because of censorship and other repressive factors tied to particular political conditions. In other words, *Global Perspectives* is strongly and distinctively attuned to the cultural and political milieu of digital literary productions and reception at a global scale.

There remains a deficit in scholarship addressing gendered, ethno-racial, and other cultural-political aspects of digital literature. Notable exceptions include *Hypertext and the Female Imaginary* (2010), where Jaishree K. Odin examines how hypertextual strategies respond to questions of gender and cultural difference. Claire Taylor's *Electronic Literature in Latin America* (2019) and Cecily Raynor's *Latin American Literature at the Millennium: Local Lives, Global Spaces* (2021) situate digital textuality within national and transnational contexts. Nele Lenze's *Politics and Digital Literature in the Middle East: Perspectives on Online Text and Context* (2019) analyzes the connections of online literature with politics in major Arabic-speaking countries in the Middle East. This book adds to these cultural critiques through a diversity of case studies, encompassing a broad range of genres (including speculative, horror, and weird fiction, autobiography, games) and using a variety of methodologies.

Murray (2018) has observed that approaches to digital literary studies remain "text-, author-, or medium-centric rather than adopting a cultural-sociological approach focusing upon the *context* or material and institutional cultural systems influencing the emergence and circulation of specific literary texts" (7). *Global Perspectives*' comparative framework, however, attends to contexts and cultural systems. By doing so, the book initiates dialogue with scholarship on not only digital literature but also other comparativist projects focused on media and mediality. Kiene Brillenburg Wurth (2018), for instance, recognizes a 'material turn' in comparative literature and Rebecca Walkowitz (2015) situates contemporary world literature in relation to digital culture. *Global Perspectives* builds on these scholarly efforts.

While criticizing colonial practices in digital humanities and articulating what a 'postcolonial' approach might look like, Roopika Risam (2019) notes that digital humanities projects including digitization initiatives in literary studies (such as Willian Blake Archive, the Walt Whitman Archive) "skew heavily towards canonical authors and histories within the Global North" and comments on the extent to which "the digital cultural record is implicated in structures that produce colonial discourse, devalue black lives, and in turn, facilitate state violence" (15). To move past these issues, Risam argues it is not only important to add more voices and perspectives to the digital cultural record but also evaluate the "circumstances surrounding knowledge production of digital humanities" (17). What Risam says of digital humanities projects applies to digital literary criticism as well. Thus, apart from identifying a multitude of texts and practices emerging in a variety of linguistic and regional contexts as subjects of interest for digital literary studies, resisting the geopolitical tug of Anglo-America, chapters in this book discuss the limitations of prevalent modes of categorizing, classifying, and critiquing in digital literary scholarship.

Chapter Outlines

This book is divided into four parts: "Reimagining Digital Literary Studies," "Digital Embodiments and Disabilities," "Forms of Resistance," and "Medial and Cultural Crossings." The chapters constituting these parts strike a balance between analyzing specific texts and literary practices and offering general overviews of significant conversations and debates about digital literature. Each part opens with a mini-introduction situating the concerns addressed in the following chapters.

In the first chapter of Part I "Reimagining Digital Literary Studies," Simone Murray revisits the claims made by early theorists of electronic literature about the radical instability of electronic texts. The instability was thought to proceed from the choices these texts offered reader-users, and the reader's process of decision-making was theorized as empowering. However, Murray notes, the choices of reader-users were restricted by the text's structure. Instead of the early hypertexts where readers were only offered the illusion of having immense control over the narrative's outcome, Murray draws attention to a type of digital literary work labelled "constructive hypertexts." These texts are created by remixing, rewriting or altering source texts. Examples include the Australian professional/amateur collaboration Remix My Lit (2007), the tag-team writing project *Lost in Track Changes* (2014), and the Italian collectively written historical novel *In Enemy Territory* (2013). Murray observes that the format shares similarities with remix practices in music and filmmaking since at least the early 1980s, but the format's slow acceptance as digital literature in academic circles has to do with the prejudices of the literary field against reworked texts. This prompts Murray to discuss how such prejudice counters electronic literature community's self-image as inclusive and democratic. Murray's chapter makes a valuable contribution to the study of collaborative authorship in digital environments as well as digital literary criticism's changing positions on reader participation. It raises questions about the relationship of collaborative authorship with aesthetic quality and exposes the limitations of digital literary criticism's commitment to a vague notion of aesthetic quality.

Mariusz Pisarski, in Chapter 2, notes that during the initial phases of digital literary scholarship, electronic literature was classified according to genres, generations, and platforms. These methods led to certain texts being considered classics. These texts' disjointed and interconnected structures were typically legible as serious literary artefacts to critics trained on poststructuralist theories. However, with the emergence of the Internet, social media, and worldwide proliferation of computing technologies, new forms of digital literary works continued to be created—these were more ludic, incomplete, generative, and collaborative. However, digital artifacts sharing many of these aesthetic features did not emerge in different parts of the world all at once. Pisarski thus sets out to discuss methods for expanding the corpus of what is regarded as digital literature, methods of canonizing and analyzing digital literary texts. Apart from tracing multiple strands of digital literary practices, his chapter categorizes texts according to formal and thematic dyads like "epistemological/ontological, multimodal/transmodal, substitutive/associative."

In Chapter 3, Souvik Mukherjee, discusses how the relationship between stories and games has become increasingly complicated with the simultaneous rise of digital games and other hypermedia narrative forms with a ludic character. Games Studies, Mukherjee observes, offers comparative frameworks for parsing ludic and narrative media (or ludonarrative media), but a persisting problem is that particular theoretical frameworks from literary studies are yet to sufficiently impact Games Studies. In this context, Mukherjee charts how postcolonialism as a theoretical framework could open ludonarrative media to questions of inequality and oppression. Postcolonial theories would facilitate alternative reading practices, attend to multiplicities and discontinuities in anticolonial thinking. Mukherjee's chapter advances postcolonial approaches to ludonarrative digital texts by comparatively considering Munshi Premchand's short story, "The Chess Players," which was adapted into a film by Satyajit Ray, and *80 Days*, a digital adventure game based on Jules Verne's novel. Mukherjee addresses the continuity of colonial logics across digital games and board games, how postcolonial reading strategies can support disruptive readings of these formats and explores alternatives to colonialist game design.

Chapter 4 by Cody Mejeur opens Part II "Digital Embodiment and Disabilities." Mejeur discusses how players are afforded unique opportunities to play with identities and rethink strategies of worldmaking in video games. The affordance of "narrative play" associated with video games has the potential to queer encounters with difference, shift strategies of embodiment, and transform conceptions of humanity. Mejeur analyzes the opportunities of narrative play and embodiment available in the game *SOMA* (Frictional Games 2015). *SOMA* is a first-person narrative game in which players are required to survive in a post-apocalyptic world and the game tackles ideas related to promises of transhumanism, politics of posthuman futures, and other issues concerned with embodied cognition and identity. Mejeur argues that *SOMA* exemplifies narrative difference and novel modes of worldmaking in games and beyond. Their chapter makes a significant contribution to conceptions of embodiment in digital media ecology.

In Chapter 5, Sara Bimo examines the digital narrative forms and phenomena grouped within the template of "creepypasta." Bimo argues that "creepypasta" is a new narrative form utilizing the technological affordances of digital environments and the World Wide Web. This new narrative form is a kind of horror fiction produced and circulated digitally. It combines various literary conventions of the past while working with the structures of the platforms and forums in which the narrative is presented. Bimo discusses the embodiment and identity-related anxieties that prompt the production of creepypasta narratives and demonstrates how these narratives blur subject–object distinctions and carry an affective charge impacting readers in unpredictable ways.

The narrative representation of embodied experiences discussed in Chapter 6 by Rimi Nandy relate to the contested illness of fibromyaglia. Nandy's focus is on how social networking sites change the genre and notion of autobiographical writing. In this context, she attends to newer forms of life writing in which selves are constituted digitally and are concentrated on the experiences of chronic pain and disabilities. Her chapter explores the collaborative and participatory dynamics of self-constitution through narratives posted on a Facebook community. Nandy herself participates in the community and her mode of participatory critique exemplifies a disability studies centered approach to digital literature.

Part 3 of *Global Perspectives*—"Forms of Resistance"—is made up of four chapters examining digital texts and practices that respond to political oppression and authoritarianism. Chapter 7 by Álvaro Seiça surveys material, literary, and visual techniques that can be understood as erasure strategies. Such strategies, Seiça notes, have gained global impetus in the last 20 years. Analyzing works of both Anglophone and non-Anglophone authors using erasure not only as an aesthetic but also political strategy to protest injustices, Seiça draws attention to new kinds of political poetry produced in the digital media ecology. This chapter also crucially discusses digital literature's engagement with systemic and structural violence, racial profiling, police brutality, state repression, and mass incarceration, among other issues. Among the digital texts comparatively discussed in this chapter are the Chilean poet Carlos Soto-Román's digitally mediated *Chile Project: [Re-Classified]*, the Iranian American author Solmaz Sharif's *Look*, and the Hong Kong-based artist Daniel C. Howe's "ChinaEye."

In Chapter 8, Kin Wai Chu considers the role of digitally circulated political cartoons in raising social awareness and mobilizing people with reference to the Hong Kong protests since 2010. Chu identifies two prominent tendencies in the production of digital political cartoons—self-censored authorship due to a fear of consequences and collaborative, participatory exchanges involved in the creation and dissemination of the protest literature. Chu discusses collaborations among political cartoonists such as Cuson Lo and Chao Yat and the initiatives of these artists to foster collectives to promote democracy. The interactivity afforded by social media engenders conditions that distinguish political cartoons in digital environments from their print counterpart and Chu's chapter effectively shows how media affordance when utilized within particular political contexts can prompt citizens to protest oppression.

Reham Hosny, in Chapter 9, undertakes a comparative study of two acclaimed texts documenting the January 25th revolution in Egypt: digital artist Amira Hanafi's e-lit piece *A Dictionary of the Revolution* (2017), winner of the New Media Writing Prize and The Public Library Prize for Electronic Literature, and director Jehane Noujaim's documentary film *The Square* (2013), winner of three Emmy Awards and an Academy Award nominee. Hosny outlines the methods of composition of both texts and their stylistic features. The chapter then argues for recognizing the ways in which the media of digital literature (*A Dictionary of the Revolution*) and cinema (*The Square*) inform the narrative techniques of both these works, which in turn culminate in significantly different representations of the 2011 revolutionary protests.

In Chapter 10, Brian Davis analyzes the American writer Bill Bly's *We Descend*, one of the longest running hypertext sagas in electronic literary history, as an instance of "archival fiction," which Davis defines as an emergent form of literature using "a poetics of documentation and preservation, of curation and transmission" to underscore how "subjectivity, knowledge, history, and memory are increasingly configured through distributed networks of people and artifacts in different social and institutional spaces." Against the backdrop of a post-apocalyptic setting, *We*

Descend presents multiple generations of archivists who are tasked with authenticating or disauthenticating a proliferating body of writings containing (and concealing) knowledge about earlier writing systems and reasons behind the global disaster. Davis traces how *We Descend* in particular and archival fictions in general mediate anxieties about ideological import of digital technologies, blurring borders between fact and fiction, document and hoax. The chapter offers insights into the political dimensions of archival practices and valuably discusses authentication practices across historical periods and cultures.

Part 4 of *Global Perspectives*, "Medial and Cultural Crossings," opens with Chapter 11 by J.B. Amissah-Arthur and Kwabena Opoku-Agyemang on digital literary expressions connected to two philosophical concepts—Sankofa and Ananse Ntontan—sacred to the Akan, an ethnic group found along the coast of West Africa, particularly present-day Ghana and parts of la Cote d'Ivoire. Amissah-Arthur and Opoku-Agyemang explore the relation of oral and digital traditions of storytelling involving these philosophical concepts while also interrogating prior approaches to African digital literature. Their chapter then offers an alternative framework for understanding African digital literature based on the philosophy underlying symbols like Sankofa and Ananse Ntontan. Amissah-Arthur and Opoku-Agyemang also demonstrate how such a framework might be successfully applied to the study of specific case studies by closely analyzing the YouTube series *Ananse Tales* by Parables Animation Studios, a content creating company based in Accra, Ghana.

In Chapter 12, Hazel Smith studies the uses of voice and music in digital literary texts. Smith's chapter offers a wide-ranging view of voice-based digital literature across cultures. Along with distinguishing between different types of sound in digital literature (environmental, acoustic, electronic, vocal), the varying ways sound is juxtaposed or merged with words, the chapter attends to the emotional and cultural import of what Smith calls "musico-literary miscegenation." The chapter also analyzes works by several artists, including Jeff Morris and Elisabeth Blair, Jeneen Naji, Claire Fitch, Jörg Piringer, Roger Dean, and Smith herself, and shows how voices summon particular identities and subjectivities as well as destabilize them. In addition, Smith comments on how digital literature is gesturing toward a new kind of oral culture, founded upon algorithmic approaches and artificial intelligence, among other techniques.

In Chapter 13, Jarkko Toikkanen and Mari Hatavara advance the study of aural aspects of digital literature by attending to how voice serves as vehicle for characterization. Combining literary narratology with media critical thinking around intermediality, Toikkanen and Hatavara discuss the mediation of a short story by the American author H.P. Lovecraft in digital audio drama and podcast formats. The chapter shows how audio drama adds layers of meaning to the written text and how an interactive literary podcast further complicates the situation, both productions contributing to interpretive ambiguities. Toikkanen and Hatavara are also concerned with audiences' experiences across media and the nature of their interactions with the story as the text moves from print to vocalized and dramatized formats produced and circulated digitally.

Global Perspectives ends with notes on the limitations and potentials of the comparative, interpretive approaches to digital literature exhibited in the volume and speculates about directions for future scholarship.

Bibliography

Anam, Nasia. 2019. "Forms of the Global Anglophone." *Post45*. http://post45.org/2019/02/introduction-forms-of-the-global-anglophone/

Anderson, Benedict. 2006. *Imagined Communities*. New York: Verso.

Baucom, Ian. 2001. "Globalit, Inc.; Or, the Cultural Logic of Global Literary Studies." *PMLA* 116, no. 1: 158–172.

Bell, Alice, Astrid Ensslin, Dave Ciccoricco, Hans Rustad, Jess Laccetti and Jessica Pressman. 2010. "A [S]creed for Digital Fiction." *Electronic Book Review*. https://electronicbookreview.com/essay/a-screed-for-digital-fiction/

Bell, Alice, Astrid Ensslin, and Hans Kristian Rustad (eds.). 2014. "From Theorizing to Analyzing Digital Fiction." In *Analyzing Digital Fiction*. New York: Routledge, 3–16.

Bly, Bill. 1997. *We Descend, Volume One: Writings from Archives Pertaining to Egderus Scriptor*. Eastgate Systems.

———. 2017 [2015]. *We Descend, Volume Two: New Selected Writings from Archives Pertaining to Egderus Scriptor*. *The New River: A Journal of Digital Writing & Art*. www.cddc.vt.edu/journals/newriver/17Fall/WeDescend/index.html

———. 2020 [2019]. *We Descend, Volume Three: A Preliminary View of Further Selected Writings from Archives Pertaining to Egderus Scriptor*, forthcoming from *The New River: A Journal of Digital Writing & Art*. www.wedescend.net/WDvol3_ImpA1a/

Brillenburg Wurth, Kiene. 2018. "The Material Turn in Comparative Literature: An Introduction." *Comparative Literature* 70, no. 3: 247–263.

Ciccoricco, David. 2007. *Reading Network Fiction*. Tuscaloosa: University of Alabama Press.

Cole, Teju. 2014. "Hafiz." *Twitter*. https://twitter.com/tejucole/timelines/437242785591078912

Coover, Robert. 1999. "Literary Hypertext: The Passing of the Golden Age." Keynote Address, *Digital Arts and Culture*, Atlanta, Georgia. https://nickm.com/vox/golden_age.html

Damrosch, David. 2006. "World Literature in a Postcanonical, Hypercanonical Age." In *Comparative Literature in an Age of Globalization*, edited by Haun Saussy. Baltimore: Johns Hopkins University Press, 43–53.

Delany, Paul, and George P. Landow. 1991. *Hypermedia and Literary Studies*. Cambridge: MIT Press.

Edmond, Jacob. 2021. "Against Global Literary Studies." *New Global Studies* 15, no. 2: 193–226. https://doi.org/10.1515/ngs-2021-0028

Ensslin, Astrid. 2007. *Canonizing Hypertext: Explorations and Constructions*. New York: Continuum.

Hanafi, Amira. 2014–2017. *A Dictionary of the Revolution.* http://qamosaltha wra.com/

Harpold, Terry. 2009. *Ex-Foliations: Reading Machines and the Upgrade Path.* Minneapolis: University of Minnesota Press.

Hayles, N. Katherine. 2008. *Electronic Literature: New Horizons for the Literary.* Notre Dame: University of Notre Dame.

Howe, Daniel C. 2016. "ChinaEye," Browser plug-in. https://rednoise.org/daniel/chinaeye

Kushner, Scott. 2015. "Comparative Non-Literature and Everyday Digital Textuality." Paradigms. *ACLA.* https://stateofthediscipline.acla.org/entry/comparative-non-literature-and-everyday-digital-textuality-0#_ednref2

Landow, George. 1997 [1992]. *Hypertext 2.0: The Convergence of Contemporary Critical Theory and Technology.* Baltimore: Johns Hopkins University Press.

———. *Hypertext 3.0 : Critical Theory and New Media in an Era of Globalization.* Baltimore: Johns Hopkins University Press, 2006.

McNulty, Tess. 2019. "Close Shaves with Content." *Post45.* https://post45.org/2019/09/close-shaves-with-content/

Montfort, Nick. 2000. "Cybertext Killed the Hypertext Star." *Electronic Book Review.*

———. 2003. *Twisty Little Passages: An Approach to Interactive Fiction.* Cambridge: MIT Press.

Moraru, Christian. 2014. "'World,' 'Globe,' 'Planet': Comparative Literature, Planetary Studies, and Cultural Debt after the Global Turn." Paradigm. *ACLA.* https://stateofthediscipline.acla.org/entry/%E2%80%9Cworld%E2%80%9D-%E2%80%9Cglobe%E2%80%9D-%E2%80%9Cplanet%E2%80%9D-comparative-literature-planetary-studies-and-cultural-debt-after

Murray, Simone. 2018. *The Digital Literary Sphere: Reading, Writing, and Selling Books in the Internet Era.* Baltimore: Johns Hopkins University Press.

Nelson, Theodor Holm. 1982. *Literary Machines.* New York: Mindful Press.

Noujaim, Jehane. 2013. *The Square.* Noujaim Films and Worldview Entertainment.

Odin, Jaishree K.. 2010. *Hypertext and the Female Imaginary.* Minneapolis: University of Minnesota Press.

Pandey, Manoj. 2016. *Tales on Tweet.* New Delhi: HarperCollins Publishers India.

Poster, Mark. 2001. *What's the Matter with the Internet?.* Minneapolis: University of Minnesota Press.

Press Trust of India. 2016. "Now a book of stories that are not more than 140 characters long." *Deccan Chronicle.* www.deccanchronicle.com/lifestyle/books-and-art/160816/now-a-book-of-stories-that-are-not-more-than-140-characters-long.html

Pressman, Jessica. 2014. *Digital Modernism: Making It New in New Media.* Oxford: Oxford University Press.

———. 2020. *Bookishness: Loving Books in a Digital Age.* New York: Columbia University Press.

Pressman, Jessica, and N. Katherine Hayles (ed). 2013. *Comparative Textual Media: Transforming the Humanities in the Postprint Era.* Minneapolis: University of Minnesota Press.

Raynor, Cecily. 2021. *Latin American Literature at the Millennium: Local Lives, Global Spaces.* Lewisburg: Bucknell University Press.

Rettberg, Scott. 2018. *Electronic Literature.* Cambridge: Polity Press.

Risam, Roopika. 2019. *New Digital Worlds: Postcolonial Digital Humanities in Theory, Praxis, and Pedagogy*. Evanston: Northwestern University Press.

Roig-Sanz, Diana, and Rotger, Neus. 2022. "Global Literary Studies Through Concepts: Towards the Institutionalisation of an Emerging Field." *Global Literary Studies: Key Concepts*. Berlin: De Gruyter.

Rotger, Neus, Diana Roig-Sanz, and Marta Puxan-Oliva. 2019. "Introduction: Towards a cross-disciplinary history of the global in the humanities and the social sciences." *Journal of Global History* 14, no. 3: 325–334. doi:10.1017/S1740022819000147

Sharif, Solmaz. 2016. *Look*. Minneapolis: Graywolf Press.

Simanowski, Roberto, Jörgen Schäfer, and Peter Gendolla (eds.). 2010. *Reading Moving Letters: Digital Literature in Research and Teaching. A Handbook*. Berlin: De Gruyter.

Soto-Román, Carlos. 2013. *Chile Project: [Re-Classified]*. San Francisco: Gauss PDF. www.gauss-pdf.com/post/60951201700/gpdf082-carlos-soto-roman-chile-project

Tabbi, Joseph. 2017. *The Bloomsbury Handbook of Electronic Literature*. New York: Bloomsbury Publishing.

Taylor, Claire. 2019. *Electronic Literature in Latin America: From Text to Hypertext*. New York: Palgrave MacMillan.

Vadde, Aarthi, and Jessica Pressman. 2019. "Web 2.0 and Literary Criticism." *Post45*. https://post45.org/2019/09/web-2-0-and-literary-criticism/

Walkowitz, Rebecca L. 2015. *Born Translated: The Contemporary Novel in an Age of World Literature*. New York: Columbia University Press.

Yeung, Heather H. 2019. "Thinking the Global with Literature: Introduction." *New Global Studies* 13, no. 1: 1–12. https://doi.org/10.1515/ngs-2019-0009

Part I
Reimagining Digital Literary Studies

The chapters in Part I of *Global Perspectives* call into question the cultural and aesthetic assumptions constraining our studies of digital literature within the present-day globalized culture. Taking into account the evolving dynamics of the web, emerging screen-based and textual media, the participatory and collaborative dynamics of cultural expressions in Web 2.0, the following chapters explore alternatives to dominant ways of grouping, critiquing, and engaging with digital literary texts and practices.

Understanding how digital literature is influencing our world today requires us to map the multidirectional trajectories literary expressions take in the twenty-first century, the decentralized and unpredictable circumstances of their production and distribution. In other words, we are required to move past the traditional, hegemonic ways of thinking about digital literature in which genres and types of literary expressions are believed to have originated in Europe and North America, supported by academic institutions and corporate platforms in these regions, before spreading out to the rest of the world. A colonial vision of the world underlies such a hegemonic model of thinking. While scholars interested in archiving and studying digital literary expressions have long recognized the desperate need to challenge such a vision, their approaches have tended to be additive. For instance, notwithstanding the much more "diverse" contributor list of *Electric Literature Volume* 3 (2016), the editorial statement framing the volume does not examine its curatorial logic at any length. The editors simply note, "we disseminated an open call inviting communities from across the web and across the globe to submit their work to this collection" (Boluk et al. 2016, n.pag.). There is no discussion about the historical forces driving the creation and dissemination of digital texts across the globe in the note and no mention of the transnational, translational, and cross-cultural encounters involved in the presentation of a variety of digital literary texts in a volume side by side. The problem with the additive approach is that it obscures why the global majority of writers—non-European, non-White, and without institutional affiliations—were left out from conceptions of digital literature for decades. That is to say, the dominant rationale running through generations of digital literary scholarship goes unexamined.

Ryan Ikeda (2021) has observed that logics of White supremacy "linger among electronic literature" (n.pag.). Databases, fellowships, publications, and genealogies privilege Eurocentric White aesthetics and experiences. Despite the electronic literature community extolling virtues of open source, collaboration, and decentralization, structural racism persists in the methods used to produce and organize knowledge. The canonization and anthologizing of specific digital literary texts purport the aesthetic value of these texts and implies their widespread reception. However, the unequal distribution of resources that govern the production of texts and determine their worldwide reach also needs to be considered when grouping and classifying them. As John Guillroy (2013) observes,

> if the socially unrepresentative content of the canon really has to do in the first place with how access to the means of literary production is socially regulated, a different history of canon formation will be necessary, one in which social identities are historical categories determined as much by the system of production as by consumption.
> (18)

One of the many ways in which not only White but also other privileged perspectives stay at the center of digital literary studies is through the continued emphasis on the legacy of the twentieth century avant-gardes as antecedents of contemporary hypertextual and fragmented digital writing. While insisting on the legacy, digital literary criticism refuses to interrogate how the very notion of avant-garde writing is systematically regulated. For example, Scott Rettberg's (2019) *Electronic Literature*, which "attempts to place the most significant genres of electronic literature in historical, technological, and cultural contexts to make the subject more readily accessible," traces the debt of these genres to "Dada, Surrealism, modernism and postmodernism, Situationism, Fluxus, and others" (3). These movements are largely associated with White authors, more men than women, trans*, or nonbinary authors. As Timothy Yu (2009) notes, White poets (such as the Language poets) were generally understood as practicing formal experimentalism while authors from other ethno-racial communities (Yu's focus is on Asian American poets) were not seen as avant-garde. By framing literature produced in the digital sphere in terms of the legacy of the twentieth-century avant-gardes, without interrogating the notion itself or recognizing competing experimental practices and histories, digital literary criticism perpetuates the same systemic biases.

Against this backdrop, Simone Murray, Mariusz Pisarski, and Souvik Mukherjee propose distinct methods for grouping and studying digital texts. Instead of simply proposing additions or noting exclusions in existing scholarship, Murray and Pisarki examine the logics guiding and regulating scholarly attention. While discussing how literary remix collapses distinctions between amateur and so-called professional artistic expressions, Murray identifies fan fiction and other popular cultural forms rather than the avant-garde as predecessors of innovative, collaborative digital literary practices. Pisarski tracks the multiple temporalities of digital literary and cultural trends while suggesting ways to reorient the directions of canon formation.

Mukherjee has previously discussed how borders drawn around electronic literature leave out the complex, heterogeneous ecology of digital texts produced outside United States and Europe and the historical relations of those texts with regional cultural forms. For instance, Mukherjee notes,

> Electronic literature, as it is understood in Europe and the U.S.A, does not have a presence in Indian literary and cultural traditions yet. The few Digital Humanities programmes that have developed in the country might be engaging with electronic literature in their curriculum. If so, the beginnings of e-lit are already evident in older cultural traditions and the process of remediation is certainly.
>
> (2017a, n.pag.)

The chapter Mukherjee contributes to this volume discusses the failings of digital literary and game scholarship to engage with Postcolonial criticism and anticolonial thinking (also see Mukherjee 2017b). By attending to the value and power of literary works as well as scholarly approaches that are often sidelined in digital literary studies and comparatively studying textual practices and technological cultures, the chapters in this section signal ways to reimagine the field.

Bibliography

Boluk, Stephanie, Leonardo Flores, Jacob Garbe, and Anastasia Salter. 2016. "Editorial Statement." *Electronic Literature Volume Three*. Cambridge: Electronic Literature Organization. https://collection.eliterature.org/3/about.html

Guillory, John. 2013. *Cultural Capital: The Problem of Literary Canon Formation*. Chicago: University of Chicago Press.

Ikeda, Ryan. 2021. "Excavating Logics of White Supremacy in Electronic Literature: Antiracism as Infrastructural Critique", *Electronic Book Review*, January 3, 2021, https://doi.org/10.7273/cctw-4415

Mukherjee, Souvik. 2017a. ""No Country for E-Lit?" – India and Electronic Literature." *Hyperrhiz: New Media Cultures*, no. 16. https://doi.org/10.20415/hyp/016.e08

———. 2017b. *Videogames and Postcolonialism: Empire Plays Back*. London: Palgrave Macmillan.

Rettberg, Scott. 2019. *Electronic Literature*. Medford: Polity Press.

Yu, Timothy. 2009. *Race and the Avant-garde: Experimental and Asian American Poetry Since 1965*. Redwood City: Stanford University Press.

1 Textual Instability
Paradoxes of Literary Remix

Simone Murray

One of the hallmarks of digital literature since its emergence in the late 1980s has been that it offers unstable, individually customizable texts, in contrast to the linear uniformity of print. Practitioner-theorists of the first, euphoric wave of electronic literature (eLit) in the early 1990s hailed as revolutionary texts that changed with each reading, and in which the 'tyranny' of the Romantic-style print author was overthrown by the participatory agency of reader-users (Bolter 1991; Landow 1992; Coover 1992; Aarseth 1997). Would-be reader-authors could assert influence over hypertext fictions by choosing from a number of possible paths through the text, usually by selecting from among numerous text blocks ('lexia') via links provided at the end of a prior section. Thus, reading was allegedly transformed from a passive trudge along a singular, author-demarcated path to a unique, freewheeling trespass across a textual landscape, with reader-poachers free to explore whatever byways took their fancy. For eLit enthusiasts, the triad of downgraded author, liberated reader, and ever-evolving text represented the medium's unique selling proposition (USP). It demonstrated that this "new medium for thought and expression" marked a decisive, epoch-defining break from literature's print-dominated, lamentably quiescent past (Slatin 1991 qtd. in Bolter 2011, 44).

Yet, by the turn of the millennium, such revolutionary rhetoric rang increasingly hollow as hypertext fiction failed to attract mainstream readerships and critics began to challenge some of eLit boosters' more hyperbolic claims. Sometimes these critiques took issue with the ostensible 'freedom' accorded to readers, suggesting that it felt more like an onerous imposition, exemplified by Laura Miller's tetchy riposte that "I already have a life,…and it is hard enough putting that in order without the chore of organizing someone else's novel" (1998). More theoretically, other critics charged that the alleged agency accorded to hypertext readers was in truth only the freedom to explore within pre-determined authorial confines (Manovich 2001, 61). The reader of Storyspace hypertexts had no ability to add to or meaningfully change the text, a powerlessness underlined by publisher Eastgate Systems' anomalously stern copyright warnings on their floppy-disc and CD-ROM packaging. In truth, such an eLit reader more closely resembled a toddler free to roam only within

DOI: 10.4324/9781003214915-3

the confines of their playpen, mistaking the appearance of freedom for its reality. Still more damningly, critics began to point out that even the much-disparaged, 'passive' print reader is free to flip forward or back in the text, and knows from a glance at a codex how much of the story is still to be consumed—basic orienting devices denied the frequently confused and aimless electronic reader (Parks 2002; Solway 2011). Such critique of digital environments' false freedom reaches its apogee in the literary computer game *The Stanley Parable* (2011), a walking simulator in which a hapless corporate drone named Stanley ('employee 427') endlessly wanders the halls of his deserted office building while being told by a faceless Narrator which choices he has already made (Wreden and Pugh 2011). Total compliance to this omniscient Narrator results in the controls being metaphorically wrested out of the player's hands, while repeated defiance prompts first gentle coercion, then sarcastic putdowns and, in one ending, revelation of the game's mind-control room. Granted, exploring the building and provoking the Narrator hold a certain adolescent appeal yet, ultimately, the game foregrounds that "choice in video games is an illusion" (Heron and Belford 2015, 17).

Faced with such theoretical pushback, the eLit community of writers, academics, and visual artists regrouped and returned to a distinction first drawn by literary hypertext pioneer Michael Joyce: one between 'exploratory' and 'constructive' hypertexts (1988).[1] Hypertext fictions of the 1990s had typically conformed to the author-scripted exploratory model, but an alternative 'constructive' kind would permit readers to edit and add to the existing text, thus realizing eLit's holy grail of reader as co-author. This would go beyond the kind of AI-driven recombinatory poetics deployed in works such as Nick Montfort's *Taroko Gorge* (2009), where details inputted by users result in random algorithmic remixes of the original text.[2] Rather, constructive hypertexts would allow deliberative, artistic co-creation of contemporary eLit works by ceding to readers the right to expand, condense, or radically alter a text that was formerly the sole province of authors. Clearly, such a radically appropriative approach to cultural property owes much to postmodern creative practices like sampling in rap music, fan video-editing, computer-game modding, and internet memes (Navas 2012; Navas, Gallagher, and burrough 2018; Middleton 2020). Even during the Web 1.0 era of predominantly one-way communication, such literary practices were already recognizably akin to fan fiction (aka fanfic), where amateur writers create further adventures for characters drawn from established literary, filmic, or televisual universes (Hellekson and Busse 2006). Yet such mass-access, popular culture-aligned practices clash fundamentally with the avant-garde, neo-Modernist aesthetics eLit has cultivated as its entry ticket to academic respectability (Pressman 2014; Flores 2019; Berens 2020). Can the two impulses be reconciled? This chapter explores three case-studies that attempt to straddle eLit's theoretical commitment to democratic textual remixing with its residual attachment to the concept of Romantic author-genius and experimental aesthetics: the Australian-based Remix My Lit project (2007–09); the Italian collaboratively written historical novel *In Territorio Nemico* [*In Enemy Territory*] (2013); and the more recent Australian literary tag-team writing experiment *Lost in Track Changes* (2014). Each of these deliberately unstable, 'processural' texts strikes a different balance between the eLit values of community participation and literary artistry, with varying degrees of success (Ensslin 2007, 34).

'Remix My Lit'/*Through the Clock's Workings*

The early years of the new millennium witnessed a number of eLit experiments that attempted to harness network technologies to realize the ideal of highly participatory, mass-authored creative writing. The 2007 experiment *A Million Penguins*, co-organized by the UK's Penguin Books and De Montfort University, was a wikinovel where anyone on the internet was able to amend and add to an evolving, ever-mutating text during a five-week period. Despite its founders' hopes that this would undermine the authority of the singular author by encouraging participants to 'leave their egos at the door', in practice the experiment resulted in a mostly unreadable mishmash of styles and narratives, with some participants seemingly motivated more by vandalism and 'griefing' than collaborative goodwill (Pauli 2007; Mason and Thomas 2008; Rettberg 2018, 174). As a result of the project being deemed an interesting failure (or, more euphemistically, a 'diverse, riotous assembly'), proponents of subsequent collaborative digital narratives have looked to alternative structures that impose greater editorial control upon users in the interests of generating legible and coherent texts.[3]

One such experiment was the Brisbane-based Remix My Lit (2007) which, as its name suggests, aimed to introduce remix music culture principles to the traditionally staider world of short fiction (Murray 2010). Project leaders Amy Barker and Elliott Bledsoe elicited short stories from nine 'established' Australian authors who agreed to post their works to the project's website for remixing by all and sundry (Barker 2009, 5). Rather than venturing into the grey area that is fanfic's status in copyright law, the project used a Creative Commons (CC) 'Attribution-NonCommercial-ShareAlike' license that permitted anyone to rework the stories so long as they acknowledged the first creator, did not exploit the work for commercial purposes, and permitted others to rework their remixes in turn (Jenkins 2006; Lessig 2008; Tushnet 2017). Remix My Lit's coordinators specifically positioned the project as a challenge to print-culture concepts of textual fixity and the superior status of the singular Author:

> Read/Write has traditionally been a dichotomy in literature. The author is on one side of the production process, toiling away in solitude to produce the manuscript which is read by many, in solitude. But is there a more collaborative space for literature? Can your pages

be Read&Write? Remix My Lit, a Brisbane-based, international remixable literature project thought so.

(Barker 2009, 5)

The original stories covered a broad range of genres: sci-fi; campus fiction; young adult (YA); realism; fantasy/horror; literary fiction; feminist poetics; magical realism; and crime. Predictably, the content of the remixes was even more diverse with sequels/alternative endings, gender inversions, and radical shifts in format prevalent. The original stories and the 'best' of the remixes as chosen by Barker were subsequently published as a print-on-demand anthology titled *Through the Clock's Workings* (2009), with the full text remaining freely available from Remix My Lit's website, in keeping with CC's spirit of open access.

The project's aim was to reimagine literary authorship as interactive, collaborative, and digitally distributed. As Larry Friedlander notes, "the digital environment...integrates authorship back into community," suggesting an analogy between the 'flat' structures of the internet and dismantling of print-ordained cultural hierarchies (2008, 191). In its positing of texts as innately mutable and possessing at most permeable boundaries, Remix My Lit is closer to a manuscript-era conception of authorship than a post-Gutenberg, copyright-based one (Pettitt 2007). Participating short-story writers seem to have relished this idea of innate intertextuality, where stories are understood not as self-contained, proprietary entities but rather as interlinked, perpetually fecund sources of others' inspiration. Short-story writer Cate Kennedy echoes eLit theorists of the early 1990s in drawing attention to the democratizing potential of reader-as-writer implicit in this form of interactive fiction:

> I was very keen to see what people would do because it's quite a playful thing to do and...it takes away some of that threat level or intimidation level where you look at a work of fiction as being something that's carved in stone and totally finished. It helps us understand I think that fiction is never totally finished, that there's always these open-ended things that happen in a good piece of fiction or a good story where someone else with a fresh pair of eyes can pick up some thread you've left or some character's perspective that you haven't seen and make something that's totally new out of it, which is a great idea.
>
> ('Remix' 2008)

The resulting anthology is a notable hybrid, and not only because it exists at the interface of digital and print mediums. While avowedly committed to democratizing literary culture by lowering barriers to entry for new writers, it nevertheless preserves some of the established/amateur distinction in the contributor biographies bound into the book's final pages. There is, moreover, an undeniable quality gap between many of the original short stories and their remixes, especially when taking into account that those print-published represent the editor's winnowing of the online crop. The overall impression is of a precarious balance being struck between public accessibility and editorial quality control, between the speed and reach of online publication on one hand and the formalizing and archival affordances of the printed codex on the other.

In Territorio Nemico

At the start of the new millennium's second decade, Italy's Scrittura Industriale Collettiva [Industrial Writing Collective] set out to explore whether a community was capable of writing a quality, full-length novel. The SIC's motto *'Tutti scrivono tutto'* [everyone writes everything] encapsulates the group's opposition to the 'author function' that has lain at the heart of western aesthetics since the Romantic period, and which is codified internationally in the 1886 copyright treaty, the Berne Convention for the Protection of Literary and Artistic Works (Foucault 2006 [1969]; Santoni 2014, 14; Murray 2019). The group's chosen subject matter – the Nazi occupation of Italy and the country's Resistance during World War II – is a politically charged topic still within living memory. To strengthen the novel's claims to historical veracity, the collective crowdsourced oral-history accounts from Italians who had lived through the war or their descendants. They then passed these to the eight editorial members of the collective (known as 'composers') who drew on them to construct a high-level 'treatment' of a multi-linear fictional narrative (Santoni 2014, 15). The composers then coordinated the drafting of individual narrative sections by over 100 writers, and took responsibility for selecting, arranging, and editing the patchwork sections into a tonally consistent overarching plot. Significantly, members of the editorial collective did not themselves write, as "writers can have a tendency towards egocentrism" (Santoni 2014, 14).[4] After three years of writer-composer back-and-forth, the completed novel, credited only to SIC on its cover, was published under CC license and enjoyed substantial critical and commercial success in Italy, being deemed as good a narrative as could be produced by so many hands.

The design of the project was based on "observation of the pros and cons of many collective writing practices" and strikes interesting contrasts with the principles underpinning Remix My Lit (Santoni 2014, 14). Firstly, the genre of historical fiction (as opposed to purely imaginative writing), and especially on so controversial and complex a subject, predisposed the project to a more collectivist mode, as in a sense this was a narrative already 'owned' by a significant proportion of the population. Secondly, all sections of the novel appear to have been produced by writers with some degree of publishing experience, in contrast to the many literary neophytes who participated in Remix My Lit. Thirdly, SIC's editorial cadre played a highly interventionist role in the planning and construction of the narrative, unlike the coordinators of Remix My Lit who initiated the project and then selected the best of the submissions at its close, but during its mid-stages took a largely hands-off approach. The scale of the resulting products is of course a factor here, as a short-story anthology can withstand a greater degree of tonal variation than can a traditionally structured, full-length novel. The lessons of earlier participatory writing experiments, especially the willful anarchy resulting from sandbox undertakings like *A Million Penguins*, appear to have been learnt. If multiple hands are to collaborate successfully on producing a literary work, the project will only succeed with a predetermined narrative arc, a high degree of editorial oversight, and strictly demarcated writer roles.

Lost in Track Changes

The final of this chapter's collaborative writing case-studies is the remix anthology *Lost in Track Changes*, coordinated and edited by Simon Groth for Brisbane's if:book Australia, an organization committed to exploring the potential of digital technology for rethinking books and writing. Groth recruited five well-regarded Australian writers (including the previously mentioned Cate Kennedy) to write a brief piece of memoir, which would then be passed along to the next writer for remixing until all of the original pieces had been remixed four times, round-robin style. The authors would only have access to the version of the story immediately prior to them in the writerly chain and would not know a text's provenance, nor what other authors had made of their own contribution, until the project's completion (v). The format for the rewriting experiment was, as flagged in the project's title, Microsoft Word's Track Changes editing function, and snippets of the 'typographical soup' resulting from the 'all-markup' display were bound into the subsequently published print version, although the body of each story is (mercifully) shown in 'no markup' for ease of reading (v). The completed anthology (now in its second edition) was published in numbered spiral-bound and later perfect-bound print copies, as well as being made available in toto from the project's website as a pdf for free download.

Groth's Introduction notes that the choice of the memoir genre was deliberate, as the (presumably) factual content of autobiography prompts a greater sense of transgression when rewriting another's work; in his phrasing it brought "a personal and emotional punch to what would have otherwise been a purely intellectual exercise" (ii). In theoretical terms, the project thus represents a heightened experiment in literary ownership and whether the link between a particular work and its author is inviolable or expendable. One interesting observation when reading the resultant anthology is that more minimalist remixes (where only a small proportion of the preceding text has been altered) are less creatively satisfying than the maximalist rewrites, which obviate any sense of déjà vu and replace it with an earnest search to find what connection, if any, there might be between the original story and its subsequent remixes. On this point, the contributions of Ryan O'Neill especially merit attention. His wildly inventive remixes included an automatic short story–generating software program with drop-down menus, a category-5 cyclone scrambling of a previous memoir snippet, and a spoof dictionary of biography entry for a fictitious, virulently racist Australian science fiction author. The remixing mandated by Groth even exceeded the boundaries of this project, as O'Neill appears to have so enjoyed writing his spoof biography of Rand Washington that he reworked and expanded it into the first in a whole volume of parodic Australian literary biographies titled *Their Brilliant Careers* (2016). This metafictional tour de force the following year won the country's lucrative Prime Minister's Literary Award for Fiction. Stories here really do appear to generate new stories, leaving loose threads to be reworked, in best postmodern style.

While *Lost in Track Changes* appears superficially to subscribe to postmodern remix orthodoxies, on closer inspection the printed version gives off mixed signals. The reverse title page shows that the project as a whole operates, as might be expected, under a CC license but that it *also* reserves standard copyright to each author for their "original texts and remixes" (2014, n.pag.). This seeming anomaly – the equivalent of having a bet each way – could be attributable to the logos of various national, state, and university cultural funding entities also listed on the reverse title page and may have been a precondition of their support. More intriguing from the perspective of digital literature's long championing of textual instability is Groth's insistence in his Introduction that remixing is "not fan fiction" but rather "a creative act," as though the pop-cultural, low-status associations of fanfic might tarnish the literary aspirations of his project, its funders, and (presumably) its writers (iii). This is in spite of the fact that the remixing techniques that underpin the project are immediately reminiscent of the kinds of fanfic practices engaged in by millions of writers on portals such as Archive of Our Own[5] and Fanfiction.net.[6] It seems a pointed instance of eLit experimentalism cutting adrift popular culture practices in its insistence on its own elevated artistic status, implicitly positing popularity as incompatible with avant-garde aesthetics. Granted, *Lost in Track Changes* is alert to the fact that its invitation-only authorial roll-call appears exclusionary, and takes pains in its paratextual matter to invite broader readerly participation. Groth's Introduction challenges readers to scribble in the margins, "cross this sentence out" or even "while you're at it, cross this whole paragraph out" if they feel they could write a better one (i). Similarly, an afterword appended to the print version offers a flash-fiction challenge for readers to write their own remix of a given 150-word story (216). Nevertheless, all of this metafictional breaking of the fourth wall cannot quite disguise the fact that the anthology's commitment to democratic participation is more theoretical than actual, and that the quality of the remixes preserved between its covers depends upon a stringent degree of editorial exclusion. Unstable texts and a free-for-all attitude to cultural property are all very well but, as Michael Joyce wrote of his original

Storyspace hypertext fiction *afternoon*, seemingly only "according to some scheme I had predetermined" (1995, 31).

Fanfic/Print/eLit Interplay

Over roughly the last decade, one publication above all others has brought fanfic to mainstream attention and highlighted its potential interplay with the print publishing industry: the transmedial phenomenon that is E.L. James's *Fifty Shades of Grey* (2011). Yet, for the eLit community, this sets a problematic precedent both because the book's origins in the world of collaborative writing are complex, and because its flagrant indifference to literary standards runs counter to the high-Modernist aesthetic underpinning the Electronic Literature Organization (ELO).[7] If anything, the extraordinary commercial success of the *Fifty Shades* five-book series (2011–17) suggests that collaborative authorship and artistic standards exist in inverse proportion, and that eLit adherents cannot pursue both goals simultaneously.

Over 100 chapters of the erotic *Twilight* fanfic that became *Fifty Shades of Grey* were first released during 2009–10 on fanfiction.net under the title *Master of the Universe* by a writer using the pseudonym 'Snowqueens Icedragon' (Guthrie 2013). The chapters generated such high levels of site traffic, word-of-mouth publicity, and online reviews by beta-reader editors that James (another pseudonym) secured a hardcopy publishing contract with an Australian self-publishing outfit, and later with the Vintage imprint of conglomerate Random House, which bought out the rights from the previous publisher (Jones 2014). As a condition of corporate publication, all James's fanfics were taken down so that rival content was not available for free, and the title and character names were changed to minimize the *Twilight* connection (and hence the risk of litigation for copyright infringement by Stephanie Meyer or her publisher). Vintage claimed that *Fifty Shades* was a distinct and separate work, despite amateur comparisons using Turnitin antiplagiarism software finding an 89% similarity with *Master of the Universe* (Jones 2014; Mulligan 2015).

Such 'filing the serial numbers off' *Fifty Shades* to disguise its fanfic origins caused disquiet within the fan community because James had benefitted from its gift economy, but then appropriated the financial benefits of print publication under a decidedly old-fashioned version of the singular author function. This was deemed especially problematic because "one of the major fannish mores is to never profit materially from one's writing" (Coker 2017). From a theoretical perspective, James's and Vintage's move appears particularly hypocritical given that *Fifty Shades* is itself an intertext of an in-copyright work—Meyer's *Twilight* series, which is in turn an intertext to the whole vampire genre from Bram Stoker's *Dracula* (1897) onwards.[8] Moreover, Meyer herself had cut her teeth writing in the fanfic community (Guthrie 2013). The manifest instability of this text and its tendency to elude singular conceptions of intellectual property foreground the key issue at stake in fanfic: can anyone ever *own* a story?

For the university-based eLit community, by contrast, the stakes were different. The *Fifty Shades* phenomenon disproves 1990s eLit theorists' assertion that digital platforms would replace print, as here digital collaborative spaces serve as incubators for products then pulled for publication at low risk by legacy print publishers. Moreover, the irredeemably trashy reputation attaching to this bestseller phenomenon threatens to undo eLit proponents' decades of lobbying to secure academic respectability for born-digital works. Certainly, *Fifty Shades* demonstrates popularity on a scale inconceivable for niche artefacts of the eLit community. However, its decidedly retrograde gender politics and willful flouting of artistic standards jeopardize the ELO's campaign of showcases at events such as the Modern Language Association Convention to have eLit works taken seriously within the academy – as texts commensurate with, though medially distinct from, the Anglo-American print canon.[9] In throwing open the doors to the popular, the quality claims on which the eLit movement is rhetorically based are destabilized, if not discredited. This tension can be perceived elsewhere in eLit circles, such as prominent eLit scholar Astrid Ensslin's confession that, "In a field as fluid as digital literature, new, groundbreaking technology as well as writerly creativity proliferate new works, most of which, sadly, do not meet the standards of an experienced literary scholar" (2006). Or consider James O'Sullivan's recent lament:

> We are seeing at present an increasing number of writers do very trivial and esthetically [sic] uninteresting things with computers and calling it electronic/digital/multimodal literature, representing the field of practice in a way that makes me, as a scholar and practitioner who has invested their intellectual time and professional labor in this space, deeply uncomfortable.
>
> (2021, 264)

Perhaps this conflict's most piquant incarnation was ELO President Leonardo Flores's positing of a so-called 'third generation' of eLit in his presentation to the organization's 2018 conference. Flores argued that, in order to survive as a field, eLit must include works made on popular social-media platforms and apps where audiences already congregate and are familiar with the interfaces' affordances. Doing so requires a shift from an aesthetics informed by hieratic Modernist difficulty to embrace of a postmodern cultural poetics of remix and pastiche (Flores 2019).[10] These sentiments met with significant pushback from ELO founders, who questioned both Flores's division of eLit into generations as well as his closing contention that eLit faced cultural extinction if it failed to effect such a pivot. The incident highlights how the eLit movement's long investment in unstable texts has been highly conditional on a singular, credentialed author pulling the strings of readerly exploration, and how texts so fluid that they evade authorial control – or even attribution – clash with the latent Romanticist precepts lingering at the movement's core.

Conclusion

Early in the eLit era, things appeared less complicated. In "The End of Books" (1992), Robert Coover, writing about activities of graduates in his MFA workshop at Brown University, introduced "Hypertext Hotel" – a "group fiction space" in which students were free to add to, rework, or "sabotage" the anonymous stories others wrote about the happenings inside the many rooms of a fictional hotel. Whether collaborative creation is in fact innately liberatory or valuable was never explicitly rationalized during this period, revealing a rather naïve faith in the novelty of interactivity that is harder to sustain amidst current calls for regulation of social media. While Coover praised the writing experiment's unfolding anarchy, attempts to replicate such principles on a mass scale, along the lines of *A Million Penguins*, have proven deeply flawed. Hence, each of the eLit collaborative writing experiments examined here has corralled reader-user participation within set confines, either by authorizing an editorial team to make final selections from submitted remixes, by reserving overall control over plotlines and characterization to an inner sanctum of non-writing 'composers', or by handpicking established literary authors to rewrite each other's work, relying on demonstrated expertise and professional respect to ensure things do not go so far off the rails as to alienate cultural policy and university funders. In the era of what John Vallier terms "post-individualistic authorship," these seem necessary concessions to preserve eLit's USP of the unstable, mutating, ever-protean text (2018, 39).

Yet, it is becoming increasingly apparent how much of eLit's *theoretical* embrace of textual instability depended in practice on unwritten understandings about project scale, participant background, and aesthetic "quality." In the era of Web 2.0, these tacit agreements can no longer be sustained nor justified. At the core of the conundrum eLit presently faces is the lag time between theoretical pronouncement and technological possibility. Theorists of the 1990s rhetorically championed empowered reader-authors, though in actuality the cost and programming complexity of eLit software erected barriers to entry for most people. This dichotomy enabled the ELO to remain vague about the exact limits to its understanding of "participation," even regarding more ostensibly open, "constructive" hypertexts. Yet now that social-media platforms and apps enable all and sundry to create and globally circulate remixed digital texts with ease, the theory–technology gap on the ELO's part has become glaringly evident. Which way should the ELO jump? Fully embracing participation threatens the neo-Modernist artistic standards in which the community has been so invested since its origins, as well as the laborious bridge-building it has undertaken to convince a frankly skeptical literary studies mainstream of eLit's value. But to continue to hold the line against mass digital creativity threatens to sideline the ELO, estranging it from potential supporters and fellow-travelers, rendering it an esoteric byway on the digital superhighway (to employ a metaphor from eLit's 1990s naissance). In such a situation, something has to give. The eLit community globally must choose between the never-entirely-disavowed cultural hierarchies of literary studies, or embrace the cultural relativism and sociological schema dominant in digital media studies – the two main tributaries from which eLit derives (Hayles 2008, 30). As recent third-generation debates highlight, it is becoming increasingly untenable for eLit to maintain a foot in both camps (Skains 2023). At a minimum, the eLit community needs to undertake a frank stocktaking and far-reaching examination of its theoretical, disciplinary, and institutional priorities to move forward into the third decade of the digital century.

Notes

1. The eLit community is centred upon the Electronic Literature Organization (ELO) and eLit as a genre has almost no profile nor constituency outside of public sector-supported spaces. This fact was indirectly acknowledged by the Reading Digital Fiction project's launch in 2016 of the Opening Up Digital Fiction Writing Competition, designed "to expand digital fiction readership to include a broader segment of the public." https://readingdigitalfiction.com/writing-competition/
2. https://collection.eliterature.org/3/collection-taroko.html
3. "What today appears not to be a novel as we know it may in time to be seen as one… . But for the moment at least the answer to whether or not a community can write a novel appears to be 'not like this'" (Mason and Thomas 2008, 20–21).
4. Refer also Santoni's comments in his joint blog interview (2016): https://readingitaly.wordpress.com/2016/10/03/collective-writing-memory/
5. https://archiveofourown.org/
6. https://www.fanfiction.net/
7. https://eliterature.org/
8. On Stoker's *Dracula* as the source for a flood of screen and print adaptations, see Leitch, 2007: 108.
9. Refer, for example: https://www.youtube.com/watch?v=YVsPu2k7khI
10. See also Flores's 2020 ELO presentation "Decentering E-literary History": https://www.youtube.com/watch?v=1f2PpLyt6jk.

Bibliography

Aarseth, Espen. 1997. *Cybertext: Perspectives on Ergodic Literature*. Baltimore, MD: Johns Hopkins UP.
Barker, Amy, ed. 2009. *Through the Clock's Workings*. Sydney: Sydney UP.
Berens, Kathi Inman. 2020. "'Decolonize' E-Literature?: On Weeding the E-lit Garden." *Electronic Book Review* 5 Jul. https://doi.org/10.7273/svqq-ab68
Bolter, Jay David. 1991. *Writing Space: The Computer, Hypertext, and the History of Writing*. Mahwah, NJ: Lawrence Erlbaum Associates.
———. 2011. *Writing Space: Computers, Hypertext, and the Remediation of Print*. New York: Routledge.

Coker, Catherine. 2017. "The Margins of Print? Fan Fiction as Book History." *Transformative Works and Cultures* 25 http://dx.doi.org/10.3983/twc.2017.1053

Coover, Robert. 1992. "The End of Books." *New York Times Book Review*, June 21, 1992. www.nytimes.com/books/98/09/27/specials/coover-end.html

Ensslin, Astrid. 2006. "Hypermedia and the Question of Canonicity." *dichtung-digital* 36 www.dichtung-digital.org/2006/1-Ensslin.htm

———. 2007. *Canonizing Hypertext: Explorations and Constructions*. London: Continuum.

Flores, Leonardo. 2019. "Third Generation Electronic Literature." *Electronic Book Review* 7 Apr. https://doi.org/10.7273/axyj-3574

Foucault, Michel. 2006. "What Is an Author?" [1969] In *The Book History Reader*. 2nd ed., edited by David Finkelstein and Alistair McCleery, 281–91. Abingdon, Oxon: Routledge.

Friedlander, Larry. 2008. "Narrative Strategies in a Digital Age: Authorship and Authority." In *Digital Storytelling, Mediatized Stories: Self-Representation in New Media*, edited by Knut Lundby, 177–96. New York: Peter Lang.

Groth, Simon, ed. 2014. *Lost in Track Changes*. Brisbane: if:book Australia.

Guthrie, Meredith. 2013. "Whatever You Do, Don't Call It 'Mommy Porn': *Fifty Shades of Grey*, Fan Culture, and the Limits of Intellectual Property Rights." *Infinite Earths* October 8, 2013. - D-Scholarship@Pitt.

Hayles, N. Katherine. 2008. *Electronic Literature: New Horizons for the Literary*. Notre Dame, IA: University of Notre Dame P.

Hellekson, Karen, and Kristina Busse, eds. 2006. *Fan Fiction and Fan Communities in the Age of the Internet: New Essays*. Jefferson, NC: McFarland.

Heron, Michael James, and Pauline Helen Belford. 2015. "All of Your Co-Workers Are Gone: Story, Substance, and the Empathic Puzzler." *Journal of Games Criticism* 2: 1. http://gamescriticism.org/articles/heronbelford-2-1

Jenkins, Henry. 2006. *Convergence Culture: Where Old and New Media Collide*. New York: New York UP.

Jones, Bethan. 2014. "Fifty Shades of Exploitation: Fan Labor and *Fifty Shades of Grey*." *Transformative Works and Cultures* 15 https://doi.org/10.3983/twc.2014.0501

Joyce, Michael. 1988. "Siren Shapes: Exploratory and Constructive Hypertexts." *Academic Computing* 3: 10–14.

———. 1995. *Of Two Minds: Hypertext Pedagogy and Poetics*. Ann Arbor, MI: U of Michigan P.

Landow, George P. 1992. *Hypertext: The Convergence of Contemporary Critical Theory and Technology*. Baltimore, MD: Johns Hopkins UP.

Leitch, Thomas. 2007. *Film Adaptation and Its Discontents*. Baltimore, MD: Johns Hopkins UP.

Lessig, Lawrence. 2008. *Remix: Making Art and Commerce Thrive in the Hybrid Economy*. New York: Penguin Press.

Manovich, Lev. 2001. *The Language of New Media*. Cambridge, MA: MIT Press.

Mason, Bruce, and Sue Thomas. 2008. *A Million Penguins Research Report*. Institute of Creative Technologies, De Montfort University, UK. www.ioct.dmu.ac.uk/documents/amillionpenguinsreport.pdf

Middleton, Kim. 2020. "Remix." *Digital Pedagogy in the Humanities*. MLA Commons Digital Pedagogy | Remix hcommons.org.

Miller, Laura. 1998. "www.claptrap.com." *New York Times Book Review*, March 15, 1998. www.nytimes.com/1998/03/15/books/bookend-wwwclaptrap com.html.
Mulligan, Christina. 2015. "The Most Scandalous Part of 'Fifty Shades of Grey' isn't the Sex and Bondage." *Washington Post*, February 12, 2015.
Murray, Simone. 2010. "'Remix My Lit': Towards an Open Access Literary Culture." *Convergence* 16, no. 1: 23–38.
———. 2019. "Authorship." In *The Oxford Handbook of Publishing*, edited by Angus Phillips and Michael Bhaskar, 39–54. Oxford: Oxford UP.
Navas, Eduardo. 2012. *Remix Theory: The Aesthetics of Sampling*. Vienna: Springer.
Navas, Eduardo, Owen Gallagher, and xtine burrough, eds. 2018. *Keywords in Remix Studies*. London and New York: Routledge.
O'Neill, Ryan. 2016. *Their Brilliant Careers: The Fantastic Lives of Sixteen Extraordinary Australian Writers*. Melbourne: Black Inc.
O'Sullivan, James. 2021. "Publishing Electronic Literature." In *Electronic Literature as Digital Humanities: Contexts, Forms, and Practices*, edited by Dene Grigar and James O'Sullivan, 253–266. New York: Bloomsbury Academic.
Parks, Tim. 2002. "Tales Told by the Computer." *New York Review of Books*, October 24, 2002. monash.edu.au.
Pauli, Michelle. 2007. "Penguin Plans 'wiki-novel'." *The Guardian* February 1, 2007. www.theguardian.com/books/2007/feb/01/news.michellepauli.
Pettitt, Tom. 2007. "Before the Gutenberg Parenthesis: Elizabethan-American Compatibilities." Plenary presentation to Media in Transition 5 conference, MIT, MA. Microsoft Word – Gutenberg.L-Plenary2.doc mit.edu.
Pressman, Jessica. 2014. *Digital Modernism: Making it New in New Media*. New York: Oxford UP.
"Remix My Lit---Literary Mashups." 2008. *The Book Show*, ABC-Radio National November 13. Australian Broadcasting Corporation.
Rettberg, Scott. 2018. *Electronic Literature*. Cambridge: Polity.
Santoni, Vanni. 2014. "Collective Writing and the Historical Novel in the Information Age: The SIC Method." *Scrittura Industriale Collettiva* (Spring): 14–15. www.scritturacollettiva.org/files/uploaded/file/sic_bm_s14.pdf
Scrittura Industriale Collettiva. 2013. *In Territorio Nemico*. Rome: Edizioni minimum fax.
Skains, R. Lyle. 2023. *Neverending Stories: The Popular Emergence of Digital Fiction*. New York: Bloomsbury Academic.
Solway, David. 2011. "On Hypertext, or Back to the Landau." *Academic Questions* 24, no. 3: 341–350.
Tushnet, Rebecca. 2017. "Copyright Law, Fan Practices, and the Rights of the Author." In *Fandom: Identities and Communities in a Mediated World*, 2nd ed., edited by Cornel Sandvoss, Jonathan Gray, and C. Lee Harrington, 60–71. New York: New York UP.
Vallier, John. 2018. "Authorship." In *Keywords in Remix Studies*, edited by Eduardo Navas, Owen Gallagher, and xtine burrough, 33–42. London and New York: Routledge.
Wreden, Davey, and William Pugh. 2011. *The Stanley Parable*. https://store.steampowered.com/app/221910/The_Stanley_Parable/

2 Diverse Mappings of Electronic Literature

Expanding the Canon(s)

Mariusz Pisarski

Everyday thousands of pieces and types of writing are born and distributed on social media. As text-based and digital-born artifacts, they are forms of electronic literature, regardless of their authors' intentions or awareness (Flores 2019). Making sense of such prolific literary production and forming bridges between the current generations of digital natives and prior literary traditions is an enormous task. While existing classifications of e-literature greatly contribute to such task by bringing order into an ever-evolving field, the sheer scale of digital works offered to contemporary audiences encourages scholars to expand established categories, propose alternative source materials, and introduce new conjunctions. It is especially true if one wants to embrace the notion of electronic literature as both a global and a local phenomenon, as world literature with divergent roots and multiple strands (Tabbi 2010, 20). Such diversification is necessary because while having a global, common denominator – the emergence of digital technologies – the field of electronic literature witnessed processes of canon formation similar to those in the print world (Ensslin 2007, 4). Consequently, a pattern of relations between hyper canon, counter canon, and shadow canon, a dynamic governed by the rule which David Damrosch describes as "the richest of the rich get richer still" (Damrosch 2006, 40), could also be observed here. Exposing divergent roots, variable timelines, and alternative classifications of e-literary practices might not in and of itself entirely prevent some authors from rising to the status of "hypercanonical celebrity" (Damrosch 2006, 53) at the expense of others, but at least these methods offer strategies to place the most often discussed works of digital poetry and fiction in particular languages (especially, English) alongside their counterparts from other languages and cultures.

My goal in this chapter is to offer alternative approaches to the established genealogies, historical models, and typological frameworks within which global community of scholars and authors discuss and practice electronic literature. The existing historical models offer either a generational (first, second, and third) or a Web-based classification (pre-Web, Web, and post-Web) of electronic literature. In my overview of these models, I will also pay attention to perhaps the most persuasive theoretical typology that

DOI: 10.4324/9781003214915-4

distinguishes between modern and postmodern e-literature. However, if one wants to look at e-literature as a global phenomenon and takes into account – for example – unequal access to digital technologies, some of the models will be of little use. What is considered the second generation of e-literature in the United States or Germany, turns out to be the first generation in Eastern Europe. Similarly, the distinction between modernism and postmodernism when used in a strictly historical sense loses its theoretical grounding when we agree on the existence of various modernisms across the global culture and the ever-changing perception of modernity, postmodernity and their relation to each other (Huyssen 2006, 1–3).

Therefore, in this chapter, I offer sets of secondary distinctions that allow for alternative groupings and ungroupings of the already established constellations of genres and generations of electronic literature. Each of these distinctions map a spectrum of approaches to artistic ideology (ontological/epistemological), medium transparency (immersive/emersive), semiotic resources (multimodal/transmodal) or semantic content (substitutive/associative). Although their use might be limited to a particular study or perspective, the strength of such categorizations lies in the ability to dismantle existing hierarchies and micro-canons within the established typologies, uncover works not widely discussed, and shed new light on diverse histories of electronic literature across the globe.

Existing Methods of Classification and Their Limitations

From its outset, electronic literature has been classified according to its software and system dependencies. In the early 1990s, for example, literary works that employed affordances of pre-Web hypertext systems could be conveniently labelled hypertext fiction and poetry. In the similar fashion one could speak of Hypercard poetry and Storyspace fiction to emphasize the specific tools in use. Software-based typology functions as fundamental feature of a work's metadata in online databases such as ELMCIP – Electronic Literature Knowledge Base or the NEXT. However, with the development of e-literary practice the community of authors and scholars moved toward more general classifications.

Genre-Based

The most accepted way of reading electronic literature as an emerging cultural form was established on the occasion of the launch of the first volume of *Electronic Literature Collection* in 2006, and it was reinforced by editors of two more volumes, from 2011 and 2015. In his monograph *Electronic Literature* (2019, 3–6), Scott Rettberg, drawing from that experience, groups cultural artefacts and new literary objects of e-literature into five major genres: combinatory poetics, hypertext fiction, interactive fiction, kinetic and interactive poetry, network writing. A sixth group – "divergent streams" – contains locative narratives, interactive installations, expanded cinema, virtual reality, and augmented reality. Genre-based classification, according to Rettberg, provides a map to a certain territory, establishes a frame of reference, and develops a shared vocabulary for practitioners and scholars in the field (Rettberg 2019, 10). In this context, genres of electronic literature are closely connected to affordances of platform they utilize. This is not surprising. According to Edward Balcerzan, Polish semiologist, a genre is a reusable combination of artistic means that determines the composition (morphology) of text geared toward some communication goals, afforded by material and medium (Balcerzan 1998, 12). We can only speak of a medium, Balcerzan adds, if it can constitute at least one autonomous genre (Balcerzan 1998, 15). The close relation between medium and genre, with an additional factor of "material", can springboard further categorizations to expand their range or depth. The usefulness of genre- and medium-based typologies is proven almost on a daily basis because it is able to encompass many new forms. Some of these new forms, if the combination of artistic means that brought them to life is accepted by audience and reused by authors, will form their own generic constellations. Instagram poetry, gifs, image macro memes – not included in Rettberg's classifications – are bound to start their own generic families that will be embraced by future collections of electronic literature. Generic classifications, well-tried by hundreds of years of literary tradition thanks to their accumulative methods and measurements of social reception, seem to guarantee a stable way of reading electronic literatures. However, there are also possible limitations of such models. Firstly, when new technologies render old technologies obsolete and along with them make obsolete the genres associated with them. Secondly, when a genre develops only in certain regions and becomes country or culture specific. Japanese cell phone novel illustrates both of these cases: as mainly a local phenomenon, tied to a specific technological context, its role as a predecessor to serialized fiction on Twitter and to literary smart phone apps might be potentially left out from classifications based on global, mainstream, and contemporary practices focused on genre.

Generation-Based Classifications

Much more contested proposals are those founded on historical models. By painting a picture of electronic literature in broad brush strokes they initiate debates and, as such, may even look more exciting than generic models, but, if one wants to treat electronic literature as world literature, then historical models soon lose their descriptive power, especially if the projected timelines are tied to specific territories.

Periodization based on the notion of generations is a dominant and polemical example of the historical approach. For example, N. Katherine Hayles (2008) draws a line between the first- and the second-generation of electronic literature. The former generation is represented by stand-alone hypertext fiction and poetry, and the latter by e-literary production on the

Web. The typology also suggests a generational divide between established pioneers and new practitioners, between the closed and copyrighted distribution formula of older works, and the free for all, open-source approach of born-digital works of the Web. "Hypertext Killed the Cybertext Star", the title of Nick Montfort' essay,[1] aptly illustrates the formative years for many of today's leading authors. While reviewing key points of Espen Aarseth's seminal *Cybertext. Perspecitves of Ergodic Literature*, Montfort challenged the literary-oriented reader by emphasizing computational roots of electronic literature, which gave rise to IF or interactive fiction and MUDs (multi-user dungeons), and which – unnecessarily were deemed – "not serious" by those members of the hypertext community who saw the roots of digital literature mainly in poststructuralism of Roland Barthes and Julia Kristeva (Montfort 2005, 9). By doing so, Montfort demonstrated how finding alternative traditions can reinvigorate the field. Fifteen years later, a similar impulse to summarize the past and anticipate the future prompted Leonard Flores to expand Hayles' initial typology and introduce a tripartite model of e-literary generations. The third generation is said to encapsulate text-based works created on social media that developed "without the need for academia and its validation" (Flores 2019).

There is a problem though with historical models based on generation count that – by definition – starts with biographies of particular authors whose works belong to a particular culture.[2] In case of Hayles and Flores such sequence has its roots in the United States, in a specific socio-technological *milieu*. The conditions might have been different in other countries, especially when the unequal access to digital technologies is accounted for. The first generation of e-literature works produced on early PC computers and stand-alone authorial platforms, such as Storyspace or Z-machine and distributed by companies such as Eastgate Systems and Infocom, found its audience mostly in the Western countries. Its reception was almost non-existent in Eastern Europe, for economic reasons, or in South and Southeast Asia, for cultural reasons. As a result, what is considered the second generation of e-literature in the United States or United Kingdom, may well be the first-generation in Eastern Europe or South and Southeast Asia. For example, a polyphonic hypertext novel by Radosław Nowakowski titled *Koniec Świata Według Emeryka* (2001) initiated the first wave of Polish e-lit, although such Web-based work would be considered a second generation just across the border, in Germany. On the other hand, the third generation of e-literature, such as Twitter bots or Instagram poetry could be seen as the first generation in some African countries, where widespread of the internet arrived only with mobile phones and social media. A representative example is Angola. First works of electronic literature appear in this country in 2016 and 2018 with digital storytelling apps distributed on mobile platforms by Zuinder Manico and Bantu Games studios (Manico 2018). Even though Leonardo Flores' periodization took into account a wide-range of works from Portuguese and Spanish speaking countries, the model they were included in worked against them, because the generation count in the historical model was relative to one specific – mostly American – history of literature and technology.

Platform-Based Classifications

The relative character of historical models aimed at mapping generations of e-literature renders the very models atemporal and as such – of limited use. Soon after Flores' presentation of the concept of the 1st, 2nd, and 3rd generation of e-literature, Montfort (2018) offered an alternative: a similarly three-tier model of pre-Web, Web, and post-Web electronic literature. Despite the apparent similarity between the generational and Web-derived approaches (both consist of three parts and adhere to timelines) though, the focus of the Web-based approaches on a single, global technology, detached from biographies belonging to specific literature, makes this approach more universal and useful.

Digital literary objects were made before the advance of the World Wide Web (from IF text games to Eastgate's stand-alone hyperfiction), during its heydays (1996–2009), and after it was incorporated into the current "digital plentitude" of products and practices (Bolter 2019, 7–9), some of which are within the confines of the "walled gardens" raised by content curators such as Android Marketplace and Apple App Store. Yet because the Web remains a reference platform, it offers any contemporary author certain choices: one can publish outside the Web, just as before the invention of Tim Berners-Lee, on the Web, and off the Web, but within the confines of popular platforms such as Twitter or Instagram. Montfort thus assigns pre-Web, Web, and post-Web affiliations to the highly computational works published in the *Using Electricity* (2017–present) series at Counterpath Press, most of which turn out to be pre-Web. And here, perhaps, lies the most important difference between Flores' and Montfort's models. Contemporary authors can create a pre-Web project but cannot be at the same time regarded as the authors of a first-generation work. The latter – in Flores' model – belongs exclusively to the first-generation of authors. Of course, one can create a hypertext fiction on an old Mac on Storyspace 1.5. But this will be a retro-computing act of an imposter because first-generation e-literature is now a closed chapter. Platform-based approach to the practice of electronic literature, especially if it derives from the meta-platform – the Web – proves to be a potent, widely understood classification built not so much on historical timelines but on artistic choices of platform or mode.

However, an approach founded on Web-derived distinction is not without its limitations. The limitations come into view when digital-born works outlive their original platforms and – without losing their identity and distinct qualities – find new audiences in a changed software/hardware ecology. *The Book of All Words* by the Polish author Józef Żuk-Piwkowski – included in the 3rd volume of *Electronic Literature*

Collection (2015) – is an excellent example of this phenomenon. Created in 1975 on the Polish office computer MERA–303, Żuk-Piwkowski's text generator belongs to the same line of pioneering works from across the globe as Jean Baudot's *La machine à écrire* (1964) or Alison Knowles and James Tenney's *A House of Dust* (1968). They are results of early literary and artistic experiments with the clunky, industrial, pre-PC machines. Yet, in contrast to the works of French and American pioneers, *The Book of All Words* transcended its pre-Web condition. Newer versions of this Borgesian generator – which produces infinite word combinations of 26 letters of Latin alphabet and prints the results on demand – have appeared over the years. First one in 1987, as a pre-Web installation piece for the international exhibition Art & Communication; second one in 2000, and third one in 2009 – both on the Web. The author does not rule out a next, post-Web version (Piwkowski 2014). Thanks to the constant curatorship of the work, *The Book of All Words*, belongs both to the first and the second generation of e-literature; and both to pre-Web and Web modes of presentation and distribution. If an app version is released it would also render Piwkowski's work as a third-generation object. As such, this single work breaks the confines of both the generation model and the Web model of historicizing electronic literature.

The case of *The Book of All Words* also illustrates a rather widespread problem that plagues any study of born-digital literature: the problem of versioning. For example, Dene Grigar identified 13 different versions of Michael Joyce's *afternoon. a story*, a highly acclaimed hypertext fiction (Grigar 2020). Are we speaking of the same work if one person reads the early Mac version from 1987 and another the Windows edition from 2001? The differences between the two editions range from the reader's visual access to the structure of the work to significant differences in the number of words and lexias? If the "1997 Norton Special Web Edition", or the Polish online edition, count as second-generation, then Joyce's text accounts for more than a single object in library catalogs, critical overviews, or even in readers' memories. This way, *afternoon. a story* turns out to be a complex constellation of its own versions, emulations, and translations. The longevity of *The Book of All Words*, along with the raised awareness about material entanglements of electronic literature that defy our habitual preconceptions of the work as a single entity (there is in fact no "Book of All Words, there are "Books..."; no "afternoon.a story" but "afternoons...") opens a Pandora's box that would make many classification models insufficient. And not only those based along chronological axis. Andrzej Pająk, for instance, demonstrates how *The Book of All Words* – if we approach all its versions with their added features – is both static and dynamic, transient and intransient, determined and undetermined (Pająk 2010). Such findings indicate that unless one treats a work of e-literature as a hybrid – of modes, genres, and generations – descriptive categories will always be inspirationally volatile and in need of revisions because they refuse to offer relatively long-lasting picture of the field. In this light,

I will offer a few alternatives to frame born-digital literary works in later sections of the chapter.

Digital Modernism vs Digital Postmodernism

The conceptual dichotomy of modern/postmodern that dominated critical theory in the 1980s and beyond, has been expanded to include e-literary practice. After Lev Manovich applied categories of modernism and postmodernism to computer art, and Jessica Pressman elaborated on the notion of "digital modernism" (Manovich 2001, 225; Pressman 2014, 5) scholars were also able to identify digital postmodernism (Pisarski 2017; Flores 2019). In the context of electronic literature, the dichotomy (unlike in the case of print literature) is not of a historical nature and refers instead to artistic strategies.

According to Flores, digital modernist poetics are summed up as "make it new, make it difficult, make it international". Digital postmodernism is characterized by the poetics of "remix, pastiche, readymade, adapt". Another major paradigm shift can be noted in the type of sociocultural connections digital modernism and digital postmodernism make: the former – according to Flores – connects to literary tradition, the latter to "fandom and internet culture". I have described digital postmodernism as ludic, short in form, fast-paced, and fast-served. Although these distinctions can be contested just as the highly debated boundaries between (non-digital) modernism and postmodernism (Connor 2017), they provide a general framework for understanding contemporary production in the field of e-literature where pre-Web, Web, and post-Web literary forms compete for attention of the global audience.

Broad distinctions between digital modernism and postmodernism are much more useful for approaching *The Book of All Words* by Piwkowski than those based on generation and the history of the Web. The modern/postmodern framework makes it clear: the Borges-inspired, pioneering computer program created on the machine that could be accessed by only a select few was a modernist work. Even the "Web 2.0" additions in later versions that allowed users to add their own textual input – definitions of the word they select out of the infinite numbers of pages – does not push the work into the postmodern group. Unless, of course, a new, post-Web app of *The Book of All Words* fully connects to fandom and internet culture by means of ludic poetics and skillful deployment of other engagement strategies. In such case, the work would represent both digital modernism, with its earlier versions, and digital postmodernism, in the app version for mobile Web. Mapping electronic literature across the divide of modern and postmodern poetics has its advantages: in an instant it assigns the object of our study a recognizable artistic tradition, preparing it for further scrutiny for which – as too general and prone to contradictions inherited from the never-ending debates about modern and postmodern cultural conditions – such method itself is not fully suitable.

Conclusions that can be drawn from the short overview of historical and cultural mappings of electronic literature support a non-monolithic and hybrid vision of born-digital literary corpora, far from synthetic clarity and distinctively marked borders. This is especially true if some works, thanks to preservation efforts or continuous curatorship by their authors, attain a relative longevity and, to reach new audiences, migrate to newer platforms. In such cases, a single work can belong both to the first and the last generation of e-literature, to pre-Web and post-Web, to digital modernism and digital postmodernism.

Mapping electronic literature across the divide of modern and postmodern poetics has its advantages: in an instant it assigns a recognizable artistic tradition to the object of our study, preparing it for further scrutiny. However, as perhaps too general and indebted in debates about historical modernism and postmodernism, one cannot rely on such method alone.

Conclusions that can be drawn from the short overview of historical and cultural mappings of electronic literature support a non-monolithic and hybrid vision of born-digital literary corpora, far from synthetic clarity and distinctively marked borders, especially if these lines are drawn across single timeline (history of American e-literature) or one single platform (the Web). This is especially true if some works, thanks to preservation efforts or continuous curatorship by their authors, migrate to new platforms. In such cases, a single work can belong both to the first and the last generation of e-literature, both to the pre-Web and post-Web. The poetics-based distinction between digital modernism and digital postmodernism, although painted in broad brush strokes, prepares a ground for formal, nonhistorical and perhaps more flexible classifications.

Alternatives: Epistemological vs Ontological; Multimodal vs Transmodal; Substitutive vs Associative

Given that existing classification models are not able to serve as exhaustive descriptive tools for a single work or a group of works, other approaches become necessary. One way of achieving this is by identifying a "dominant"[3] of a subject in question. The dominant, a category popularized by Roman Jakobson and Russian formalists, is a focusing component of semantic, semiotic, narratological, or ideological nature. If one can identify a set of opposing entities within their respective focusing component, a vector of relations can be drawn that forms a foundation for a given mapping and classification.

Within the general framework of digital modernism and digital postmodernism, and within the broad historical context of e-literary generations, a space for various alternative classifications is not hard to find. If one continues to seek value in transposing the modern/postmodern debate onto the field of e-literature, one could, for example, expand on Brian McHale's distinction between epistemological and ontological poetics specific to – respectively – modernism and postmodernism (McHale 2004, xii). It takes just a short comparative survey to discover that the epistemological mode of pre-Web, first generation *afternoon. a story* is shared with numerous post-Web, third generation production on Twine platform, such as Zoë Quinn's *Depression Quest*. Numerous Twine games that helped their creators on their coming-of-age quests for self-identity (Salter, Blodgett, and Sullivan 2018, 3) might be off from Peter's peregrinations in the labyrinth of self-denial. Both *afternoon* and queer Twine games thematize "epistemological doubt, metalingual skepticism and auto-reflection" – traits that Douwe Fokkema, McHale, and other scholars attribute to modernism. The resulting connection not only detemporalizes Flores' generation model but re-evaluates Pressmans' definition of digital modernism.

Linguistically oriented pair of opposites – substitutive and associative writing – proposed by Manuel Portela in his study of electronic poetry (Portela 2013, 12), could be applied to a broader corpus of global e-literature and bring new insights in the world of text generators, kinetic texts, and hypertexts. If one, for example, could locate substitutive hypertexts and associative generators – traits usually attributed to these genres in a reversed order – to create alternative narratives within respective strands of digital creativity, then the benefits of such new classification might be far greater than those delivered by more abstract classifications. To make their impact stronger such narratives might want to rely on their own foundational metaphors and practices. Exquisite corpse – the Dadaist and Surrealist word game and procedure (Stockwell 2017, 102) – could be considered a foundational practice for substitutive writing, where the dominant element of the work's structure is the substitution of words within a rigid syntactical structure. However, in search of poetic roots one can look even further and consider word games, and poetic riddles of the Baroque period as the substitutive writings' *ur-text*.

The framework of substitutive and associative writing would inevitably connect artistic works that used to be far apart, for geographical or political reasons, such as the visual and concrete poetry of Augusto de Campos (born in 1931) and Stanisław Dróżdż (1939–2009) – both of whom inspired many followers in e-literary practice, and not only in Brazil and Poland. Code-driven works of John Cayley and Daniel Howe – such as the *Readers' Project* (2010) – perhaps only on this occasion might come close to non-generative, almost hand-written emanative poems of Zenon Fajfer (*Ars Poetica* 2009; *Powieki* 2013) because these authors explore the domain of trans-linguistic associations (from code to text to internet "common tongues" in case of Cayley; from text to book to body, in case of Feifer). Finally, trans-semiotic approach to electronic literature would befit its own counter-canonical configurations. Contemporary artistic strategies that draw from new developments in data processing and neural networks could be matched with traditional explorations of trans-semiotic and inter-semiotic potential of the written world across languages and cultures. Works such as Allison Parrish's *Frankenstein-Genesis* (2016) where techniques of vector representations subject language to manipulations usually made on audio or visual material suggest that a whole tradition of transmodal poetics might be due for re-evaluation. A distinction between multimodal and transmodal works could bring into focus an influential but undertheorized e-literary practice, one having to do with the problem of translation. Translation in electronic literature is interlingual to some extent, but in its most innovative instances it is also inter-semiotic.

Radical projects such as Eric Zboya's visual translations of Stephane Mallarmè's *Un Coup de Dès* (Raley 2016, 115) or literary experiments in data bending (Mason 2012) are worth mentioning here. It would be interesting to study whether the emergence of accessible computation techniques, the emergence of the Web and linguistic AI accelerated transmodal productions, and to what extent European avant-garde and post-war neo avant-garde were multimodal (rather than transmodal). It would be of interest also to re-examine works that can be positioned just halfway between multimodality and transmodality, such as Maria Mencia's *Birds Singing Other Birds' Songs* (Shackelford 2014) or Katarzyna Giełżyńka's filmtexts in *C()n Du It* (Marecki and Małecka, 2016). Both works thematize media translation and inter-semiotic transfers of linguistic content. Inevitably, when selected set of traits is investigated in a broad corpus, some works that have so far stayed in shadow may come forward and perhaps overshadow those that had stayed in the spotlight. If the samples for such studies come from various cultures and languages, the result might lead to redistribution of positions on the map of electronic literature. These are further directions to explore in digital literary studies and in the classification of literary texts.

Immersive vs Emersive Dominants

Because we are faced with digital objects with medium-specific properties, I intend to close this chapter with a dominant coming from outside traditional literary studies: interface. Studies by Marie Laure-Ryan and Alexander R. Galloway (Ryan 1999, 351; Galloway 2012, 43) demonstrate how interface is central to the operational, narrative and perceptual effects of a work, making it either immersive or not immersive. This effect also relates to what Bolter and Grusin call immediacy and hypermediacy respectively. In the first scenario, the user looks through the medium (its interface), in the second at the medium. Polish game scholar Piotr Kubiński proposes to rename the phenomenon "immersion vs emersion" (Kubiński 2014, 134). To the already established conditions for immersive experience (McMahan 2013) one can add that immersive texts comply to our habitual reading rituals and deeply ingrained modes of consuming narratives. Additionally, immersion is increased by an alignment of narrative content, or narration itself, with readers' actions while engaging with the work. Radosław Nowakowski's *Sienkiewicza Street in Kielce* (2003), an accordion book, which – when unfolded – spans over 10 meters long, invites readers to walk along it when reading. The story about an Australian professor who by accident found himself in a provincial Polish town of Kielce, is metonymically enacted by readers who walk along and around the 10 meter-long book, reading snippets of main characters thoughts and interactions with an unknown environment. Although experimental, the book is immersive thanks to the implied, "programmed", contiguity between the story world and the mode of its perception (Bazarnik 2019, 493).

Samantha Gorman and Danny Canizarro's app novella *PRY* (2013) is another example of immersive text. Through a careful balance between revealing a secret (the roots of war trauma, the details of love story) and hiding it, *PRY*'s storytelling puts readers in a comfortable position in which anything that happens constitutes another attractive element that adds up to the overall story. Stuart Moulthrop's *Hegirascope* (1995), on the other hand, is an emersive text. A 20-second timer built into every lexia forces each page to refresh and transfer the reader to another page, making the text extremely hard to read. Andy Campbell and Christine Wilks' *Inkubus* (2014) is immersive, because – even before its VR version – it takes its readers down a graphically rich rabbit hole of teenage girls' mind and body while the rhythmic exchange of text messages delivers linguistic content in sync with our daily modes of communication, making it transparent and in line with our daily habits. In contrast, Nick Montfort's and Stephanie Strickland's *Sea and Spar Between* (2010) is – just as *Hegirascope* – notoriously emersive. Every move of the mouse triggers different stanzas. Once the reader moves her mouse to a point where the displayed text remains stable, the generated content itself – a mishmash of poetic vocabularies of Emily Dickinson and Herman Melville – points her toward the algorithm and raises questions about how the work was made rather than what it semantically conveys. In these works, authors place readers' experiences on strategically different planes: in case of immersive works, the reward of reading is in the story world; in case of emersive works – in the very design of the work. A much less known example from Poland, *Sienkiewicza Street in Kielce* (2009), demonstrates that a work can be pointing both to its unusual concept and design (a 10-meter-long *leporello* type book) and to its story that subtly aligns with the actions of the reader.

The immersive/emersive opposition reveals patterns that otherwise might have stayed hidden. For example, electronic literature read in physical (or emulated) space tend to be immersive, because most often it engages the body of the reader by making it part of the interface. Contiguity between the text and the body makes the text instantly familiar and the reader more perceptive. In this respect, *Sienkiewicza Street in Kielce* stands side by side with the installation classic *Legible City* by Jeffrey Shaw and – when looking for newer examples – with Samantha Gorman's *Canticle* (2010).

However, the principle of embodiment as a vehicle for immersion does not necessarily apply to locative narratives. Although they also employ our body, they do it in a way that results in emersive experience. Dragging readers from one location to another – often in public, crowded spaces and asking them to use various devices to retrieve the text, makes storytelling hyper-mediated. Do locative narratives, such as *34 North 118 West* by Jeremy Hight, Jeff Knowlton, and Naomi Spellman (2002), which made readers wander around old LA railway tracks with early tablet PCs connected to special GPS cards depart from what Marie Laure- Ryan calls "the ultimate goal of art", which is to involve the whole of the embodied mind, the intellect as well as the senses (Ryan 2012)? Not necessarily. But they engage the embodied mind in an emersive, and not immersive, manner.

Conclusions

The proposed methods of remapping electronic literature bring tremendous opportunity to re-evaluate the canon. By canon I do not only mean an established, accumulated list of most quoted works, but above all a canon of perception: how the global community of digital culture scholars perceive electronic literature and what examples each of us have at hand when speaking with colleagues from other fields or with students in the classroom.

Canons are created by classification models, which mark the territory, draw lines, and invite further explorations. Canons can also, unfortunately, result in a form of a scholarly automatism and the explorations they invite us to make quite often tread along paths that were already taken. Abolishing the notion of canon, or any discussion about it, does not seem beneficial because, as David Damrosh points out, the forces of canon formation constitute a permanent feature of the literary discourse, even in postcanonical age, just as industry is still present in the postindustrial age (Damrosch 2006, 44).

The aim of this chapter was, firstly, to question the applicability of existing models. Secondly, I aimed to offer alternate ways of reading electronic literature as a territory of global practice. The practice of electronic literature, from multicultural and multi-language perspective does not run along a single timeline. In fact, as opposed to a timeline, a more suitable metaphor would be a heat map. Some e-literatures, thanks to technological infrastructure, institutional support or a strong tradition of literary experiments in their countries, may turn out to be more visible than others. Some may progress at an accelerated speed, close to overdrive; histories of some others may develop at a steady, slower pace. We can incorporate these to create a heat map based on selected traits related to medium-specific, semiotic, conceptual, or ideological conditions of e-literary practice. If, for example, we want to see when national literatures begun in different parts of the globe, a heat map of Eastern Europe or Africa would reveal a telling mosaic of countries, some of which would bear a mark of the first generation, most that of the second generation, but there would also be spots – in Africa – that mark the third generation of e-literature as a starting point for e-literary production in a specific country. However, regardless of how useful the heat map's visual overview might be, the generations-based approach would also reveal its main weakness: dependency on a nonuniversal criterion based on the Western timeline of digital literature. Linguistic and semiotic approaches, on the other hand, introduce their own internal measures, both qualitative and quantitative. Once we determine that a work is immersive rather than emersive, or that it employs ontological rather than epistemological strategies, we are ready to feed our research samples into the visual heat map – both as a metaphor and as an exercise in big data literary studies. This will in turn deliver a truly comparative study based not on external criteria, but on aesthetic qualities of studied examples. The results of such a study would uncover differences in individual approach to digital fiction and poetry by particular authors, countries, or – timelines. It would bring together works separated by generations, by languages and culture. Diverse roots and canons of electronic literature would be revealed.

My alternatives, based on pairs of opposites such as immersive/emmersive, epistemological/ontological, multimodal/transmodal, substitutive/associative are some examples of classification strategies that can be adopted. Every scholar can approach texts with a set of such vectors, depending on the object of study. The potential list of similar tactical antonyms is unlimited because it expands together with technologies that make electronic literature possible.

Notes

1 Montfort's title paraphrases the MTV hit *Video Killed The Radio Star* by The Buggles.
2 There seems to be also a fundamental problem with Flores' theoretical gesture of embracing almost all textual production on of Instagram and Twitter (outside of practical communication) as electronic literature. A study of "secondary modelling systems", which would transpose Jurij Lotman categories of signification processes needed in order for any text to be literature could bring some clarifications in this regard. In other words, it is necessary to establish when a tweet or Instagram becomes e-literature, before assigning literariness to communication practices outside of literature. Otherwise such gesture bears traits of theoretical imperialism.
3 The dominant, as a category, was widely used in Russian formalism and remains a useful tool for reading both a single work and a group of works. As demonstrated by Brian McHale, identifying a dominant in a group of works is able to illuminate larger literary formations, such as those of modernism and postmodernism. Jakobson defined the dominant as "the focusing component of a work of art: it rules, determines, and transforms the remaining components. It is the dominant which guarantees the integrity of the structure" (Jakobson 2002, 82).

Bibliography

Balcerzan Edward. 1999. "W Stronę Genologii Multimedialnej [Eng. *Towards Multimedial Genology*]". *Teksty Drugie* 6 (59): 7–24.
Bazarnik, Katarzyna. 2019. "A Stroll Through Polish Leporellos: Some" Liberatic" and Other Accordion-Folded Works." In *Die Geschichte(n) gefalteter Büche: Leporellos, Livres-Accordéon und Folded Panoramas in Literatur und bildender Kunst*, edited by Schulz, Christoph Benjamin, 487–510. Georg Olms Verlag: Hildesheim.
Benjamin Schulz. 2015. *Poetiken des Blätterns*. Hildesheim: Georg Olms Verlag, 487–510.
Bolter, Jay David. 2019. *The Digital Plenitude: The Decline of Elite Culture and the Rise of New Media*. Cambridge MA: MIT Press.
Connor, Steven. 2017. "Epilogue: Modernism After Postmodernism." In *The Cambridge History of Modernism*, edited by Vincent Sherry, 820–34. Cambridge: Cambridge University Press.
Damrosch, David. 2006. "World Literature in a Postcanonical, Hypercanonical Age." In *Comparative Literature in an Age of Globalization*, edited by Haun Saussy, 43–53. Baltimore: Johns Hopkins University Press.
Ensslin, Astrid. 2007. *Canonizing Hypertext: Explorations and Constructions*. London: Continuum Internation Publishing.
Flores, Leonardo. 2019. "Third Generation Electronic Literature." *Electronic Book Review*. July 4th 2019. https://electronicbookreview.com/essay/third-generation-electronic-literature/
Funkhouser, Christopher, and Sandy Baldwin. 2007. *Prehistoric Digital Poetry: An Archaeology of Forms, 1959–1995*. Tuscaloosa: University of Alabama Press.
Flores, Leonardo. 2019. "Third Generation Electronic Literature", *Electronic Book Review*, April 7, 2019, https://doi.org/10.7273/axyj-3574
Galloway, Alexander. 2012. *The Interface Effect*. Cambridge: Polity.
Grigar, Dene. 2020. "Afternoon, a Story Editions At-a-glance." https://dtc-wsuv.org/afternoon-with-afternoon/docs/afternoon-at-a-glance.pdf
Hayles, N. Katherine. 2008. *Electronic Literature. New Horizons for the Literary*. Notre Dame: University of Notre Dame Press.
Hight, Jeremy, Knowlton, Jeff, Spellman Naomi. 2002. "34 North 118 West". *Electronic Literature Collection vol 3*. https://collection.eliterature.org/3/work.html?work=34-north-118-west
Huyssen, Andreas. 2006. "Introduction: Modernism After Postmodernity." *New German Critique* 99 33 (3): 1–5.
Jakobson, Roman. 2002. "The Dominant." In *Reading in Russian Poetics. Formalist and Structural Views*, edited by Ladislav Matejka and Krystyna Pomorska, 82–87. Chicago: Dalkey Archive Press.
Kress, Gunther. 2000. "Multimodality: Challenges to Thinking About Language." *TESOL Quarterly* 34 (2): 337–40.
Kubiński, Piotr. 2014. "Immersion Vs. Emersive Effects in Videogames." In *Engaging with Videogames: Play, Theory and Practice*, edited by Dawn Stobbart and Monica Evans, 133–41. Oxford: Inter-Disciplinary Press.
Lyotard, Jean-François. 1984. *The Postmodern Condition: A Report on Knowledge*. University of Minnesota Press.
Manico, Zuinder. 2018. "Angola 360°", *MAELD (Multilingual African Electronic Literature Database)*. https://africanelit.org/

Manovich, Lev. 2001. *The Language of New Media*. MIT Press.
Marecki, Piotr, and Aleksandra Małecka. 2016. "AS - C()n Du It by Katarzyna Giełżyńska–a Case of a Total Translation of an Electronic Literature Work." *Miranda* (12): 12.
Mason, Stacey. 2012. "Glitched Lit: Possibilities for Databending Literature." *Proceedings of the 2nd Workshop on Narrative and Hypertext*, 41–44. https://doi.org/10.1145/2310076.2310086
McHale, Brian. 2004. *Postmodernist Fiction*. London: Routledge.
McMahan, Alison. 2013. "Immersion, Engagement, and Presence: A Method for Analyzing 3-D Video Games." In *The Video Game Theory Reader*, edited by Mark J.P. Wolf, Bernard Perron, 89–108. London: Routledge.
Montfort, Nick. 2005. *Twisty Little Passages*. Cambridge MA: MIT Press.
Montfort, Nick. 2018. "A Web Reply to the Post-Web Generation." August 26th 2018. https://nickm.com/post/2018/08/a-web-reply-to-the-post-Web-generation/
Pajak, Andrzej. 2010. "Modern Generators." *Cybertext Yearbook*. https://jyx.jyu.fi/handle/123456789/77573?locale-attribute=en
Pisarski, Mariusz. 2017. "Digital Postmodernism." *World Literature Studies* 9 (3): 41–53.
Piwkowski, J. Żuk. 2014. "Księga Słów Wszystkich Czyli Archeologia Mediów Po Polsku (Interview By Piotr Marecki)." *Przegląd Kulturoznawczy* 1 (19): 100.
Portela, Manuel. 2013. *Scripting Reading Motions: The Codex and the Computer as Self-Reflexive Machines*. Cambridge MA: MIT Press.
Pressman, Jessica. 2014. *Digital Modernism: Making it New in New Media*. Oxford: Oxford University Press.
Raley, Rita. 2016. "Algorithmic Translations." *CR: The New Centennial Review* 16 (1): 115–38.
Rettberg, Scott. 2019. *Electronic Literature*. Cambridge: Polity.
Ryan, Marie-Laure. 2012. "Narration in Various Media." In *The Living Handbook of Narratology*. Interdisciplinary Center Narratology, University of Hamburg. www.lhn.uni-hamburg.de/node/53.html
Ryan, Marie-Laure. 1999. "Immersion vs. Interactivity: Virtual Reality and Literary Theory." *SubStance* 28 (2): 110–37.
Salter, Anastasia, Bridget Blodgett and Anne Sullivan. 2018. "Just Because it's Gay?": Transgressive Design in Queer Coming of Age Visual Novels." In *Proceedings of the Foundations of Digital Games (FDG'18)*. 10.
Shackelford, Laura. 2014. "Migrating Modes: Multimodality in E-Poetics as Another Kind of Language." *Mosaic: A Journal for the Interdisciplinary Study of Literature* 47 (4): 99–118.
Steiner, Peter. 2007. "Matejka, Ladislav and Krystyna Pomorska, Eds. Readings in Russian Poetics: Formalist and Structuralist Views." *Studies in Twentieth and Twenty-First Century Literature* 31 (2): 472–77.
Stockwell, Peter. 2017. *The Language of Surrealism*. London: Palgrave.
Stockwell, Peter. 2012. "The Surrealist Experiments With Language." In *The Routledge Companion to Experimental Literature*, edited by Joe Bray, Alison Gibbons, Brian McHale, 64–77. London: Routledge.
Tabbi, Joseph. 2010. "Electronic Literature as World Literature or the Universality of Writing Under Constraint." *Poetics Today* 31 (1): 17–50.

3 Ludonarrative Postcolonialism
Re-Playing the Colonial Discourse

Souvik Mukherjee

In October 1997, Microsoft Games released a rather unique digital game where the player controlled an entire nation and created citizens and soldiers who could work for the state or fight battles to expand influence and bring more territory under the player's control. The game was quite obviously named: *Age of Empires* (Ensemble Studios 1997). Incidentally, 1997 also marked the beginning of Games Studies as a discipline and the decade-long ludology–narratology debate regarding whether videogames could tell stories or whether they were more about formal elements of play, such as rule sets. Ludologists such as Markku Eskelinen complained that "if and when games and especially computer games are studied and theorized they are almost without exception *colonised* from the fields of literary, theatre, drama and film studies" (Eskelinen 2001, n.pag.; italics added) while critiquing the work of the so-called "narratologists" who were linking storytelling in videogames with that in older narrative media. Since then, of course, the storytelling capabilities of games have been much commented on and there are positions that have brought the two apparently disparate strands of analysing videogames on a common ground.

Despite sharing its beginnings with a game so obviously based on empire, the analyses of games fail to even acknowledge the obvious endorsement of colonialism in these early theorizations of either storytelling or the formal rule-based experience of these games. Colonization may have been used as a metaphor by Eskelinen for describing the relationship between videogame studies and older disciplines but in the analyses of videogames that actually use colonization as part of their narrative context as well as their play mechanic, it has remained a veritable elephant in the room. Only recently, after over two decades of research on videogame culture, perspectives on Postcolonialism have begun featuring regularly in Games Studies.

Why did Postcolonialism arrive so late in Game Studies and why is colonial thinking still the norm in game design and gaming cultures? What is intriguing for the purposes of this chapter is not just the delay (or deferral) of Postcolonial thinking in reading videogames; it is the perpetuation of colonial thinking in both the formal game mechanics as well as the narrative contexts of digital as well as analogue games that is an even

DOI: 10.4324/9781003214915-5

greater concern. For this, it is necessary to think across media – from a board game such as *Settlers of Catan* (Teuber 1995) to a digital game such as *Age of Empires*. Together with the story and the context, it is also important to think about the rules and the algorithms. This chapter explores colonialism across ludic media, from analogue to digital and *vice versa*, and attempts to think through the process and the main contributory factors. While doing so, I also look at alternative design and story mechanics, especially coming from contexts outside of the Global North and question the default logic of colonialism in gameplay and code.

Colonialism in Digital Games

In the 1993, videogame *Doom* (ID Software 1993), known among gamers the world over for its mindless violence and the first-person shooter mechanics, the player is an unnamed space marine shooting his way through hordes of aliens and the undead in one of the moons of Mars. In strategy games like *Age of Empires*, the player controls a nation on a map viewed from an isometric perspective, almost a God's eye view, settling in newly conquered territories and exploiting their resources (such as stone, wood, gold and food). Humans settling in alien planets or conquering unknown lands also seems to be a guiding mechanic in games such as the *Civilization* series, *Empire: Total War* (Creative Assembly 2009) as well as the many SF-based games such as *Starcraft* (Blizzard Entertainment 1998) and *Mass Effect: Andromeda* (Bioware 2017) that are about settling or resettling galaxies. In *Age of Empires*, the player is tasked with building a town-centre (which can be upgraded if resources are available) and to farm, build and mine on empty land. As soon as they start building, players also have to expect attacks from rival factions – soon the empty space or *terra nulla* is covered with walls, armies and watch-towers that increase the line of sight into the surrounding dark space. As I say elsewhere,

> The sooner the player explores the dark areas of the map to reveal what is hidden, the better are the chances of finding resources such as gold, stone, wood, and food […] this is very similar to the colonial stress on mapping and surveying.
>
> (Mukherjee 2019, 161)

The game's insistence on upgrades in the technology-tree, one might note that "imperialism also involves certain key technologies (the gunboat, quinine, steamship lines, submarine telegraph cables, colonial railroads)" (Mbembe 2019, 9). Many such empire-building games aim to present a uniform colonial logic that is very Western:

> In the case of AoE, the '"empires" it represents from ancient history – such as Babylon, Greece, and ancient Japan – are each very different from the colonial systems of nineteenth- century Europe.

The game, however, makes all of them work by the same colonialist logic [...] Victory is usually achieved in the AoE games with the overthrow of the opponent governments and/or the destruction of their entire populace. The adversaries in these games are the "Other" of postcolonialism.

(Mukherjee 2019, 160)

There is, however, a continuing colonial agenda in digital games even 20 years later.

In the recent game, *Mass Effect: Andromeda*, spaceships from the Milky Way that reach the Andromeda Galaxy with the intention of settling its planets. As Tomasz Majkowski and Magdalena Kozyra observe,

[t]he two sentient races of Andromeda galaxy can be interpreted as a heavily stereotyped depiction of the native population of the Americas, with the Plains Indians, a noble yet backward culture of high spirituality seeking communion with nature, and the 'evil native empire' of Central and South America, conventionally (and inaccurately) depicted as bloodthirsty and governed by half-mad priests. This interpretation is reinforced by how the protagonist assumes the title of Pathfinder – a clear reference to the third installment of James Fenimore Cooper's Leatherstocking Tales.

(2021, 26)

Majkowski and Kozyra also point out the similarities of *Mass Effects* with H. Rider Haggard's Victorian adventure fiction (seeing an allusion in the protagonists' last name, Rider) and Cooper's *Leatherstocking Tales*. The popular models for the narratives in digital games continue to be those of Victorian adventure fiction, such as that of Haggard and R.L. Stevenson as Majkowski and Kozyra argue. In the just-released *Far Cry 6*, for example, Phillip Penix-Tadsen observes that "What *Far Cry 6* serves up is neocolonialism and cultural appropriation—with a wink" (2021, n.pag.).

Given the fascination of digital games with colonialism and the fact that from the very first discussions around games and storytelling, a whole range of positions in critical theory, from narratology and reader-response to gender studies, have been applied to reading games, the omission of such a well-known and current theoretical framework as Postcolonialism is surprising. Admittedly, Lisa Nakamura's *Cybertypes: Race, Ethnicity and Identity* (2002) addressed some important concerns of Postcolonialism but it was only much later that it came to the forefront as a key theme in reading games. Coming much later, after almost a decade, Sybille Lammes (2010) and Shoshana Magnet's (2006) work on colonial spaces in videogames, Hanli Geyser and Pippa Tshabalala's (2011) work on colonial stereotypes in *Resident Evil 5*, and my monograph *Videogames in Postcolonialism* (2017) are some of the earlier interventions. Meanwhile, similar work is being done in connection to boardgames and tabletop games by scholars such as Will

Robinson (2014) and Aaron Trammell (2016) on *Puerto Rico* and *Dungeons and Dragons*.

Boardgames and Colonialism

Boardgames have had long history of connections with colonialism. As Megan A. Norcia points out, the deep colonial resonances in games such as William Spooner's *A Voyage of Discovery* (1836) and John Betts's *A Tour through the British Colonies and Foreign Possessions* and their similarities to the colonial underpinnings of videogames are striking:

> board games were part of this story and [...] they, too, created evocative narratives of imperial tourism, yet nonetheless also promised more practical vocational models than the flashy heroes who appear throughout the century on the beaches of R.M. Ballantyne and in the stockades of Robert Louis Stevenson.
>
> (Norcia 2019, n.pag.)

It is hardly surprising that this preference for a colonial logic is carried into later games: "*Settlers of Catan*, by allowing its settlers to find the island of Catan in a similarly [E]denic state, reifies this myth, which helped to render American Indians invisible" (Loring-Albright 2015, n.pag.).

Older games ranging from the eighteenth century such as *Geographical Game of the World* (Bowles & Carver 1797) made in Britain to the twentieth-century *Africa Tahti* (Mannerla 1951) show a preference for the colonial mechanic. The premise of Bowles's game is that the colonialist narrative is like a benign game of mastering fortune. Centuries later, the *Africa Tahti* game repeats the same formulaic logic – as Faith MkWesha and Sasha Huber observe, the game "basically teaches children about how to exploit and colonize Africa without explaining what colonialism was" (Mkwesha and Huber 2021, 235). In Victorian England, other older boardgames were also taking a different form; the metamorphosis of *Shatranj* to the nineteenth-century European Chess was similarly influenced by colonialism as will be shown later in connection or Premchand's story. Norcia's point about the links of boardgames with Victorian adventure stories is usefully compared with Majkowski and Kozyra's reading of the videogame *Mass Effect: Andromeda*, showing a remarkable continuity of the same logic of colonialism from the early nineteenth century to the twenty-first.

Procedural Rhetoric or Allegorithm: Coded Colonialism

What Norcia describes as fundamental characteristics of such games that sent a clear message to the nineteenth-century players regarding the glory of the imperialistic project of European nations has a conceptual parallel in the case of videogames. Ian Bogost calls this "procedural rhetoric." For Bogost, the art of persuasion through rule-based representations and interactions rather than the spoken work, writing, images or moving pictures. This type of persuasion is tied to the core affordances of the computer: computers run processes, they execute calculations and rule-based symbolic manipulations.

(Bogost and Losh 2017, 764)

While Bogost claims that procedural rhetoric applies to videogames in a unique way, the similarities with boardgames are also more than evident from analyses such as that of Norcia and others. In this connection, speaking of Sid Meier's *Civilization*, Alexander Galloway observes:

If Meier's work is about anything, it is about information society itself. It is about knowing systems and knowing code, or, I should say, knowing the system and knowing the code. [...] To win, you can't just do whatever you want. You have to figure out what will work within the rules of the game. You must learn to predict the consequences of each move, and anticipate the computer's response. Eventually, your decisions become intuitive, as smooth and rapid-fire as the computer's own machinations.

(Galloway 2004, n.pag.)

What Galloway calls the "allegorithm" elsewhere (a compound of allegory, rhythm and algorithm, as one may assume) is applicable in videogames as well as, arguably, in boardgames. Galloway's allegorithm is somewhat more complicated in conception:

the more one allegorizes informatic control in *Civilization* [...] and the more one tries to pin down the ideological critique, the more one sees that such a critique is undermined by the existence of something altogether different from ideology. [...] To use the concept of history as an example: the more one begins to think that *Civilization* is about a certain ideological interpretation of history (neoconservative, reactionary), or even that it creates a computer-generated 'history effect', the more one realizes that it is about the absence of history altogether.

(Ibid.)

Meier's algorithms, argues Galloway, can only be a reductive exercise in modelling history. Instead, Galloway's "allegorithm" challenges the ostensible and purported ideology or as it were, moral. I would argue that this could happen in boardgames and indeed other procedural systems as well. It is the allegorithm that needs more attention – as it makes the procedural rhetoric not one but multiple. Nevertheless, in boardgames such as Spooner's *Voyage* or videogames such as *Age of Empires*, even if the allegorithm is found, the algorithm remains paramount and the logic of the game, its procedural rhetoric dominates interpretations. In

Galloway's (2004) view, "To win means to know the system. And thus to interpret a game means to interpret its algorithm (to discover its parallel "allegorithm")"; this, however, is often optimistic. In the majority of cases connected to colonialism and its perceptions in the Global North, the allegorithm, algorithm or procedural rhetoric, whichever framework one views the issue from, shows a clear bias for empire and colonialism.

One might conclude that this is a risky assertion considering that there is such increasing awareness of such issues in the wake of critiques by Postcolonial scholars. Sadly, such an assertion is only borne out by numerous instances, made particularly obvious by scholars such as Joy Buolamwini whose notions of machine neutrality were shattered when it became

> impossible for her to ignore that the algorithm in the software she was using, along with many other algorithms, was crafted for the faces of white men, or what she calls "pale males," embedding implicit biases and, even worse, creating the potential for direct and lasting harm.
> ("The Coded Gaze: Unpacking Biases in Algorithms That Perpetuate Inequity" 2020, n.pag.)

The realisation stemmed from the experience where a face-recognition algorithm refused to track the movement of her face until she put on a white mask. Shakir Mohamed, Marie-Therese Png and William Isaac use the term "algorithmic coloniality to build upon data colonialism in the context of the interactions of algorithms across societies, which impact the allocation of resources, human socio-cultural and political behaviour, and extant discriminatory systems" (Mohamed, Png, and Isaac 2020, n.pag.). If the algorithm or the procedure determines the rhetorical stance and impact created by the game, then one needs to watch out for the bias and the default algorithmic coloniality coded into the artificial intelligence (AI) as Mohamed et al. argue. Ruha Benjamin refers to such inequities as the "the New Jim Code" or "the employment of new technologies that reflect and reproduce existing inequities but that are promoted and perceived as more objective or progressive than the discriminatory systems of a previous era" (Benjamin 2019, 5–6), a clear and grim reference to the Jim Crow laws that legalised segregation in the United States from the late nineteenth to the mid-twentieth centuries.

Applying the broader definition of procedure to the rules, play requirements, formal structure and the algorithm of the game, as observed by scholars like Henry Jenkins (2007), there are obvious connections across non-digital and digital media. Such transmediality can, however, also serve to perpetuate existing inequities in the narratives that are read and played in the older media into those in the more recent media such as videogames. Roopika Risam makes a similar observation regarding the cultural record in general:

the hallmarks of colonialism in the cultural record – fissures and lacunas, politics of representation that render subjects of the Global South under the gaze of the Global North, and complicity in the act of world making – are being ported over into the digital cultural record, unthinkingly, without malice, in part because Postcolonial critique has not made many inroads in the practices of digital humanities.

(Risam 2018, 5)

Risam advocates a conversation between Postcolonial studies and technology studies to reveal how imperialism has shaped scientific discourse. She also speaks of how "digital archives perform and resist colonial violence" (Risam, 2018, 19) by intervening in the digital cultural record, understanding and questioning what is sanctioned by digital humanities scholarship and decentring the practices of digital knowledge production. Strategies such as those recommended by Buolamwini and Risam, in their various disciplines, would also be relevant in reading games as well; one could start with the code of the digital game and look back at that of the boardgames from this perspective.

The Postcolonial Ludic: *80 Days*

This chapter will look at two ludic texts in its attempt to highlight the implicit and explicit colonial coding of digital and boardgames. In questioning the colonial procedural rhetoric of such games, it will also be necessary to engage with concepts in Postcolonial theory. Inkle Studios' *80 Days* (Inkle Studios 2011), a videogame adaptation of Jules Verne's nineteenth-century adventure story, *Around the World in Eighty Days*, engages head-on with the imperialist agenda of Verne's writing and indeed, the nineteenth-century adventure story genre, which has already been discussed earlier. Meghna Jayanth, who wrote the script for *80 Days*, with all its numerous possible combinations of dialogue states that she wanted to use the videogame's hypertextuality and multiplicity to:

[E]nable us to tell the kind of story we wanted to be able to tell, to redress some of the colonialism, sexism and racism of the period. If you're inventing a world, why not make it more progressive? Why not have women invent half the technologies, and pilot half the airships? Why not shift the balance of power so that Haiti rather than barely postbellum United States is ascendant in the region? [...] History is full of women, and people of colour, and queer people, and minorities. That part isn't fantasy—the fantastical bit in our game is that they're allowed to have their own stories without being silenced and attacked. That their stories are not told as if they're exceptional.

(Joho 2014, n.pag.)

Jayanth, who originally hails from India, makes a statement that is a timely intervention in a medium whose history has been fraught with the use and the understanding of code within a colonial framework mainly connected to the Global North. The fact that *80 Days* factors in those who are silenced and attacked for telling their stories is significant. For those unfamiliar with the game, it is one where the player (in the persona of Passepartout, the French manservant of Phileas Fogg in Verne's novel) arranges the luggage, plans the itinerary and makes decisions from among options provided in a decision-tree. The player often encounters characters who would have been rendered "minor" and voiceless within the colonial apparatus. Gayatri Chakravorty Spivak's (2010) seminal essay, "Can the Subaltern Speak?" raises this question in Postcolonial Studies. By providing a voice to the otherwise minoritarian groups, Jayanth is addressing a key concern of Postcolonialism. In *80 Days*, one comes across a freed slave who pilots an airship, a version of the fabled city of Atlantis, which is a refuge of escaped slaves inspired from the mythical continent whose citizens have modified their bodies to allow them to survive under the ocean and a strong Zulu emperor who averts the European Scramble for Africa using an army of automatons. Jayanth also plays with the conventional procedure of videogames as Sabine Harrer notes, "the player can choose to ignore the implicit goal of traveling around the world in eighty days or fewer. [...] Exploration and the discovery of different endings supplant a clear win/loss dichotomy" (Harrer 2018, n.pag.). Harrer rightly identifies the postcolonial and post-binary identity politics of *80 Days* where the player may meet a former slave in New Orleans who has an ambiguous response to his family's history of enslavement or a gay love interest who offers to take the player to the North Pole.

Contrast this with the original novel by Verne, where the protagonist barely has time to observe the places through which he travels because as Mohit Chandna writes, the logic of colonial capitalism is that time is money and Fogg does not have time to waste. According to Chandna,

> [T]he novel is in many ways an excuse for putting on display the vast British colonial empire. No wonder that at times the journey takes the adventurers into locales that are nothing but exact replicas of British counties. At other times, the level of savagery or civilization of the stopovers is a function of their relationship to the colonizer.
>
> (Chandna 2021, 20)

The colonial premise of such popular and ostensibly innocuous adventure stories such as Verne's stories is important to highlight and as Peter Aberger notes, despite assertions to the contrary "[Verne] remains in the tradition of the eighteenth-century philosophes who, while deploring slavery, did not consider blacks as the white man's equals" (Aberger 1979, 201). Jayanth also picks up on this element as well as the way in which Fogg is described as the "white saviour" of the Princess Aouda. She writes that she loathes Aouda and that one of her first thoughts in writing this adaptation of the game was to address the problem with Verne's Aouda: "Aouda is not just Indian, she is an imperialist's vision of India: rescued from savagery and ignorance by the cool-headed rationality of an Englishman; a grateful bounty that delivers itself willingly into the hands of the benign master" (Jayanth 2014, n.pag.). In Jayanth's adaptation (or remediation), Aouda is a "sabre-wielding revolutionary leader, where she is not only not in need of rescuing, but in fact, sees herself as rescuer" (Ibid.). The *80 Days* takes full advantage of this ambiguity, and it recodes the procedural rhetoric of Verne's novel and adventure videogames in general to create a counter-discourse to colonialism.

Premchand's Colonial Gambit: Playing *Shatranj ki Khiladi*

If code can be described as "a cultural logic, a machinic operation or a process that is unfolding" (Berry and Pawlik 2005, n.pag.), *80 Days* provides a recoding in that it intervenes in the conventional logic of videogames. Such cultural coding does not necessarily have to be digital. Chess is well known as the favourite game of semioticians and mathematicians such as Ferdinand de Saussure and Lewis Carroll as well as pioneers of cybernetics and artificial intelligence such as Norbert Wiener (1948) and Claude Shannon (1950). Like the digital games discussed earlier, Chess has its own procedural rhetoric and its allegorithm.

Originating in ancient India as *chaturanga*, Chess later became popular in India as *shatranj*, which is what it is still called in Hindi and Urdu. Premchand's short story "Shatranj ki Khiladi" (Premchand 1994) translated as "The Chess Players" (Davis 2015), an important analysis of the procedural rhetoric of Chess. A reading of the game's colonial procedural rhetoric is quite unique to Premchand's story and its famous cinematic adaptation by Satyajit Ray. In Premchand's story, two chess-obsessed aristocrats in the kingdom of Oudh in India are playing the game near a riverbank as they spot the army of the East India Company advancing towards the capital, Lucknow, to depose its ruler, the Nawab Wajid Ali Shah. As they play on, their comments are of interest:

> Mir: "Yes, indeed it is – take that, check again! That's it, this time check is mate, you can't escape.//" Mirza: "Good God, you're very hard-hearted. You can witness such a great catastrophe and feel no grief. Alas, poor Wajid Ali Shah!"
>
> (Davis 2015)

Satyajit Ray commenting on Premchand's novel notes that "the beauty of the story lies in the parallel that Prem Chand draws between the game and the moves of the crafty Raj leading to the 'capture' of the king" (Ray 1989). A factor in the East India Company's success in annexing Oudh, as Derek Davis describes it, is the inaction of the Awadhi aristocracy in saving their king: "Two beings who had shed not a teardrop for their king surrendered their being in defence of a chess queen" (Davis 2015). Davis, however, mistranslates Premchand's text. Premchand's text mentions the *wazir* and not the Chess queen. The mistranslation is significant as the Chess queen is a Western import and not part of the original game of *Shatranj*. Ray captures the way in which European chess rules alter the experience and culture of Chess-playing in India and how this also symbolises other kinds of cultural coding:

> Nandalal: [...] The piece we call the Minister is called the Queen in the British game. And the Queens are placed facing each other. [...] And the Pawn can move two squares in its first move. When a Pawn reaches the eighth rank it can be exchanged for a Queen. [...] Mirza: But why change the rules?// Nandlal: It's a faster game. /. Mirza: So they find our game too slow?// Meer: Like our transport: now we're to have railway trains, and the telegraph.
>
> (Ray 1989)

Nandalal's intervention in the chess-game, here, is crucial. Absent in Davis's translation but keenly observed by Ray is the transition from the *wazir* (minister or vizier) to queen and the changes in the moves of the pawn (the same moves that allow Alice to become a queen and escape the Looking-Glass world). The game changes with the arrival of the queen, or in the parallel world of British colonial politics, the arrival of Queen Victoria, who would be crowned Empress of India in the years to come. The characters in Premchand's story compare the speed of the game to the introduction of the railway and the telegraph, both viewed as tools to hasten the reach of British colonial power across India. The rules of the Indian game are recoded to suit the European colonisers and this recoding takes place also on the level of the cultural coding and politics.

Conclusion: Playing Beyond Colonial Logic and Over(writing) Code

The two aristocrats in Premchand's story kill each other in defence of their chess *wazirs* but in Ray's film they survive and start playing the game with the new rules of European chess, as the British soldiers lead away their king into exile. Through the examples of a digital game remediating a nineteenth-century adventure novel and a short story about Chess that connects directly to a political narrative, what is obvious is how in both cases, the ludic code not necessarily be colonial by default and how it can be challenged when the game is, as it were, played using different rules. Jayanth plays with Verne's original story and creates a multiplicity of possibilities in digital media wherein counterplay to the implicit colonial agenda is made possible. Premchand and Ray both point towards how the analogue chess-game can represent a real-life situation of colonial oppression but in Ray's film adaptation, it is clear that colonialism is not part of the default code of the game but it is always already a possibility that is waiting to be actualised. Like in Jayanth's adaptation, however, both Premchand and Ray are also creating a scenario of counterplay where they are shaking up the notions of chess, life and colonial oppression by making connections and offering parallels between them. Analysing counterplay, Tom Apperley states that:

> Counterplay challenges the validity of models of play that suggest digital games compel the players' to play according to encoded algorithms, which they must follow exactly in order to succeed. Instead, it opens the possibility of an antagonistic relationship between the digital game and player. An antagonism that is considerably more high stakes than the player overcoming the simulated enemies, goals and challenges that the game provides, rather it is directed towards the ludic rules that govern the digital games configurations, processes, rhythms, spaces, and structures. Counterplay is evident where during the course of play the player produces results that were otherwise unanticipated during the design process.
>
> (Apperley 2010, 102–3)

Such counterplay is not just against the grain of encoded algorithms but it forms an allegorithm, something that lays bare the contrary logic to algorithms and ambiguities that cannot be resolved in the overt procedural rhetoric of the game. The way in which meaning is ascribed to games in their procedural rhetoric is ultimately a signification.

The colonial bias in the rules of a large number of videogames and boardgames, as shown at the very outset, is the result of such a forced signification. Just like the tyranny and despotism that is often connected with colonial regimes, the despotism of the colonial procedural rhetoric is overcoded in the rules of these games and the conventional play practices. Such signification can easily be overwritten and problematised with the making playful of the codes of such games and examples of counterplay can be seen in both analogue and digital games. Therefore, together with those who protest against algorithmic coloniality or the proponents of Postcolonial digital humanities, it is also necessary for games researchers, developers and players to employ processes of counterplay to unsettle the implicit colonial coding of games and also extend the disruption caused by play to fixed cultural codes of empire and colonialism. While the implicit colonial logic may explain the delay in the arrival of Postcolonial critiques of digital games and the continuation of such rhetoric in games today, it is also evident that such logic is neither originary nor final and that it is continually being challenged through the very process of play.

Bibliography

Aarseth, Espen J. 1997. *Cybertext: Perspectives on Ergodic Literature.* UK edition. Baltimore, MD: Johns Hopkins University Press.

Aberger, Peter. 1979. "The Portrayal of Blacks in Jules Verne's Voyages Extraordinaires." *The French Review* 53 (2): 199–206.

Apperley, Thomas. 2010. *Gaming Rhythms: Play and Counterplay from the Situated to the Global.* Amsterdam: Institute of Network Cultures.

Benjamin, Ruha. 2019. *Race After Technology: Abolitionist Tools for the New Jim Code.* 1st edition. Cambridge: Polity.

Berry, David M., and Jo Pawlik. 2005. "What Is Code? A Conversation with Deleuze, Guattari and Code by David M. Berry and Jo Pawlik." *Kritikos* 2 (December). https://intertheory.org/berry.htm

Bogost, Ian, and Elizabeth Losh. 2017. "Rhetoric and Digital Media." In *The Oxford Handbook of Rhetorical Studies*, edited by Michael J. MacDonald, 1st edition. New York, NY: Oxford University Press. 759–772.

Bolter, Jay David, and Richard Grusin. 2000. *Remediation - Understanding New Media.* Reprint edition. Cambridge, MA: MIT Press.

Calleja, Gordon. 2011. *In-Game: From Immersion to Incorporation.* 1 edition. Cambridge, MA; London: The MIT Press.

Chandna, Mohit. 2021. *Spatial Boundaries, Abounding Spaces: Colonial Borders in French and Francophone Literature and Film.* Leuven: Leuven University Press.

Davis, Derek. 2015. "Premchand Plays Chess." *Journal of the Royal Asiatic Society* 25 (2): 269–300.

Eskelinen, Markku. 2001. "Game Studies 0101: Eskelinen: The Gaming Situation." *Game Studies* 1 (1). www.gamestudies.org/0101/eskelinen/

Fernández-Vara, Clara. 2014. *Introduction to Game Analysis.* 1 edition. New York: Routledge.

Galloway, Alexander R. 2004. "Alexander R. Galloway: Playing the Code / Radical Philosophy." *Radical Philosophy* 128 (December). www.radicalphilosophy.com/article/playing-the-code

Geyser, Hanli, and Pippa Tshabalala. 2011. "Return to Darkness: Representations of Africa in Resident Evil 5." *DiGRA Conference 2011.* www.digra.org/wp-content/uploads/digital-library/11312.58174.pdf. [accessed 02 February 22].

Harrer, Sabine. 2018. "Casual Empire: Video Games as Neocolonial Praxis." *Open Library of Humanities* 4 (1). https://doi.org/10.16995/olh.210

Jayanth, Meg. 2014. "Don't Be A Hero - 80 Days the Game." *The Literary Platform.* July 30, 2014. https://theliteraryplatform.com/news/2014/07/dont-be-a-hero-80-days-the-game/

Jenkins, Henry. 2007. "Transmedia Storytelling 101." Henry Jenkins. March 21, 2007. http://henryjenkins.org/blog/2007/03/transmedia_storytelling_101.html

Joho, Jess. 2014. "80 Days Is the Alternate-Reality, Anti-Colonialism Adventure We All Deserve." *Kill Screen.* August 5, 2014. https://killscreen.com/previously/articles/80-days-alternate-reality-anti-colonialism-adventure-we-all-deserve/

Loring-Albright, Greg. 2015. "The First Nations of Catan: Practices in Critical Modification | Analog Game Studies." *Analog Game Studies* 2 (November). https://analoggamestudies.org/2015/11/the-first-nations-of-catan-practices-in-critical-modification/

Magnet, Shoshana. 2006. "Playing at Colonization Interpreting Imaginary Landscapes in the Video Game Tropico." *Journal of Communication Inquiry* 30 (2): 142–62.

Majkowski, Tomasz Z., and Magdalena Kozyra. 2021. "Lost Worlds of Andromeda. Mass Effect: Andromeda and the Victorian Adventure Novel for Boys." *Studia Humanistyczne AGH* 2021 (2): 23–40. https://doi.org/10.7494/human.2021.20.2.23

Mbembe, Achille. 2019. *Necropolitics*. Durham, NC: Duke University Press.

Mkwesha, Faith, and Sasha Huber. 2021. "Rethinking Design: A Dialogue on Anti-Racism and Art Activism from a Decolonial Perspective." In *Feminisms in the Nordic Region: Neoliberalism, Nationalism and Decolonial Critique*, edited by Suvi Keskinen, Pauline Stoltz, and Diana Mulinari. Cham: Springer International Publishing. https://doi.org/10.1007/978-3-030-53464-6_11. 223–45

Mohamed, Shakir, Marie-Therese Png, and William Isaac. 2020. "Decolonial AI: Decolonial Theory as Sociotechnical Foresight in Artificial Intelligence." *Philosophy & Technology* 33 (4): 659–84. https://doi.org/10.1007/s13347-020-00405-8

Mukherjee, Souvik. 2017. *Videogames and Postcolonialism: Empire Plays Back*. New York, NY: Palgrave Macmillan.

Mukherjee, Souvik. 2019. "Age of Empires." In *How to Play Video Games: 1*, edited by Matthew Thomas Payne and Nina B. Huntemann. New York: New York University Press. 157–164.

Murray, Janet. 1997. *Hamlet on the Holodeck: The Future of Narrative in Cyberspace*. New York; London: Free Press.

Nakamura, Lisa. 2002. *Cybertypes: Race, Ethnicity, and Identity on the Internet*. London: Taylor & Francis.

Norcia, Megan A. 2019. *Gaming Empire in Children's British Board Games, 1836–1860*. 1st edition. London: New York: Routledge.

Payne, Matthew Thomas, and Nina B. Huntemann, eds. 2019. *How to Play Video Games: 1*. New York: New York University Press.

Penix-Tadsen, Phillip. 2021. "What Far Cry 6 Gets Wrong About Cuba." *Wired*, October 9, 2021. https://www.wired.com/story/far-cry-6-cuban-representation/

Premchand. 1994. *Premchand Rachna Sanchayan*. Edited by Nirmal Varma and Kamal Kishore Goenka. New Delhi: Sahitya Akademi.

Ray, Satyajit. 1989. *The Chess Players and Other Screenplays*. Edited by Andrew Robinson. New edition. London: Faber & Faber.

Risam, Roopika. 2018. *New Digital Worlds: Postcolonial Digital Humanities in Theory, Praxis, and Pedagogy*. Evanston, IL: Northwestern University Press.

Robinson, Will. 2014. "Orientalism and Abstraction in Eurogames | Analog Game Studies." *Analog Game Studies* 1 (December): 55–63.

Shannon, Claude. 1950. "Programming a Computer for Playing Chess." *Philosophical Magazine* 41 (314). 256–275.

Spivak, Gayatri Chakravorty. 2010. "'Can the Subaltern Speak?' Revised Edition, from the 'History' Chapter of Critique of Postcolonial Reason." In *Can the Subaltern Speak?: Reflections on the History of an Idea*, edited by Rosalind C. Morris. New York: Columbia University Press. www.jstor.org/stable/10.7312/morr14384.5. 21–78.

Trammell, Aaron. 2016. "How Dungeons & Dragons Appropriated the Orient | Analog Game Studies." *Analog Game Studies* 3 (1). https://analoggamestudies.org/2016/01/how-dungeons-dragons-appropriated-the-orient/

"The Coded Gaze: Unpacking Biases in Algorithms That Perpetuate Inequity." 2020. *The Rockefeller Foundation* (blog). December 16, 2020. www.rockefellerfoundation.org/case-study/unpacking-biases-in-algorithms-that-perpetuate-inequity/

Wiener, Norbert. 1948. *Cybernetics – Or Control and Communication in the Animal and the Machine.* Cambridge, MA: MIT Press.

Ludography

Betts, John. 1853. *A Tour Through the British Colonies and Foreign Possessions.* London: Betts.
Bioware. 2017. *Mass Effect: Andromeda.* Electronic Arts.
Blizzard Entertainment. 1998. *Starcraft.* Blizzard Entertainment.
Bowles & Carver. 1797. *Bowles's Geographical Game of the World: In a New Complete and Elegant Tour through Known Parts Thereof, Laid down on Mercator's Projection World Maps.* London: Printed for the proprietors Bowles & Carver.
Creative Assembly. 2009. *Empire: Total War.* Sega.
ID Software. 1993. *Doom.* ID Software.
Inkle Studios. 2014. *80 Days.* Inkle.
Mannerla, Kari. 1951. "Afrikan Tähti." Helsinki: Peliko.
Spooner, William. 1836. *A Voyage of Discovery or The Five Navigators.* London: Lefevre and Kohler.
Teuber, Klaus. 1995 *Settlers of Catan* Stuttgart: Cosmos.

Part II
Digital Embodiments and Disabilities

Digital technologies offer new sensory experiences, novel possibilities for imagining bodies and corporeal relations. This idea is foundational to artistic and narrative visions of living in a globalized, digital world. The idea is realized through myriad practices. A "cyborg antenna" attached to the skull of the Spanish-born British-Irish artist and transspecies rights activist Neil Harbisson converts color to sound. South Asian transdisciplinary artist Aminder Virdee's project *Exosomatic Echoes* (2021) disrupts ableist perceptions of the body through bio-digital, audiovisual art. Virdee notes that *Exosomatic Echoes*

> is an embodied audio-visual stim, transforming sensory experiences of medical rituals, pain, biodata, imagery, routines, sounds, memories, and the post-traumatic, into cultivated sites of radical crip agency. Here, the crip (disabled) cyborg body and technology is a site of wider possibility, and way(s) of being, that transcend preconceived ideals of able-bodiedness, aesthetics and normativity, and fuel re-making, re-worlding, and allow the re-imagining of disability futures.
>
> (n.d., n.pag.)

Both Harbisson's and Virdee's art expand the scope of embodiment in the current media ecology, though they differ significantly in their approaches. Narrative visions of digital embodiment spawning across a variety of modes and media oscillate between the utopic and the horrific. For example, the Netflix anthology series *Black Mirror*, focused on how emerging technologies impact societies, generally leans toward the bleak end of the spectrum with episodes like "Metalhead" where artificial intelligence (AI) is presented as monstrous, but the series also presents utopic visions in certain episodes, most notably "San Junipero," where simulation enables a blissful afterlife.

The cluster of chapters constituting Part II of *Global Perspectives* outline the contours of digital bodies populating narratives produced and experienced on digital platforms. Mejeur, Bimo, and Nandy, the contributing authors, are concerned with how digital media not only expand and extend bodies but also fundamentally reconstitute the idea of embodiment.

DOI: 10.4324/9781003214915-6

They are also interested in contemplating how digital media alter one's sense of self and mapping the affective attachments shaped by interactions in digital environments. Susan Broadhurst and Sara Price (2017) have observed that the digital body is "a body of infinite variability and creativity that is still linked with our everyday mode of 'being' tied to our locatable and temporal existence" (2). The variability of digital bodies challenges assumptions about the singularity and boundedness of the individual. In this light, Mejeur, Bimo, and Nandy chart the extent to which the experience of embodiment is both fragmentary and dispersed in digital spaces, reliant on co-creation and collaborative participation of others. At the same time, their chapters recognize the inequities and bodily vulnerabilities involved in digital role playing and self-making. That is, collaborative and interactive possibilities afforded by digital technologies are not beatific by default nor are they uniformly accessible. As C. Newell and G. Goggin (2003) have noted,

> the sorts of embodiment and subjectivity implied by hyperbolic claims about interactivity need to be scrutinized. The way interactivity is constructed discursively often naively purports to include people with disabilities, suggesting that the Internet offers us opportunities to be more active. However, the way that interactivity is framed creates new circumscribing ways of managing people with disabilities.
>
> (130)

Mejeur's chapter on the game *SOMA* critically examines hypotheses about the accommodation of bodily differences in digital futures. Mejeur considers how power and control obstruct the realization of utopic visions of embodiment presented in prior scholarship on post- and transhumanism. Nandy, on the other hand, performs a participatory critique about the possibilities and limits of inclusion in social media communities. She discusses how collaborative life narration produces knowledge about disabled bodies and transforms understandings of contested illnesses as well as one's experiences of one's own body.

As opposed to the discussion of social and ethnocultural identities in some of the other chapters of this book, Bimo's chapter analyzes the viral "creepypasta" narratives that make it difficult to pin down the origins of storytellers and thereby destabilize notions of authorship. The emotional cost of viral phenomena has been considered in discussions of politics and online activism. Anu Koivunen, Katarina Kyrola, and Ingrid Ryberg (2018), for example, discuss how campaigns like #MeToo and #BlackLivesMatter "mobilized enormous and powerful waves of feeling from compassion to guilt, from shame to rage" (3). While digital activism is considered at length in the third part of this book, the transmission and transmutation of affect come up in Bimo's chapter in relation to the virality of a narrative structure that materializes anxieties about surveillance and the loss of control over one's data.

Questions guiding this section of *Global Perspectives* include: what part does digital media play in the way we experience bodily differences and disabilities? How are practices of embodied self-narration and self-experience regulated and transformed in digital environments? How do digital fictions and practices of self-narration prompt and manage the hopes, anxieties, and fears related to bodily transformation and bodily autonomy across real and imagined geographies?

Taken together, the three chapters in Part II show how experiences and processes of embodiment prompt repetitive ruptures in one's sense of identity and reflect upon issues of empowerment, equity, and justice. Given their choice of case studies, Mejeur, Bimo, and Nandy also comment on long established literary genres like speculative fiction, horror fiction, folklore, and autobiography and the shape these take in digital environments.

It is worth noting that despite their overlapping focus on bodies, interplay of subjectivity and social life in a networked culture, the chapters adopt distinct methodologies. Mejeur uses play as method alongside other theoretical frameworks, Bimo performs a media-historical inquiry, and Nandy participates in the social media community she studies. Ultimately, this cluster of chapters sheds light on forms and strategies of bodily representation to comment on infrastructures governing and regulating the contemporary globalized culture.

Bibliography

Broadhurst, Susan and Sara Price. 2017. "Introduction." In *Digital Bodies: Creativity and Technology in the Arts and Humanities*, edited by Susan Broadhurst and Sara Price. London: Palgrave Macmillan. 1–7.

Koivunen, Anu, Katariina Kyrölä and Ingrid Ryberg. 2018. "Vulnerability as a Political Language." In *The Power of Vulnerability: Mobilising Affect in Feminist, Queer and Anti-Racist Media Cultures*, edited by Anu Koivunen, Katariina Kyrölä and Ingrid Ryberg. Manchester: Manchester University Press.

Newell, Christopher, and Gerard Goggin. 2003. *Digital Disability: The Social Construction of Disability in New Media*. London: Rowman & Littlefield.

Virdee, Aminder. 2021. "Exosomatic Echoes." *Aminder Virdee*. www.aminder-virdee.com/exosomatic-echoes-2021

4 Games as Critical Literature

Playing with Transhumanism, Embodied Cognition, and Narrative Difference in *SOMA*

Cody Mejeur

One of the great advantages of literature is how it allows us to examine the worlds we know and imagine ones quite different at the same time. Speculative fiction in particular has proven to be a broad genre across many media forms that is adept at addressing present realities through other futures, pasts, and dimensions. In this sense, to engage in speculative fiction (as reader, writer, audience, or player) is to engage in world-building—the process of generating *different* possible worlds, and through those differences to better understand our own (Ryan 1991, 51; Ryan 2015, 17). While instances of speculative fiction and world-building abound in novels, films, comics, and television shows, video games provide especially changeable and potentially transformative experiences of these literary processes because they allow players to become active agents in their possible worlds, determining to variable extents what characters will do and where, how their stories will proceed, and what the final outcomes of the narrative will be. In video games, the player is embodied in the possible world as either a preset character or one of their own choosing or making, and the player's actions as the character will determine what form and meaning the possible world will take. One game that exemplifies this using speculative fiction is *SOMA* (Frictional Games 2015), a science fiction survival horror game that questions what life and humanity would look like after humans as we know them today become extinct.[1] *SOMA* plays with the ideas of posthumanism, life after humans, and transhumanism, the evolution of humanity with technology, and provides a critical perspective on each.

SOMA takes place primarily in a postapocalyptic setting, specifically a research facility at the bottom of the ocean off the coast of the Iberian Peninsula after the surface world has been annihilated by a comet strike. The player character is a man named Simon Jarrett who underwent an experimental brain scan after a car accident in 2015 and wakes up to discover his consciousness has been duplicated and put into a new, female body in 2104. As Simon explores the research facility he (and the player) realizes there are no humans present, but only the imprints of human consciousness that have been imported to many of the facility's machines or preserved in human–machine hybrid bodies that are often enemies, providing much of the terror and danger in the game. Broadly, one can already detect some of the major themes of *SOMA*'s possible world: posthumanism in the life that exists after humanity, transhumanism in the transitions between human bodies toward a posthuman world, minds and cognition in the neuroscience and digital copies of consciousness, embodiment in the focus on bodies and experiences they have, and difference in how the game portrays different bodies inhabiting and navigating the world differently. The theme of difference in *SOMA* is an essential part of what makes the game a piece of critical literature. By representing how different bodies have different positionalities, experiences, and capabilities, *SOMA* provides a possible, speculative world that can reflect on the social, cultural, and political realities of our world. We are all embodied differently, meaning that to at least some extent we all think, play, and narrativize our experiences differently, a phenomenon I refer to as narrative difference (Mejeur 2020). Through its story and gameplay, *SOMA* reveals how the embodied, cognitive process of narrative works, including how it works differently for different people and what it might look like in the future.

Of course it is difficult to speculate about worlds completely other to, outside of, or after the human species, as *SOMA* does, and perhaps even more difficult to imagine how humanity could continue in such spaces. These questions have animated discourses in posthumanism and transhumanism for decades, and some recurring themes have emerged in speculative fiction playing with these ideas. Broadly speaking, the posthuman is the concept that a person or entity exists in a state beyond or after being human, and transhumanism is the process of human enhancement through technology that might lead to becoming posthuman. Donna Haraway's much-cited "A Cyborg Manifesto," for example, provides a vision of hybrid, fluid identities and coalitions that become possible when the lines between human and animal or human and machine become blurred, and a posthuman, postgender future emerges (2016, 5, 8). Similarly, N. Katherine Hayles (1999) posits that who we are and how we think is changing through technogenesis, a potentially transhuman process by which we coevolve with our technology into new forms of the human or posthuman (3). Some scholars, such as Martine Rothblatt, have noted the trans connections between transhumanism and transgender, suggesting that the process of transitioning from one state to another, including the freedom and fluidity of form that implies, contains liberatory potential for the human (2011, 2014, 317). In some cases, theorizations of the posthuman and the transhuman offer utopian visions of a world where divisions of race and gender no longer matter, and humans attain eternal life through technology (Blascovich and Bailenson 2011, 10). In each iteration of posthumanism and transhumanism, the concepts question what it means to be human and why humanity is or is not worth preserving.

Yet a question often elided in posthumanism and transhumanism is what or who is at stake in imagining posthuman futures. As critical race studies scholars have noted, it is conspicuous that these discourses emerged at roughly the same time (the latter half of the twentieth century) that critical race studies, feminist and queer studies, and postcolonial and decolonial studies were finally gaining footholds in academia. It is further conspicuous that many theorizations of posthumanism and transhumanism are built almost exclusively on the ideas of white, Western scholars (DeCook 2020, 1158). To put it another way, it seems convenient and dangerous to be imagining posthuman, post-gender, and post-race worlds at exactly the time when there was finally active, critical efforts to account for these concepts and inequities. How could we be posthuman, when so many were still left out of even being fully human? As Zakiyyah Iman Jackson notes, the concept of the posthuman is built on top of those it excludes, silences, and leaves behind, just as the concept of the human was built through appropriating and controlling peoples deemed lesser or nonhuman, such as Black peoples (2020, 1–3). There remain serious concerns about who will pay the price for the glittery posthuman utopias imagined in scholarship and speculative fiction, and the answer seems to be an all too familiar one: the peoples, life-forms, and resources who have been marginalized and exploited to build the world we know today. Part of what makes *SOMA* an intriguing work of critical literature is that these questions animate its narrative play spaces, and its posthuman world is a desperate bid for survival for a few built on the nightmares of others.

SOMA is a play space for critical reflection on what it means to be human, who gets to be human, and how human consciousness can continue or transform once humans are extinct. There is ultimately a horrible price of posthuman or transhuman futures—the characters in game who are left behind and die so that others can live, reminding players that identity and humanity have deeply social, political, and ethical dimensions. Even in the futures of speculative fiction the category of human is constructed through its exclusions, and technologies like cyborg bodies, virtual reality, and AI serve some at the expense of others. The ruins of *SOMA*'s facility herald the tattered remains and refuse that humanity leaves behind, and in this regard the game mirrors actual world inequalities wherein technology is an escape from environmental disaster afforded to some, while others are left to pay the price. Yet *SOMA*'s dystopian posthumanism also points to other forms of life, identity, and cognition that become possible when we embrace narrative difference and let go of the need to control and preserve humanity.

Dreams/Nightmares of Posthumanism

When Simon Jarrett, the player character, wakes up in the year 2104, he and the player are initially very confused. As far as they know, they were just in a doctor's office in Toronto, Canada in 2015, and suddenly they are in a dark, damp, metallic room with no clear indicators of where or when they are. As they start to explore their surroundings, they realize that the technology they are interacting with, including a multipurpose Omnitool personal computer, is quite different and more advanced than 2015's technology, and they find mentions of PATHOS-II, which they will discover is the name of the underwater research facility where they are. As they stumble around in the darkness of the ruined facility, Simon and the player soon encounter their first human/robot hybrid body: a Mockingbird, which they later learn is one of the facility's robots imprinted with a brain scan of one of the crew (and a copy of their consciousness) and often augmented with a substance known as Structure Gel (see Figure 4.1). Many of the Mockingbirds encountered serve as enemies in *SOMA*—while they take different forms and move and sound differently in the game, they will attack Simon as soon as they detect him, and either injure or kill him. The minds of the crew members implanted in the Mockingbirds appear disoriented, delusional, and/or angry, and the short utterances from some of them make it clear they are not aware that they are no longer in their human bodies.

The Mockingbirds embody many elements of the cyborg and posthuman identity, but they twist them and reveal the limitations and dangers of these ideals. Of course, they are quite literally cyborgs in that they are combinations of technological and biological components with human consciousness, and with many of them it is not clear where the cybernetics end and the organic matter begins. In this sense the Mockingbirds reflect the blurred boundaries between human and machine that Haraway (2016) posited as essential to hybrid cyborg identities, wherein one is not essentially human, technology, or any one stable thing (5). The Mockingbirds further represent the blurred boundary between human and animal, particularly in those that appear to have lost the ability to speak and instead communicate largely through guttural grunts, screams, and roars (32). This becomes particularly apparent in the areas where Mockingbirds stalk Simon like prey and will roar at him when they find him, giving chase with the intent to subdue and kill. In each of these ways and more, the Mockingbirds are hybrid entities that are something beyond human, even as they preserve copies of human consciousness that can still interact with and affect the world around them. Yet the Mockingbirds are not necessarily better off or more enlightened for being cyborgs. While they do present the challenge to categories and dichotomies that Haraway envisioned, they remain trapped in a purgatory of hybridity, wherein their different components, minds, and identities become something new but not something free.

The limitations of the Mockingbirds' cyborg bodies are not merely inherent in their forms, but are imposed on them by an AI called the WAU that seeks to preserve and control human life on PATHOS-II. The WAU is a station-wide, biologically engineered computer system that oversees all activity in the station's various sites, and one of its primary directives is to safeguard human life, though it lacks an operable definition of what human life is. After the comet eradicated life on the surface world, the WAU began implanting brain scans of crew members into robots around

Figure 4.1 The Construct, a Mockingbird enemy encountered several times throughout the game. This Mockingbird is slow and makes loud, disturbing noises as it moves that are similar to garbled radio, static, sharp cracks, and screaming.

the facility, creating the Mockingbirds but also causing many of them to become catatonic, delusional, or aggressive from the disjointed connection between human consciousness and robot body. For example, at one point in the game the WAU implants a brain scan of an unknown crew mate into a DUNBAT submarine, and upon realizing what they have become the cyborg begins lashing out, screaming, and finally destroys itself. To prevent this, the WAU uses Structure Gel to enhance the Mockingbirds and even the human corpses on PATHOS-II, controlling, reanimating, and preserving them though in limited states. One could argue that the limitations of *SOMA*'s cyborgs stem more from the evil of the fictional WAU than anything inherent in cyborgs themselves, but this misses an essential point at the heart of the game's horror: the same technology that can preserve, evolve, and free humanity can also be used to dominate and control. In other words, through its cyborgs the game presents an implicit critique of the assumption that hybridity brings with it agency and freedom, and shows instead how the dream of the posthuman can quickly become a nightmare if we view technology as an unmitigated, universal good, engaging in what Evgeny Morozov calls "cyber-utopianism" (2011, 10).

SOMA's most direct critique of posthuman, transhuman, and cyborg discourses is Structure Gel, which as its name implies provides the research station with form and support but is also fluid and adaptable. Structure Gel is a black, liquid biological substance that can conduct electricity and carry signals, and can be encoded with instructions for different functions and contexts. Its original use was to repair any structural damage or leaks in the underwater research station, as the gel could easily fill any size gaps or holes and further relay information back to the WAU. As the WAU began experimenting with preserving human life, however, it began flooding the facility with Structure Gel in order to communicate with, augment, and control both the machines and biological life in PATHOS-II. This led of course to the cyborg Mockingbirds, but also to reanimated human corpses, disfigured and mutated animals, and organic material overgrowing and embedding in computers throughout the facility. What is interesting about Structure Gel is that it is a substance without any essential or static form—it has no clear boundaries, it has no set purpose or function, and while it is biological it is also computational and technological. It is the fluid, hybrid, evolving, adaptable form that posthuman and transhuman ideals are made of, at least in speculative fiction. Yet it is also the means the WAU uses to achieve a pernicious and totalizing type of control that none of the remaining life at PATHOS-II can escape. Even if Simon chooses to destroy the WAU later in the game by injecting it with Structure Gel encoded to kill it, the implied outcome of this action is that all remaining life on the station will also die without the WAU to preserve it. The only freedom in *SOMA*'s posthuman dystopia is death.

The Mockingbirds, the WAU, and Structure Gel are all pieces of speculative fiction that challenge the utopian visions often traded in posthuman, transhuman, and cyborg futures. They point to how fluidity, hybridity, and the blurring of boundaries has great emancipatory potential, but also great potential for harm. Neither preserving the human nor evolving beyond it has any guarantee of making life better, more just, more agential, or freer. It is only by paying critical attention to longstanding, difficult, philosophical questions of what it means to be human, what it means to live, and who technology is for that we can keep our posthuman and transhuman dreams from becoming nightmares. Thankfully, as we shall see, *SOMA* has some suggestions for this too.

Narrative Difference and Cyborg Bodies

The key technology that enables survival in the harsh, post-apocalyptic setting of PATHOS-II is a brain scan that creates a copy of a person's consciousness and allows that copy to be transferred to new bodies, computers, and eventually a virtual reality called the ARK. The ability to move a person's mind, consciousness, or soul between bodies is a popular theme in speculative fiction, including classic science fiction novels such as Roger Zelazny's *Lord of Light* (2010) and more recent film and television such as the series *Westworld* (2016), both of which provide visions of a future where immortality is possible through digitized, transferrable consciousness. *SOMA* provides a noticeably darker take on this trope, instead asking players to encounter the dangers and costs of inhabiting new and different bodies. The transfer of consciousness *across* bodies also brings new meaning to the transhuman, wherein the transhuman is no longer just enhancing the human but also moving it between different states of being.

The first time the player encounters the movement between bodies in *SOMA*, they are not immediately aware it has happened. When they wake up in PATHOS-II, they appear to be the same Simon Jarrett that they just played as in a Toronto doctor's office—the voice is the same, the camera perspective and movement appear the same, and the only indicator that they might not be the human Simon Jarrett in Toronto is the fact that they are now in a very different time and place from where he last was. As Simon explores the facility, interacting with documentation of brain scans and the Pilot Seats that allow humans to mentally control the PATHOS-II robots, there is a growing suspicion that the Simon the player is playing as is not the same Simon from before, and specifically that the body the player is controlling is not the human Simon's. This suspicion is confirmed at one point in the game when Simon can finally see himself in a mirror and it becomes obvious he is now a cyborg body (see Figure 4.2). This moment can be an unsettling one for the player because they are forced to encounter how the player character and the body they have been navigating through the game are not the human they thought they were. In

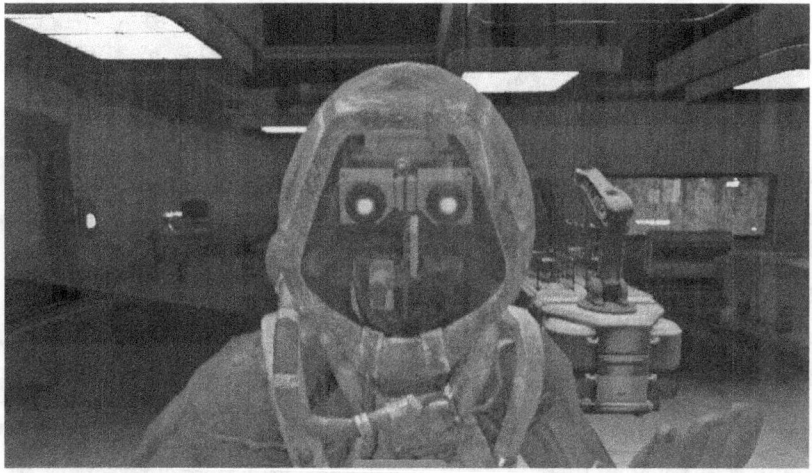

Figure 4.2 Simon Jarrett's robot body, visible in a mirror in a later area of PATHOS-II.

other words, their embodiment is not what they assumed it to be, and this shifts their narrative of who they are and how they relate to the world around them.

This rupture in the player's sense of identity and embodiment in the game also reveals how narrative operates in games. When players play video games, they take control of and are embodied as a player character that might be a person, an animal, an entity, or an object, and they experience the game world through that character. As Adrienne Shaw (2014) notes, players sometimes (but not always) identify with the player character, and every player must interact with the game world through a player character that may or may not be themselves (215). In a game like *SOMA*, the player is embodied as the player character (Simon Jarrett) through the first-person camera perspective—what the player sees is what Simon sees, and vice versa. With this first-person perspective, the player gets a window on the game world, experiencing space, objects, characters, enemies, audio, narration, and signs, interpreting them, and putting them together into their own personal narrative of the game. This narrative helps them understand the world around them, anticipate what might happen next, and make decisions about what their next action in the game will be (Upton 2015, 223). In this sense, narrative in a game is an embodied cognitive process of constructing a mental model of the game world and its events. Every player will engage in this process, but they will also do so differently based on their own values, identities, and experiences. Thus every player will have at least a slightly different narrative of the game based on the choices they made and the actions they performed, and that narrative difference will affect how they understand and respond to the game.

For example, consider the possible ways a player can interpret the environment in Figure 4.3, and how they might choose different actions and construct different personal narratives based on their interpretations. This scene takes place when the player as Simon is navigating the ocean floor and facing the entrances to site Delta, one of the PATHOS-II research facilities, and the Zeppelin Transport to site Theta. A player encountering this might choose to head to the transport hub first and look for any operational vehicles to get away from this area quickly and hopefully advance further into the game and its story. They might choose to examine or potentially flee one of the robots or cyborgs in the area, such as the one ahead and slightly to the right. They might scan the ground for objects or tools to interact with, as much of the narrative in the game is delivered through documents, recordings, and computers left behind. They might head straight to the door to site Delta, and try to get back inside as quickly as possible. Some of these options are more likely than others, particularly since effective game design often involves drawing player attention to particular areas and objects as they play, such as the lights and signs in Figure 4.3. Yet all of these and more are viable options that different players might choose, and each could subtly but significantly alter their experience and understanding of the game's narrative. This image is a snapshot of

Figure 4.3 An underwater scene on the ocean floor outside of Site Delta and the Zeppelin Transport Theta locations in *SOMA*. The lighting is dim and tinted green, and there are numerous objects, tools, and plant life strewn around the ground.

one moment among thousands in a game like *SOMA*, and over time these small, often unconscious decisions can create extremely different personal narratives for different players even if they are playing the same game.

The cognitive narrative process players use to construct their personal narratives in *SOMA* is common to all players, but the content, feeling, and outcome of this process will be quite different for different players. These differences can come from different past experiences, different beliefs or values, different levels of familiarity with games or game genres, and many other places. *SOMA* directly represents one particular source of difference in cognitive narrative processing: embodiment. For much of the game, the player plays as Simon in what appears to be his own nondisabled body of approximately expected human height with a standard first-person view. The moment with the mirror mentioned earlier reveals that this is in fact a cyborg simulacrum of human first-person visual experience, but generally speaking, the player will experience much of the game as they might experience their own first-person lives in the actual world. Yet there are moments in the game when Simon and the player's embodiment changes, which also changes how they sense and experience the game world around them. The most common of these is when Simon is injured either by enemies or by the environment, which causes him to breathe heavily and move slowly and lurchingly. These changes in embodiment alter the player's sense of the surrounding environment and likely cause them to adjust their strategy, such as favoring shorter, direct routes between cover and trying to play more stealthily because outrunning any enemies is less of an option. They might diverge from the main path and explore other areas to find a way to rest or heal, in the process encountering parts of the game other players might not. Less common, but more significant, are the times when Simon changes bodies by transferring his consciousness to a new cyborg body. As seen throughout the game, different cyborg bodies have different sensory, motor, and vocal abilities, and experiencing the game world through different bodies changes how one moves, fights, thinks, and plays. Ultimately being embodied as different cyborgs in *SOMA* shows us how embodiment is an essential determining factor in experiencing the world around us, and consequently how different bodies will have different personal narratives of the same events.

As much as *SOMA* shows us how these embodied, cognitive, narrative processes work, however, the game also points to how they can fall apart or, even worse, be used to controlling and authoritarian ends. While it is clear that different cyborg bodies experience and narrativize the world differently, it is significant that many of the cyborgs in this transhuman speculative future did not choose their bodies and are forced to live with them against their will. Most of the cyborgs at the PATHOS-II research station were created by the WAU AI using Structure Gel to force copies of human consciousness into bodies that are amalgams of technology and human corpses. The disconnect between the human consciousnesses and the different embodiments of the cyborg bodies created without their awareness or consent seems to cause intense, acute dysphoria, driving many of the cyborgs to flee, lash out violently, or even seek death. Yet the WAU uses the Structure Gel to keep the cyborgs alive, trapping them in an embodiment they do not desire and cannot survive. There are parallels here between the transhuman nightmare of the WAU's forced existence and transgender experiences in the actual world, with many transgender people experiencing immense dysphoria when denied treatment and forced to live with a disjointed embodiment.

Even Simon is affected by this disconnect, and as the player progresses through the game, they increasingly encounter hallucinations and distortions of their senses and first-person perspective. Whenever Simon and the player need to heal themselves in the game, they have to plunge Simon's hand into a pod of Structure Gel. This restores Simon and heals all of his injuries, but it also causes dark cracks to spread across his vision and bright lights to flash. The player later discovers that these are signs of the WAU's influence over Simon growing, and if Simon does not destroy or escape the WAU he will likely suffer the same fate as Mockingbirds and other cyborgs. The moments when Simon and the player's first person experience of the world are disrupted reveal two key aspects of embodied, cognitive, personal narrative, according to *SOMA*. The first is that our sensory experience of the world—our perspective and window on the world—appears coherent, natural, and objective, but is in fact subjective and constructed. Just as the fiction of being in a different body can change how we navigate and think about the world around us, when our own embodied senses shift then our personal narrative and sense of reality can shift too. Proceeding from this, the second aspect is that our embodied narratives can be disrupted, influenced, and even controlled, particularly in moments when the boundaries to our selves, the world around us, and reality are frayed. Extended exposure to Structure Gel would continue to warp Simon's sense of self and reality to the point where the WAU would be able to manipulate and dominate him. Of course the speculative fiction of *SOMA* simplifies and exaggerates this possibility that may never be possible in the actual world, but it does so to make a point. Specifically, the game's embodied narratives demonstrates how the hybridity, fluidity, and difference of cyborg bodies might not be as necessarily or inherently liberatory as transhumanism and posthumanism often claim. The ability to experience the world differently could itself become a mechanism of power and control, especially when it is forced on individuals and removes their agency.

Transhuman Refuse

SOMA's narrative embodiments and cyborg bodies paint a stark picture of transhuman and posthuman futures, but the game's most dramatic reveal points to the power, politics, and possibilities that remain. Simon and the player's ultimate goal is to reach and launch the ARK, a virtual reality capsule that contains brain scans of the PATHOS-II crew and other humans and can run indefinitely in outer space off of solar power. The ARK was created by Dr. Catherine Chun, a Taiwanese computer scientist working at the research station before the comet impact event. Dr. Chun's consciousness (brain scan) accompanies Simon on the journey to the ARK, serving as a deuteragonist, explaining events at the research station, helping him to solve problems, and guiding him around barriers on his way. It is Dr. Chun who helps Simon realize he is not the original Simon from Toronto, but a copy of his consciousness in a cyborg body.

Eventually Simon encounters an impasse: he must proceed deeper into the ocean, but his current body cannot withstand the crushing pressure of the depths. Dr. Chun helps Simon locate a dive suit that can resist the pressure and serve as his new body, and she transfers him over. It is at this point that Simon faces a terrible reality. Simon's consciousness is not just moved from one body to the next, with only one Simon in the process. His consciousness is *copied*, meaning a new version is created in the next body, and the preexisting version is left behind in the old body. This effectively means that every time Simon changes bodies in order to reach the ARK and survive, he is leaving behind a Simon who will die. The transfer of consciousness is a central plot point in *SOMA*'s narrative and it is also a metaphor for the cost of transhuman progress. Just as Simon's transhuman jumps leave people behind to die, the expensive and inaccessible technologies used to imagine and create posthuman worlds also exclude and leave people behind in the actual world. In the runaway inequality of global capitalism, poor and working-class people can barely afford virtual reality games, let alone ride on billionaire space ships or have elite access to protections and resources in the wake of climate devastation. This is all the more true for colonized peoples who continue to be exploited for cheap labor and natural resources, often under the guise of nice-sounding phrases like free trade. *SOMA* thus posits that there is a dark, hidden cost to transhuman and posthuman futures––that the escape and survival of the wealthy and privileged few often comes at the cost of the lives and livelihoods of many. Who gets to be human in the future is built and defined by who is exploited and excluded now.

There is further a racial politics to *SOMA*'s posthuman future. It is up to Dr. Chun, an East Asian woman, to guide Simon, a North American white man, to his salvation. This dynamic becomes especially apparent in the moments when Simon transfers to new bodies, when he repeatedly becomes confused and angry, lashing out at Dr. Chun. Each time she tries to explain to him, yet again, that someone gets left behind when he moves ahead: "Simon. I can't keep telling you how it works; you won't listen. You know why we're here, you were copied." The expectation that Dr. Chun patiently explain to Simon something he should already know and refuses to accept recalls Audre Lorde's theorization of the politics of difference. Specifically, Lorde points out how it is often the "responsibility of the oppressed to teach the oppressors their mistakes" (2007, 114). Here Dr. Chun is not educating Simon about what it is like to be an East Asian woman, but she must continually remind Simon of a political reality in the game's posthuman world that she knows well: when someone lives, someone else dies. Through the lens of *SOMA*'s transhuman metaphor, she is revealing to Simon and the player a dynamic present in posthuman discourse in the actual world as well.

SOMA's critique of transhumanism and posthumanism culminates in what appears to be a dark ending. After Simon's consciousness is copied into the ARK, Dr. Chun launches it into space, and the Simon the player has played as is left behind on Earth. He is once again confused and angry, and one final argument with Dr. Chun causes her computer to overload, deleting her and ending her life. Simon is alone in the depths of the Atlantic Ocean, partly by his own doing after attacking Dr. Chun again, and he remains as the refuse of transhumanism that will not live to see the posthuman world on the ARK. Yet a post-credits segment shows the copies of Dr. Chun and Simon in the virtual world of the ARK, where they finally have some safety and agency in choosing how they will live and play. This scene offers some hope for a posthuman future beyond the authoritarian constraints of the WAU or the forced hybridity of cyborg bodies, though the game remains critical of how the ARK's freedom is only afforded to a select few. Ultimately, then, what *SOMA*'s speculative play offers us is a critical warning about where transhumanism and posthumanism could take us if we are not careful, while providing a glimpse of what such futures could offer if they are available to all.

By doing so, *SOMA* is an excellent example of how games can function as critical, digital literature. Games can show us that no form of digital literature or play is neutral or apolitical. The narrative processes of world-building, identity formation, and experience are thoroughly contested and political all the way through, as they are with the cyborg bodies and posthuman worlds of *SOMA*. That might be disheartening, as though we have to constantly retread the same debates and arguments over and over again. Yet games also demonstrate how politics and identities are always changing, growing, and playing. Because of this, there is always the possibility for something different to emerge—the possibility of building and playing something otherwise. *SOMA* points to this possibility, but also demands we reckon with the cost to those who are excluded, exploited, or left behind along the way.

Note

1 Survival horror games are ones that prioritize fear, suspense, and terror by placing players in dangerous situations where they are threatened by monsters, powerful enemies, and/or their own psyches. They often limit the player's abilities and resources in order to heighten the sense of danger and fear.

Bibliography

Blascovich, Jim, and Jeremy Bailenson. 2011. *Infinite Reality: Avatars, Eternal Life, New Worlds, and the Dawn of the Virtual Revolution*. New York: William Morrow.

Caracciolo, Marco. 2018. "Posthuman Narration as a Test Bed for Experientiality: The Case of Kurt Vonnegut's Galápagos." *Partial Answers: Journal of Literature and the History of Ideas* 16, no. 2: 303–14. Project MUSE, https://doi.org/10.1353/pan.2018.0021

DeCook, Julia R. 2020. "A [White] Cyborg's Manifesto: The Overwhelmingly Western Ideology Driving Technofeminist Theory." *Media, Culture & Society*: 1158–67. https://doi.org/10.1177/0163443720957891

Haraway, Donna Jeanne. 2016. *Manifestly Haraway*. Minneapolis: University of Minnesota Press.

Hayles, N. Katherine. 1999. *How We Became Posthuman: Virtual Bodies in Cybernetics, Literature, and Informatics*. Chicago: University of Chicago Press.

Jackson, Zakiyyah Iman. 2020. *Becoming Human: Matter and Meaning in an Antiblack World*. New York: New York University Press.

Lorde, Audre. 2007 [1984]. "Age, Race, Class, and Sex: Women Redefining Difference." *Sister Outsider: Essays and Speeches*. Feasterville Trevose: Crossing Press. 114–23.

Mejeur, Cody. 2020. "Playing with Playthroughs: Distance Visualization and Narrative Form in Video Games." *Digital Humanities Quarterly* 14, no. 3.

Morozov, Evgeny. 2011. *The Net Delusion: The Dark Side of Internet Freedom*. PublicAffairs.

Rothblatt, Martine. 2011. *From Transgender to Transhuman: A Manifesto on the Freedom of Form*. United States: Martine Rothblatt.

———. 2014. *Virtually Human: The Promise—and the Peril—of Digital Immortality*. New York: St. Martin's Publishing Group.

Ryan, Marie-Laure. 1991. *Possible Worlds, Artificial Intelligence, and Narrative Theory*. Bloomington: Indiana University Press.

———. 2015. "Texts, Worlds, Stories: Narrative Worlds as Cognitive and Ontological Concept." *Narrative Theory, Literature, and New Media: Narrative Minds and Virtual Worlds*, edited by Mari Hatavara et al. London: Routledge. 11–28.

Shaw, Adrienne. 2014. *Gaming at the Edge: Sexuality and Gender at the Margins of Gamer Culture*. Minneapolis: University of Minnesota Press.

Upton, Brian. 2015. *The Aesthetic of Play*. Cambridge: MIT Press.

Zelazny, Roger. 2010 [1967]. *Lord of Light*. New York: Eos HarperCollins.

5 The Horror of Networked Existence

Affect, Connection, and Anxiety in Classic Creepypasta Narratives

Sara Bimo

In 2014, a disturbing and unusual case emerged out of Waukesha, Wisconsin: two 12-year-old girls had attempted to murder their classmate in order to appease the fictional Creepypasta monster Slenderman, whom the two perpetrators believed to be real (Hanna and Ford 2014). For many, this was the first-time hearing of the term "Creepypasta," which refers to a relatively niche subgenre of digital horror fiction that emerged from the depths of Internet forums in the mid-2000s. Suddenly thrust into the spotlight, the Slenderman stabbings (and the media moral panic that ensued) brought to popular attention the particular power of the Creepypasta genre, providing an extreme example of the powerful affect that drives the creation and consumption of these stories.

While Slenderman remains the most well-known character with regards to pop culture recognition, the canon of Creepypasta is vast and provides ample entry points for scholarly inquiry. Past scholarship can be broadly divided into examinations of the formal stylistic and narrative conventions of this genre, with particular attention having been paid to its similarity to folklore (e.g. Tolbert 2015) and urban legend narratives (e.g. Henriksen 2018), as well as theorisations on the particular narrative practices and thematic preoccupations that characterise Creepypasta as a generic mode and their relation to contemporary digital cultures (e.g. Balanzategui 2019).

In this chapter, I build upon this latter area of research and undertake a broad analysis of the narrative elements and themes of a variety of classic Creepypasta – stories that are held by the community to be in some way foundational to the genre. While Creepypasta engages with a wide-ranging variety of content, I identify three themes that consistently appear in earlier examples of the genre; I term these as *Haunted Objects*, *Haunted Memories*, and *Haunted Systems*. I suggest that classic Creepypasta can be considered a microgenre of Internet horror characterised in part by a preoccupation with and anxiety over the large-scale networked communication practices that distinguished early Web 2.0 cultures and the threat that networked existence poses to the ontological stability of *the self*.

This preoccupation is reflected in the particular techniques that Creepypasta stories deploy in order to induce affective responses in

DOI: 10.4324/9781003214915-8

readers. Creepypasta narratives enact the deconstruction of traditional subject/object boundaries through the exploitation of the affordances and imaginaries of their digital medium. Through this enactment, Creepypasta are effective in eliciting fear not through the sympathetic identification of the reader with some external fictional other (as seen in more traditional horror narratives), but rather through engendering a sense of "risk" on the part of the reader which is produced by the encroachment of narrative elements upon the world of the "real."

The Emergence of Creepypasta

The term "Creepypasta" appeared on the Internet for the first time in 2007, and derives from the earlier term "copypasta," a portmanteau of the words "copy and paste" which refers to viral digital content that is copy-pasted widely across the web (Blank and McNeill 2018, 6). While copypastas include any digital text that is widely disseminated across (typically) online forums and social networking sites, Creepypasta are explicitly horror themed and can incorporate a number of modalities, with authors often deploying hyperlinks, videos, images, and gifs in their stories.

While there is debate over what exactly counts as the "first" Creepypasta (with scholars pointing out similarities between Creepypasta and the older "chain email" format which dates back to the 1990s), the term originated on the anonymous image-based web forum 4chan, and it was in this environment that many characteristics of the style were established (Balanzategui 2019, 194). It is likely that many of the underpinnings of the Creepypasta style arose as a result of the particular mechanics, affordances, and social dynamics of 4chan, which in many ways emblematised early Web 2.0 communication conventions.

4chan requires anonymity from all users – as a result, many take on the common username "Anonymous." In addition, content is time-bound, with older threads being deleted after a certain period of inactivity. As a result, user identity is distinctly ephemeral, and it becomes impossible to pinpoint authorship to any particular user; rather, stories belong to the "collective," and authorial control is dispersed among the wider community in a way comparable to traditional folk tales, which are characterised in part by obscure or unknown origins (Ben-Amos 1971, 6). This effect is only intensified as stories are further copied and modified across different digital contexts, which aids in the creation of a "folkloric process of repetition and variation" (Blank and McNeill 2018, 72). This imitation of folkloric processes is to some extent intentional on the part of the Creepypasta community, as members often capitalise on these folk elements in order to add authenticity, plausibility, and gravitas to their stories (Blank and McNeill 2018, 8).

In an effort to preserve Creepypasta in light of the impermanence of *4chan*, archival websites such as Creepypasta.com were created as a repository for early stories. Such websites now provide a valuable reference for classics of the genre – stories that are widely agreed upon as providing foundational and widely replicated themes, narrative elements, and story beats that are still deployed in more recently created Creepypasta.

In the modern day, authenticity, plausibility, and obscure or unknown authorship remain essential to the Creepypasta genre, reflecting a continued commitment to the simulation of folkloric and legendary narrative forms. Yet, as a result of the changing locales of the Creepypasta community, the unchecked virality and genuine sense of mystery facilitated by ephemeral and anonymous forums such as 4chan is greatly diminished. Moving through the 2000s, Creepypasta forums gradually migrated to Reddit, with boards such as the r/nosleep subreddit becoming a major source for the creation of new stories. However, Reddit lacks both the enforced anonymity and the time-boundedness of 4chan; users are free to pick a username of their choice, and threads are preserved for posterity. As a result, the folkloric spirit of Creepypasta is now maintained through a more intentional kind of community wide role-play, with r/nosleep enforcing certain "rules of conduct" that are meant to preserve the early Creepypasta spirit. For example, r/nosleep forum rules inform users that "everything is true here, even if it's not," and posting guidelines require users to comment "in character" in order to preserve the suspension of disbelief.

While modern Creepypasta are still dedicated to the preservation of the conventions of the genre, shifts in the digital environment have inevitably resulted in modifications to popular narrative conventions and themes. In this chapter, I specifically focus on what I term "classic Creepypasta" – that is, stories that emerged in the early Web 2.0 era – in order to establish an overview of the foundational generic conventions of this form.

Identity Anxiety in the Networked Age

As mentioned, 4chan provides an example of early Web 2.0 communication cultures, which were distinguished from those of Web 1.0 in part by the introduction of "technologies of the self" which lead to a shift in the understanding of the stability and autonomy of user subjecthood (Bakardjieva and Gaden 2012, 159). Scholarly inquiries into the nature of and constitution of selfhood have long established the importance of continuous cross-boundary interaction between the ego and exterior others in the emergence of "self" (e.g. Mead 1934). However, the shifts in technological affordances, functionalities, and user practices that occurred between what is commonly referred to as the Web 1.0 era of the Internet (referring loosely to the period up until the early 2000s) and the early Web 2.0 era resulted in a technologically aided distribution and dispersal of identity that was unprecedented. Web 1.0 was characterised by a "read only" functionality which allowed users to access static web pages joined by hyperlinks (Van Dijck 2013, 5). While its global reach facilitated the "intrusion of distance events into everyday consciousness" (Giddens 1991, 27), the lack of interactivity meant that early users could only integrate such events into their local contexts: in other words, the pre-established local selfhood of the user was left relatively intact. As a result, Web 1.0 experience was largely atomised, with each user integrating the symbolic resources of the network in isolation (Bakardjieva and Gaden 2012).

With the development of Web 2.0 emerged a distinctly "networked self" that was enabled by the various technologies of self-making furnished by new Internet environments (Papacharissi 2011). Functionalities such as message boards and social networking sites facilitated the shift from an isolated and atomised user subjectivity into a truly networked one in which the self is created through the "reflexive process of fluid associations with social circles" (Papacharissi 2011, 305).

This shift in the ontological nature of selfhood between Web 1.0 and Web 2.0 was met with a fair share of suspicion. Anxieties over the egocentric nature of the new web manifested as derision over the so-called narcissism that drove social network usage (Bakardjieva and Gaden 2012, 159). In addition, there emerged an awareness of the vulnerabilities and risks incurred by networked self-making technologies, as Web 2.0 users were accused of exposing too much of their innermost selves to a vast, unknown, and potentially dangerous audience. While users often intentionally deployed Web 2.0 self-making technologies in the interests of developing and expanding their own identities, critics pointed to the inherent lack of user control that is an inevitable consequence of networked existence.

In addition, the phenomenon of convergence culture (Jenkins 2006) resulted in self-making technologies becoming intertwined with other cultural technologies such as the mass media and cultural industries. This convergence results in the interpellation of exterior ideologies into ostensibly neutral self-making processes, introducing the threat of invisible "foreign elements" encroaching upon the autonomy and stability of user selfhood. In addition to the threat of foreign ideology penetrating user identities, networked systems themselves constitute ideological interventions; in the environment of Web 2.0 social networks, conditions for existence, perception, and creation are structured by a preselected set of symbols and interaction pathways which are determined by some agent exterior to the user (Van Dijck 2013, 6–7). Thus, the constitution of the self in such networked systems is always influenced and guided by an exterior rationality – the invisible hand of an unknown other.

To further explore the connection between the identity anxieties of the early Web 2.0 era and the narrative mechanisms of classic Creepypasta, I delineate three common sub-categories of Creepypasta and, via an analysis of a few emblematic stories, draw attention to the ways in which their narratives enact and reflect anxieties over the loss of self in the face of networked existence.

Haunted Objects

This category centres around the digital dissemination of an object (oftentimes, a digital image) that possesses the agency to in some way act upon the reader. Crucially, the dissemination of this object occurs both diegetically and extra diegetically, in a move that deploys the folkloristic practice of *ostension* to bypass the barrier of representational narrative and induce the direct experience of a narrative moment and allow readers to encounter the "experiential substrate" of the story (McDowell 1982, 122; Dégh and Vázsonyi 1983).

A well-known example of this category is found in the classic story "The Curious Case of Smile.jpg" (also known as "Smile Dog"). While the exact provenance of this story is unknown, it possibly originated on 4chan sometime in 2008. As is typical for Creepypasta of this era, the author is unknown. The most commonly found iteration of this story is written in the first person, and follows an amateur writer who is gathering information for a college assignment. The author details his attempts to get in contact with a woman known only as Mary E. Mary E. is purported to be a victim of smile.jpg, a supposedly cursed image which dooms those who have seen it to a gamut of horrific experiences, beginning with nightmares, and ending with insanity or death. Within the diegesis smile.jpg is viewed as an urban legend, and the author is a consummate sceptic, believing the whole thing to be merely an Internet hoax. Sometime after rejecting his initial request to interview her, Mary E. sends the author an email in which she claims to have been haunted by smile.jpg for 15 years. She explains that for all this time, smile.jpg had come to her in her sleep and demanded that she "spread the word"; that is, forward the image to other people, so that they may too "experience the horror." By spreading the word, victims of smile.jpg are able to escape its hold, as they have passed the curse on to others.

Mary E. ends her email with a warning to the author to not pursue his investigation any further. She ultimately ends up dying under mysterious circumstances. Sometime later, the author receives an anonymous email from a person with the pseudonym "elzahir82." The subject line is "smile" and the email reads:

> Hello
>
> I found your e-mail address thru a mailing list your profile said you are interested in smiledog. I have saw it it is not as bad as every one says I have sent ti ti you here. Just spreading the word. [sic]

Smile.jpg is included as an attachment, and the author debates downloading the image. The story ends with him hypothesising about what he would do if he became a victim of the curse. Would he be strong enough to keep the image to himself, or would he be "capricious enough" to "spread the word," saving himself while dooming others? The Creepypasta concludes by finally revealing the smile.jpg image, implying that the author has attached the image to his blog post, thus forcing readers to witness smile.jpg in an effort to save himself from the horror.

The smile.jpg image is in equal parts silly and disconcerting: it is a polaroid of a strange-looking grinning husky dog in a darkened room with a reaching hand in the background, smeared with what appears to be bloodied fingerprints. However, readers might feel about the actual content of the image, the moment of affect generated upon the intrusion of a fictional narrative element into the world of the "real" is genuinely disturbing, and brings about the momentary sensation that the reader is actually at risk from the horrific events described in the narrative.

Such *haunted object* Creepypasta weaponise ostension and combine it with the affordances of networked communication in order to induce a forced re-enactment of the key plot elements of the story on the parts of readers. In this moment of boundary crossing, readers affectively experience the horror of the story, and are subsumed within the purview of the diegesis. This sense of "real" risk is enabled by the particular affordances of the medium of digital communication, which is deployed both diegetically and extra diegetically; it is both the subject of and the vehicle of the story.

In "haunted object" stories, the true horror lies in the deconstruction of the subject/object boundary that typically characterises narrative. Suddenly, observed objects become capable of acting upon observing subjects, and directly threatening the mind and body of the ostensibly isolated subject. In addition to demonstrating and enacting the dangers that networked existence poses to the ontological stability of the reader's selfhood, this type of Creepypasta also implicitly suggests that the degree *of one's involvement with and embeddedness in networked digital life* corresponds to the level of risk one might incur. After all, for those who are only casually online, there is a relatively low chance that they will stumble across and be forced to witness such a haunted item. Thus, one's disembeddedness from digital worlds is a kind of protection. However, the more engagement and knowledge you have of the Internet, the more likely you are to stumble across one of these cursed objects – the more likely it is for foreign elements to "cross over" from the realm of the narrative and the realm of objecthood and act upon bodies in "real life," where we think we are safe from the influence of networked technologies. As a result, the virality of these stories, which is inherent to the genre, is in itself a threat.

Haunted Memories

While *haunted object* stories threaten readers by presenting a direct existential threat to their safety and sanity, "haunted memory" stories threaten selfhood by estranging foundational childhood memories, thus destabilising ostensibly immutable pillars of one's history and identity. Stories in this category most often involve "lost episodes" of popular TV shows (which, according to Creepypasta.com, is one of the most popular Creepypasta tropes).

The best-known example of this category (and arguably one of the most popular Creepypasta ever created) is "Candle Cove." This story is quite unusual in that its authorship is well documented: it was written by Kris Straub and published on his website in 2009 under a Creative Commons license. However, soon after its publication "Candle Cove" was copied onto a variety of message boards and over the course of its viral dissemination, its authorship and original context became gradually obscured. In this way, its reproduction quickly became aligned with the anonymous folklore cycle that characterised Creepypasta, an element that only intensified as subsequent readers made modifications and augmentations to the story. As a result of this history, "Candle Cove" evokes a sense of authenticity that has fooled many readers into believing the subject matter of the story is nonfictional.

Adding to the authentic feel of the story is "Candle Cove"'s particular aesthetic presentation. The story is presented as a digital epistolary, and consists of a series of forum posts on a site entitled "netnostalgia.forum." The conversation begins with a user named Skyshale033 inquiring about a show they vaguely recalled from their childhood:

> Does anyone remember this kid's show? It was called Candle Cove and I must have been about 6 or 7. I never found reference ot it anywhere so I think it was on a local station around 1971 or 1972. I lived in Ironton at the time. I don't remember which station, but I do remember it was on at a weird time, like 4:00 PM. [sic]

Other users reply, and gradually, a collective memory of this mysterious show is reconstructed from their fragmented recollections and their conversation sparks further memories. Initially, the posters are overjoyed that they aren't the only ones who remember this obscure TV program ("YES! Okay I'm not crazy!") and find comfort in the confirmation that their memories were real and not just their imaginations.

Soon, however, this sense of warm nostalgia gives way to a pervasive uncanniness as the users' recollections grow more and more strange. It begins with user mikepainter65's description of the character "Pirate Percy," who was built from "parts of other dolls," and had the head of an "old porcelain baby doll." The posts become more and more disturbing, and Skyshale033 comments on an "awful dream" they had in which the puppets and marionettes from the show were "just screaming" and "flailing spastically," and a little girl was "moaning and crying." Other users respond that this wasn't just a dream; they too remember this disturbing episode. The story culminates with a post from mike_painter65, which reads:

> i visited my mom today at the nursing home. i asked her about when i was littel in the early 70s, when i was 8 or 9 and if she remebered a kid's show, candle cove. she said she was suprised i could remember

that and i asked why, and she said "because i used to think it was so strange that you said 'i'm gona go watch candle cove now mom' and then you would tune the tv to static and juts watch dead air for 30 minutes. you had a big imagination with your little pirate show." [sic]

This ambiguous ending leaves readers to wonder if the television show "Candle Cove" really did exist, whether it was in fact the product of supernatural forces, or whether it was merely the collective delusion of a collection of terminally online, overly media-saturated users. Just as with *haunted object* stories, the sense of authenticity in *haunted memory* stories is crucial in engendering a sense of real risk in the reader. While the "Candle Cove" TV show is fictional, the story deploys the norms of Internet communication in order to make readers seriously question the veracity of what they are reading. From the outset, the aesthetic presentation of the narrative as a series of forum posts (reminiscent of "found footage" horror films, which in turn draw inspiration from the epistolary format) imbues the story with a sense of authenticity that is further supported by the realistic and vernacular tone of the posts and the familiarity of the opening subject line (after all, turning to the Internet to dredge up information on a hazy childhood memory is a widespread phenomenon). Just as Skyshale033 opens with a sense of insecurity regarding the trustworthiness of their own memory and the reality-status of Candle Cove, readers enter the narrative with a sense of insecurity regarding the "diegetic status of the exchange" (Balanzategui 2019, 199).

It is this sense of authenticity that makes the destabilising and estranging effects of this type of Creepypasta so potent. At their core, *haunted memory* stories operate by mobilising a sense of the uncanny in order to defamiliarise nostalgia and deconstruct the continuity and cohesiveness of our memory and history. While nostalgia is initially presented as a means by which to access past selves and to establish a continuity of identity by bridging the temporal gap between the child self and the adult self, it instead becomes a means to expose the perennially disjointed and doubled nature of the self as the initially comfortable and familiar pillars of the childhood subject are revealed to be nightmarish, strange, and dangerous (Balanzategui 2019, 196). Instead of establishing a unity and stability of identity, nostalgia results in the fracturing of selfhood. Similar to *haunted object stories*, *haunted memory* Creepypasta implicitly warn that the unity and stability of selfhood is threatened by increased presence on and engagement with the network; the more that we disperse bits of ourselves across networked communication channels, the higher the risk of irrevocably losing control over our identities.

Haunted Systems

Haunted systems Creepypasta include stories which in some way defamiliarise the infrastructures and architectures within which we perform the practices of our daily lives. Such stories cast all systems of communication and networked social behaviour into question by suggesting they are secretly animated or structured by an invisible malevolent force. This suggestion has the effect of destabilising and estranging the social self-making practices that occur within them.

While *haunted object* and *haunted memory* stories deploy a relatively consistent set of narrative tropes and plot elements, *haunted system* stories are considerably more broad. Examples include "The Elevator Game," which falls under the popular "ritual list of instructions" format which eschews classic narrative structures and instead only presents readers with a list of instructions pertaining to the completion of an esoteric ritual. Possibly originating from Japan sometime in 2008 ("The Elevator Game" 2021), this story consists of an instruction manual for accessing an alternate world via an ordinary elevator. The game instructs reader-players to press certain floors of an elevator in a particular order, and to follow very precise instructions in order to ultimately access the "other world." The story warns readers to follow instructions precisely lest they be trapped in this other world (the consequences of which are left ambiguous, but are framed as appropriately horrific). By alienating a mundane infrastructure through the suggestion that it is animated by underlying supernatural forces, "The Elevator Game" engenders a sense of threat to the real bodies and minds of players by bestowing agency upon an ostensibly inert architecture.

Another example of this genre can be found in the story "Normal Porn for Normal People," which follows the narrator's experiences viewing a series of disturbing videos on a website called normalpornfornormalpeople.com ("Normal Porn for Normal People" n.d.). The story opens with the line "everybody knows that if you surf the web long enough, you'll see some pretty sick shit," and proceeds to describe how the narrator received an email from an unknown address, which read:

> Hi there
> found this site is very nice thought u might like
> Normalpornfornormalpeople.com
> pass it on, for the good of mankind [sic]

Upon clicking the provided URL, the narrator is brought to a "very average, very generic looking site," from where they eventually navigate to a white page with a long list of links. These links bring up a collection of short videos. While the first videos are relatively benign, if strange, the final few become increasingly disturbing and violent. The narrator brings this web page to the attention of an image board they frequent, and the thread explodes with activity as other users uncover the gruesome videos.

When the narrator returns to check the discussion thread the next day, they find that it has been deleted. Upon attempting to start another thread, the narrator is banned from using the image board. They attempt to get in touch with the person who initially sent them the link to normalpornfornormalpeople.com, but never get a response. Every time the narrator attempts to discuss the website, they get banned from whatever site they are using. As a result, basically all traces of normalpornfornormalpeople.com have been wiped from the web. On this note, the story abruptly ends with no resolution or explanation. In absence of an explicit perpetrator, readers are left with the unsettling feeling that the very basic structure of Internet experience – the underlying hyperlink connections that constitute the network – is loaded with hidden dangers.

Once again, authenticity is key to the affective success of the narrative. Much like "Candle Cove," the content described in "Normal Porn for Normal People" feels starkly realistic; by playing upon readers' existing knowledge and fears of the dark web, the story constructs a digital environment that seems like it could exist even in the modern day. This verisimilitude is reflected in the multitude of forum comments from users describing how, upon first reading, they fully believed the story to be true.

This sense of authenticity, augmented by the multimodal incorporation of hyperlinks which suggest that readers are only a click away from accessing the website described in the narrative, brings the realm of the fictional uncomfortably close to crossing over into the world of the real. As they experience the Creepypasta on the very same infrastructure which is depicted within the diegesis of the story, reader's proximity to the narrative puts them in harm's way. We feel as though we are only separated from the horror of the story by our decision to not click a particular hyperlink or to stay away from certain web pages; we are protected only by a thin veneer of normalcy and wilful ignorance of the malevolent forces that underpin the network.

Unlike *haunted object* and *haunted memory* stories, which position networked existence as threatening in that it provides the opportunity for and means through which the self is psychically or physically harmed, *haunted systems* stories assert that it is the network *itself* which is the source of danger. Far from being a neutral object or a tool through which users may enact social processes of identity formation, the network is instead depicted as possessing agency; it has the power to act upon subjects and manipulate or inform their everyday behaviours. As such, the networked self is continually at risk of becoming interpellated or compromised by external forces.

Such fears harken back to anxieties surrounding technologically mediated social interaction in the early Web 2.0 era (anxieties that are arguably only more relevant today). In their capacity to structure conditions of existence and interaction through the preselection of a discrete set of symbols and interaction pathways, social networking technologies constitute a system of social rationality. Instead of merely providing environments in which the human processes of social self-making may occur, networked environments exert an agentic role in their capacity to guide user behaviour and structure meaning.

In addition to capitalising upon the fears surrounding social networking technologies, *haunted systems* stories reflect an anxiety that surrounds the Internet (and all digital systems) more generally. Sandra Robinson (2014) points out that a "disturbing present absence" is engendered by the advanced systems that support digital media but remain hidden below the interface (Henriksen 2018). While digital media networks can be encountered through intermediaries such as cell phones and software applications, which provide an interface through which we can momentarily experience the network, we can never truly apprehend it; it is too vast, complex, and ephemeral. Its presence is always felt, yet we can never see the "submerged, agential, autonomous capacity for control" (Robinson 2014, 221).

Conclusion

Through the mobilisation of affect and the exploitation of the technological affordances of the Internet, classic Creepypasta narratives are invested in the deconstruction of traditional subject/object boundaries in the interests of generating in readers a feeling of risk that threatens the autonomy, stability, and safety of their selfhood. As a microgenre that is intimately intertwined with place and time, classic Creepypasta can be seen as a microcosm of early Web 2.0 cultural anxieties relating to the large-scale shift to a truly networked mode of existence.

In the modern day, changes in digital culture and dissemination patterns mean that the folkloric qualities of anonymity and authenticity which characterises classic Creepypasta are difficult to reproduce; as a result, the conventions and stylistic norms of Creepypasta have changed significantly. In addition, it can be argued that modern networked existence comes with a new set of anxieties relating to the stability, autonomy, and unity of the self. As users become increasingly aware of the big data analytics and algorithmic architectures that contribute to the abstraction of their digital selves into discrete data points and informational patterns, the threat to the cohesion and autonomy of user identities posed by large-scale networks is felt even more acutely. In the wake of these environmental shifts, and moving into the third generation of web technologies, tracking the development of Creepypasta conventions may prove invaluable in understanding the underlying anxieties that motivate and mobilise contemporary users.

Bibliography

Bakardjieva, Maria, and Georgia Gaden. 2012. "Web 2.0 Technologies of the Self." In *Cultural Technologies: The Shaping of Culture in Media and Society*, edited by Göran Bolin, 1st ed., 153–69. Routledge.

Balanzategui, Jessica. 2019. "Creepypasta, 'Candle Cove', and the Digital Gothic." *Journal of Visual Culture* 18, no. 2: 187–208. https://doi.org/10.1177/1470412919841018

Ben-Amos, Dan. 1971. "Toward a Definition of Folklore in Context." *The Journal of American Folklore* 84, no. 331: 3–15. https://doi.org/10.2307/539729

Blank, Trevor J., and Lynne S. McNeill, eds. 2018. *Slender Man Is Coming: Creepypasta and Contemporary Legends on the Internet.* Logan: Utah State University Press.

Dégh, Linda, and Andrew Vázsonyi. 1983. "Does the Word 'Dog' Bite? Ostensive Action: A Means of Legend-Telling." *Journal of Folklore Research* 20, no.1: 5–34.

Dijck, José van. 2013. *The Culture of Connectivity: A Critical History of Social Media.* Oxford; New York: Oxford University Press.

"Elevator Game." n.d. G. Hide and Go Kill Wiki. Accessed August 1, 2022. https://hideandgokill.fandom.com/wiki/Elevator_Game

Giddens, Anthony. 1991. *Modernity and Self-Identity: Self and Society in the Late Modern Age.* Stanford: Stanford University Press.

Hanna, Jason, and Dana Ford. 2014. "12-Year-Old Wisconsin Girl Stabbed 19 Times; Friends Arrested." CNN. Accessed June 3, 2014. www.cnn.com/2014/06/03/justice/wisconsin-girl-stabbed/index.html

Henriksen, Line. 2018. "'Spread the Word': Creepypasta, Hauntology, and an Ethics of the Curse." *University of Toronto Quarterly* 87, no. 1: 266–80. https://doi.org/10.3138/utq.87.1.266

Jenkins, Henry. 2006. *Convergence Culture: Where Old and New Media Collide.* 1st ed. New York: New York University Press.

McDowell, John H. 1982. "Beyond Iconicity: Ostension in Kamsá Mythic Narrative." *Journal of the Folklore Institute* 19, no. 2/3: 119–39. https://doi.org/10.2307/3814009

Mead, George Herbert. 1934. *Mind, Self, and Society: From the Perspective of a Social Behaviorist.* Edited by Charles W Morris. Chicago: University of Chicago Press.

"Normal Porn for Normal People." n.d. Creepypasta Wiki. Accessed August 1, 2022. https://Creepypasta.fandom.com/wiki/Normal_Porn_for_Normal_People

Papacharissi, Zizʻi, ed. 2011. *A Networked Self: Identity, Community and Culture on Social Network Sites.* New York: Routledge.

Robinson, Sandra. 2014. "Vital Networks: The Biological Turn in Computation, Communication, and Control." Order No. NS27951, Queen's University (Canada). https://ezproxy.library.yorku.ca/login

Straub, Kris. n.d. "Candle Cove." Accessed August 1, 2022. http://ichorfalls.chainsawsuit.com/

"The Curious Case of Smile.Jpg | Creepypasta." n.d. Accessed August 1, 2022. www.Creepypasta.org/Creepypasta/the-curious-case-of-smile-jpg

"The Elevator Game." 2021. Accessed November 3, 2021. www.Creepypasta.com/the-elevator-game/

Tolbert, Jeffrey. 2015. "'Dark and Wicked Things': Slender Man, the Folkloresque, and the Implications of Belief." *Contemporary Legend Series* 3, no. 5 (January): 38–61.

6 Networked Chronic Pain Narratives

Locating Disability through Fibromyalgia Facebook Community

Rimi Nandy

The emergence of digital technologies has greatly transformed the concept of autobiography. The representation of "digital selves" introduces newer forms of life narration. This chapter proposes to study the Facebook community page *Women with Fibromyalgia* as a form of digital pain narrative. I analyse the narratives of chronic pain from within the field of feminist disability studies and autobiography studies. Moreover, in keeping with my chapter's focus on self-narration, I bring together theoretical knowledge and personal experience of illness and disability to bear upon my analysis.

According to Theresa Sauter (2013), social networking sites typify how the practice of self-writing evolves in the digital space. A Facebook community can thus be studied as a kind of collaborative life narrative constituted by the interaction of several "authors" and "readers." As opposed to traditional autobiography, such a digital life narrative is not restricted to written elements alone. It uses visual as well as audio elements to represent the self. A private community space, *Women with Fibromyalgia* structures its narrative around the female, disabled body. Women's shared experience of chronic pain leads to the creation of a community linked together by the idea of double marginalisation.

Narrating Selves

> Sleep is something I can't do
> My body's aching like the flu
> So fatigued I can not stand
> Fingers numb on every hand
> Muscles hurt from inside out
> Work today?
>   (Block 2022, n.pag)

Storytelling is an element which is intertwined with the process of meaning making in human life. With the advent of the postmodern age, the furthering of digital technology has restructured the concept and the

DOI: 10.4324/9781003214915-9

characteristic features of narratives. Marie-Laure Ryan comments on the "distinctive properties of digital media" (Ryan 2004, 338) and elaborates on five different properties, including its reactive and interactive nature coupled with "multimedia capabilities," networking capabilities, volatile nature of digital texts and modularity. These features of digital media allow for the flourishing of fluid and fragmented narrative structures. Social media, as an integral part of the digital media ecology, influence the narrative stance used for personal storytelling. This in turn transforms the genre of autobiography.

Of course, autobiography was not a monolithic literary genre before the advent of social media. However, various types of autobiography emerging outside digital environments shared overlapping patterns, particularly in their assumptions about the self as a relatively unified, singular entity. A change in the attitude to such self-conception was already evident in the late twentieth century. In keeping with the fragmented and chaotic nature of postmodernist late capitalist culture, the construction of self also became multifaceted. Frederic Jameson, for instance, discussed the idea of the "death of the subject" and commented on the absence of an inner self and an outer self demarcating an individual. There was no longer a singular subject as the age of consumerism gave rise to multiplicity. The very idea of the self became fluid. At present, the idea of a single self seems even more irrelevant with most digital media users having multiple identities and avatars across different social media platforms. The ever-changing self is now constructed through narrative interactions across these platforms (Georgakopoulou, Iversen, and Stage Carsten 2020).

This chapter thus concentrates on the role of social media platforms such as Facebook in constructing a self out of disability. The specific condition discussed in this chapter is that of a diseased body resulting from the chronic pain disorder, fibromyalgia. In the following sections, I discuss the changing concepts of self, disease, and narrative evinced in the private Facebook community page, *Women with Fibromyalgia*. I also want to note here that the words "story" and "narrative" represent different aspects of storytelling. A story refers to an incident whereas a narrative refers to a sequence of episodes arranged in a specific order and my analysis looks at narratives.

Modern medicine dictates and delineates symptoms and concrete changes in the body for the classification of diseases. To a certain extent, advancements in medical technologies change the manner in which disease or illness is perceived in society. Moreover, what is to be considered a disease has also changes with time. The transformation in the perception of disease and illness redefines the narratives of illness.

The notion of disability remains closely linked with the idea of disease and illness. Disability studies focuses on how "disability" is a social construct based around how the society distinguishes between an able body and a disabled body (see Schalk 2021). Living with any form of illness is challenging as society "others" any form of difference, whether psychological or physiological. This challenge gets accentuated further in case of contested illnesses. According to Diane Lynn, Diane Driedger, and Michelle Owen (2008), "Contested illness are illness considered controversial because medical practitioners, researchers, the media and the public disagree whether these illnesses are psychological and/or organic in nature, or even exist at all" (88). Fibromyalgia is one such contested illness, which means digital narratives tackling the illness also confront questions of legitimacy and allegations of fictionality. In social media narratives, the tellability is an essential element. The narrative value of a particular story shared on social media marks the tellability of the same. The tellability of a story changes with context (Georgakopoulou, Iversen, and Stage 2020, 138). Within the Facebook community page *Women with Fibromyalgia*, the day-to-day struggle involved in performing mundane acts are of higher value than a story based on a large-scale transformation. The legitimacy of social media narratives is based on sharing "life-in-the moment," which makes recent everyday experiences tellable content. As Georgakopoulou, Iversen, and Stage observe, "Mining the mundane and presenting an ordinary, non-polished self in everyday life, we saw, is a hallmark of the directive for authenticity" (2020, 139–40). It is through leveraging these markers of authenticity intrinsic to storytelling practices across social media that participants of the community page contend charges of fictionality and falsehood.

Locating Disease and Illness Narratives

The concept of disease and illness has undergone immense change over the centuries. There are three different terms that have come to be associated with pathological states, namely

> illness, which identifies the personal emotional state connected to the loss of health; disease, which refers to the objective, biological and measurable dimension of it – strictly linked to the physician's activity – and sickness, which refers instead to the public dimension of the disease and highlights the link between illness and society.
> (Rovesti et al. 2018)

Illness in the present context refers to "the subjective sense of feeling unwell: illness does not define a specific pathology, but refers to a person's subjective experience of it, such as discomfort, tiredness, or general malaise" ("Chapter 1 Concepts of Health and Illness | AFMC Primer on Population Health," n.d.). However, illness as a part of the medical domain is a relatively recent development. Modern medicine used to be entirely dependent on factual procedure. Within the practices of modern medicine, the voice of the patient could only be represented through the description of physical symptoms. In his pivotal work *The Wounded Storyteller* (1997), medical sociologist Arthur Frank discusses how the approach and attitude to disease and illness was transformed in the late twentieth century. Frank further notes that, "The postmodern experience of illness begins when ill people recognize that more is involved in their experiences than the medical story can tell" (1997, 6). He mentions how illness narratives began to focus more on the experience of living with illness rather than on social expectations. Frank uses the phrase "tell the doctor what hurts" to depict the change in narrative style. Earlier, narratives describing illness could only resort to the description of concrete physical symptoms – the chart maintained by the doctors was the only story of illness that was available. At present though, the subjective experience of illness has become the most essential element in illness narratives. In this context, we can think of the term "disease" as aligned with the "biomedical model" wherein physical and mental abnormalities are diagnosed through various pathological tests. By contrast, illness is connected to the sphere of "biopsychosocial model" which links the psychological state and social perception with disease or pathological changes in the body. In the words of Kleinman: "In the practitioner's act of recasting illness as disease, something essential to experience of chronic illness is lost; it is not legitimated as a subject for clinical concern, nor does it receive an intervention" (Kleinman 2020, 29).

In the twenty-first century, digital platforms offer further transformative possibilities to illness narratives, and indeed, experiences of illness. The digital space provides a means for narrating stories using multimedia elements. Locating this form of storytelling within the purview of digital literature is a key interest of this chapter.

Digital literature varies from traditional literature and print culture as a tool that simultaneously routes information from many-to-many in contrast to traditional literature that follows the path of one-to-many. As Ruth Page has observed,

> social media is often distinguished from forms of mass media, where mass media is presented as a one-to-many broadcasting mechanism. In contrast, social media delivers content via a network of participants where the content can be published by anyone but is still distributed across potentially large-scale audiences.
>
> (Page 2013, 5)

Social media enables the construction of collaborative narratives that are perpetually incomplete. The Facebook community page *Women with Fibromyalgia*, based around women who have been suffering from fibromyalgia, creates a narrative which looks at fibromyalgia as an illness that is at the same time an individual experience as well as a community experience. Members from across the world come together to form and participate in the community space where everyday experience of living with chronic illness is discussed. The narratives, apart from sharing personal experience, also provide information and "alternative" remedies.

As I have indicated earlier, there is a long-standing debate regarding the acceptance of fibromyalgia as a clinical condition. The term "fibrositis" was first coined by Sir William Gowers in 1904 to describe widespread inflammation and muscular pain along with tender points. Tender points were first noted by a physician in Edinburgh in the year 1824 (Says 2013). This formed the basis for fibromyalgia as a medical condition. According to the American College of Rheumatology, fibromyalgia affects 2 to 4 percent people globally among which women are affected in a larger number than men:

> Fibromyalgia is characterized by widespread pain and tenderness (sensitivity to touch). The pain and tenderness tend to come and go and move about the body. Other symptoms include fatigue, sleep, memory, and mood issues. The diagnosis can be made with a careful examination. Fibromyalgia is most common in women, though it can occur in men. It most often starts in middle adulthood, but can occur in the teen years and in old age
>
> ("Fibromyalgia" n.d.)

There are no diagnostic tests for fibromyalgia. The only way it can be diagnosed is based on symptoms. Some of the main symptoms identified to diagnose fibromyalgia are tenderness (across different parts of the body, marked by 18 possible trigger points), depression, anxiety, fatigue and cognitive problems. As the diagnosis is based on how the patient feels instead of concrete diagnostic tests, fibromyalgia is often considered a disorder of the mind (Häuser and Fitzcharles 2018).

Disease and illness are very often looked at as conditions that can be cured with the help of biomedical intervention. However, chronic illness, which can never be cured, may fall outside the definition of disease, giving rise to "contested illness." In the words of Lynn, Driedger and Owen, "While tests and guidelines for evaluating and diagnosing contested illness have been developed, acceptance and widespread application of these evaluation measures is still lacking" (2008, 88). As a result, most often patients suffering from Fibromyalgia are not taken seriously by medical practitioners. In such scenario, patients are left to experience the pain on their own. Chronic illness results in the construction of a monadic body (constricted within oneself), as there are no concrete elements for diagnosing the disease, but the monadic body can connect to other individuals through dyadic relationship which can help in the establishment of a "community of pain." Collaborative narratives on social media facilitate the construction of such a space.

Facebook and Digital Pain Narratives

Facebook's appearance resembles a book – specifically, perhaps, a scrapbook. The structure and characteristics of the platform make it amenable to constructing narratives of different length. These narratives need not be created by a single user. Indeed, the interaction of various users adds layers of mediation and intricacies to stories shared on Facebook. The social media platform also provides various community spaces which can be joined irrespective of geographical boundaries. I first came across the community page *Women with Fibromyalgia* while I was looking for a space where I could discuss the pain and suffering I was encountering on a daily basis. Having been diagnosed with fibromyalgia, I have often been questioned about the credibility of the disease. This constant interrogation is a result of the "preponderance of the biomedical model in medical practice. The model attributes a key role to biological determinants and explains a disease as a condition caused by external pathogens or disorder in the functions of organs and body systems" (Häuser and Fitzcharles 2018, 22). In this context, the Facebook page has provided constant support to me and many others like me, who have to experience this debilitating illness.

Fibromyalgia can be categorized as an invisible disability as there are no concrete visible manifestations of the disease on the physical body. As fibromyalgia most commonly affects women, the resulting disability can be studied through the discourse of feminist disability studies. An able body is defined by the society as fulfilling certain roles and appearing in certain ways. Failing to perform actions deemed normative pushes the body into the category of the disabled. As fibromyalgia affects the body's ability to work at the same pace as "normal" individuals, in effect it causes disability among the patients. Frank (1997) has discussed and categorized the problems faced by a suffering body: these problems include issues of body control, body relatedness, other relatedness and desire of the body. The narratives in the Facebook page *Women with Fibromyalgia* can be analysed through such a framework.

The welcome note of the page *Women with Fibromyalgia*, states.[1,2]

WELCOME!!***WOMEN ONLY***A support group, sharing good and bad days, information, blog posts, articles, gossip, and chat, positively, what you are having for tea, what book you enjoyed...all things fibro in complete private.
(This group is closed so only members can see our chat.)
So many women all sharing the same illness can help and support each other. It is so difficult at times to feel listened to. Our own chat group for women of all ages who have Fibromyalgia.

Figure 6.1 Women with Fibromyalgia community page "About" ("(5) Women with Fibromyalgia | Facebook" n.d.).

This note situates the discussion in the community within the purview of an invisible disability which is at the same time a contested illness. This community helps the monadic bodies form a dyadic relationship with others which enables the patients to experience the pain of the disease as a community. Talcott Parson has theorized that illness does not signify a biological condition alone but a social condition (Varul 2010)(). In other words, illness is co-constructed through the interaction of an individual to the society. The Parsonian model focuses on the roles and responsibilities of a sick person to enable them to get better. *Women with Fibromyalgia* is a platform where women suffering from fibromyalgia come together to share their experiences as well as exchange information for their well-being. Although chronic illness cannot be cured, the discussions in the page appear to be in line with the Parsonian model of moving towards well-being. A recurrent theme in the posts shared on the community page is the will to fight against the pain and overcome it at some point of time. The following post (see Figure 6.2) verbally and visually captures the supportive role played by the community page where the daily struggle of enduring the pain caused by fibromyalgia becomes a shared experience.[3]

In another post, a member shares how much her legs hurt. She talks about the intensity of pain leading to a sleepless night. She further gives a list of medicines she took to overcome the pain and yet the pain persisted. The post ends with a question to the other members of the community asking if anyone else experienced a similar pain. This post shows how the quoted woman desires to get better but also that she desires to learn if anyone already shares her experience. In other words, she is not looking for medical cure alone but for understanding.

Body problem or the lack of control over the diseased body is an important element tackled in illness narratives posted in the community. For example, a member shares how difficult it is to endure the pain without crying out and pitying herself. She tries to come to terms with her life transformed by the chronic pain. Her question to the community members is whether one could find a positive aspect hidden beneath the excruciating pain which has disabled her. This post not only narrates the experience of feeling a loss of control over one's own body but also invites commentary on the condition predicated on the assumption of belonging to a shared community.

A second category of the body problem referred to by Frank is that of body relatedness. Most of the posts in the page narrativize the earlier days when the disease had still not set in. The narratives often fondly remember the past in contrast to the debilitating state of the present. In one particular post, a member depicts the problems faced by her after being diagnosed with fibromyalgia. In her post, the member describes how she was treated indifferently by a doctor, after being made aware that she had been diagnosed with fibromyalgia. The doctor stated that all her symptoms were associated with her poor mental health condition. She was prescribed antidepressants in spite of her protests that she had already been

Figure 6.2 Women with Fibromyalgia post ("(5) Women with Fibromyalgia | Facebook" n.d.).

on antidepressants earlier with no major changes in her condition. She further states that the doctor refused to prescribe her any pain medications. She ends the post by sharing how the doctors refuse to acknowledge her condition. As evident, such posts have an underlying temporal logic. Apart from distinguishing between the past (before the disease set in) and the present, the narratives also underscore chronicity and recursivity of the experience of illness.

Other relatedness is the third category devised by Frank and this concept is connected to the ideas of the dyadic body, community feeling, and storytelling. In Frank's words, "Storytelling is one medium through which the dyadic body both offers its own pain and receives the reassurance that others recognize what afflicts it. Thus storytelling is a privileged medium of the dyadic body" (Frank 1997, 36). The various posts and comments in the Facebook community showcase the network of support that has been created to overcome the pain and suffering caused by fibromyalgia.

Finally, Frank talks about the lack of desire. Most of the posts shared in the page talk about the reluctance and disinclination to complete minimal tasks as bathing or washing the hair. This is due to the lack of energy and a constant feeling of fatigue which characterizes fibromyalgia. These posts, too, invite participation and commiseration.

The participatory dynamics of the Facebook community generate a specific type of narrative that "celebrates the potential of contemporary cultures to allow users to generate and share content freely" (Thomas 2016, 126). The following post I shared in the community page while working on this chapter exploits the platform's affordances of self-representation while inviting collaborative knowledge production. The responses to my post attest to the participatory and vibrant nature of the community wherein members continue conversations about topics raised in the post through comments and reactions.[4]

In response to my post, I received 29 comments and 15 "reacts." Among the 15 "reacts," 7 are "care" emoticons, 3 heart emoticons and 8 "likes," showing the different ways the responders affectively connect to my post. Almost all the comments stated that the private nature of the community page enabled the members to share more freely. This sense of freedom, according to the comments, grows out of the absence of acquaintances and family members who challenge the credibility of our self-narrated experiences of fibromyalgia. The absence of any external manifestation of the disease and conventional diagnostic mechanisms complicates the acceptance of our illness narratives outside the community space. One

Figure 6.3 My post on the community page of Women with Fibromyalgia.

comment specified how a presence of a deep scar would make life more tolerable as it would then act as evidence of the presence of the disease. A few posts also suggested remedies to counter the pain and help me through my writing process.

As my examples and analysis of some posts show, the digital space provided by a platform like Facebook has significantly transformed the strategies used to construct and experience illness narratives. Illness narratives now also include collaboratively constituted subjective experiences. The attitude towards dealing with an illness as well as the perception of chronicity has also undergone a massive change with the introduction of social media platforms since these offer patients informal support networks and a space to share as well as better understand their own experiences with the illness.

Conclusion

I took a multidisciplinary approach to understand the possibilities of constructing and sharing digital illness narratives in this chapter. Utilising practices from the fields of literature, sociology, psychology and disability studies, my chapter scrutinized the Facebook page *Women with Fibromyalgia* in order to depict the formation of a newer kind of illness narrative entangled with newer practices of self-narration. The digital illness narratives challenge medical stories (usually regulated by people and systems that do not share the disability) about the legitimacy of invisible disabilities and contend allegations of fictionality by appealing shared experiences and a sense of community. Furthermore, the feeling of sharing comes from not only the written content of posts but also pictures and various kinds of emoticons and reactions offered in the digital environment.

It is important to recognize illness narratives (and other narratives of shared experiences) emerging in community spaces *as* literature because these narratives clearly realize the potential of digital environments as engendering novel forms of writing. Only by identifying and studying these burgeoning forms of digital texts and their dispersals can we move beyond a conception of digital literature that is too closely tied to single authors, traditional and bounded texts, and established social identities. Of course, inclusive studies of digital illness narratives also call for imagining new methodologies and, as I have shown, the participation of the disabled body in the analysis and transparency about the kind of embodied labour entailed in the production of knowledge about contested illnesses is one way to step away from conventional critical methods.

Notes

1 The screenshots used in this chapter were taken with the consent of the respective members.
2 See Figure 6.1.
3 See Figure 6.2.
4 See Figure 6.3.

Bibliography

"(5) Women with Fibromyalgia | Facebook." n.d. Accessed June 20, 2022. www.facebook.com/groups/1682166835441728

Block, Stacey Lynn. 2022. "Women with Fibromyalgia (Chronic)." www.facebook.com/groups/1682166835441728/user/565164263.

Briones-Vozmediano, Erica. 2017. "The Social Construction of Fibromyalgia as a Health Problem from the Perspective of Policies, Professionals, and Patients." *Global Health Action* 10, no. 1: 1275191. https://doi.org/10.1080/16549716.2017.1275191

"Chapter 1 Concepts of Health and Illness | AFMC Primer on Population Health." n.d. Accessed June 20, 2022. https://phprimer.afmc.ca/en/part-i/chapter-1/

"Fibromyalgia." n.d. Accessed June 12, 2022. www.rheumatology.org/I-Am-A/Patient-Caregiver/Diseases-Conditions/Fibromyalgia

Frank, Arthur. 1997. *The Wounded Storyteller*. Chicago: University of Chicago Press.

Georgakopoulou, Alex, Stefan Iversen, and Carsten Stage. 2020. *Quantified Storytelling: A Narrative Analysis of Metrics on Social Media*. New York: Palgrave MacMillan.

Häuser, Winfried, and Mary-Ann Fitzcharles. 2018. "Facts and Myths Pertaining to Fibromyalgia." *Dialogues in Clinical Neuroscience* 20, no. 1: 53–62.

Inanici, Fatma, and Muhammad B. Yunus. 2004. "History of Fibromyalgia: Past to Present." *Current Pain and Headache Reports* 8, no. 5: 369–78. https://doi.org/10.1007/s11916-996-0010-6

"International Day of Disabled Persons: I Have Fibromyalgia and It's My Lived Reality." 2018. *SOAS Blog* (blog). Accessed December 3, 2018. https://study.soas.ac.uk/fibromyalgia-my-lived-reality/

Kadar, Marlene, Linda Warley, Jeanne Perreault, and Susanna Egan. 2005. *Tracing the Autobiographical*. Waterloo: Wilfrid Laurier University Press.

Kleinman, Arthur. 2020. *The Illness Narratives: Suffering, Healing and the Human Condition*. New York: Basic Books.

Lynn, Diane, Diane Driedger, and Michelle K. Owen. 2008. *Dissonant Disabilities: Women with Chronic Illnesses Explore Their Lives*. Toronto: Women's Press of Canada.

Marson, P., and Pasero G. 2008. "[Historical Evolution of the Concept of Fibromyalgia: The Main Stages]." *Reumatismo* 60, no. 4. https://doi.org/10.4081/reumatismo.2008.301

Mintz, Susannah B. 2007. *Unruly Bodies*. Chapel Hill: University of North Carolina Press.

Page, Ruth E. 2013. *Stories and Social Media: Identities and Interaction*. New York: Routledge.

Rovesti, Miriam, Massimo Fioranelli, Paola Petrelli, Francesca Satolli, Maria Grazia Roccia, Serena Gianfaldoni, Georgi Tchernev, et al. 2018. "Health and Illness in History, Science and Society." *Open Access Macedonian Journal of Medical Sciences* 6, no. 1: 163–65. https://doi.org/10.3889/oamjms.2018.056

Ryan, Marie-Laure. 2004. *Narrative across Media: The Languages of Storytelling*. United States of America: University of Nebraska Press.

Sauter, Theresa. 2013. "'What's on your mind?' Writing on Facebook as a tool for self-formation." *New Media and Society* 16, no. 5.

Says, Michael Pfirrman. 2013. "History of Fibromyalgia." News-Medical.Net. Accessed July 10, 2022. www.news-medical.net/health/History-of-Fibromyalgia.aspx

Schalk, Sami. 2021. "Disability." In *Keywords for Gender and Sexuality Studies*, edited by Keywords for Gender and Sexuality Studies Collective. New York: New York University Press. https://keywords.nyupress.org/gender-and-sexuality-studies/essay/disability/

Thomas, Bronwen. 2016. *Narrative: The Basics*. Routledge.

Varul, Mathias Zick. 2010. "Talcott Parsons, the Sick Role and Chronic Illness." *Sage* 16 (2): 72–94. https://doi.org/10.1177/1357034X10364766.

Wagner-Egelhaaf, Martina (ed.). 2019. *Handbook of Autobiography/Autofiction vol. I: Theory and Concepts*. Berlin: De Gruyter.

Part III

Forms of Resistance

Digital media has emerged as a vital modality for transnational activism. A growing number of monographs and edited volumes attest to this phenomenon, including Fidèle A. Vlavo's *Performing Digital Activism: New Aesthetic and Discourses* (2017), Veronica Barassi's *Activism on the Web: Everyday Struggles against Digital Capitalism* (2015), and Lukas Schlogl's *Digital Activism and the Global Middle Class: Generation Hashtag* (2022). Contemporary scholarship has also begun to track what digital activism means within specific regional contexts. David Faris' *Dissent and Revolution in a Digital Age: Social Media, Blogging and Activism in Egypt* (2013), Shola A. Olabode's *Digital Activism and Cyberconflicts in Nigeria: Occupy Nigeria, Boko Haram, and MEND* (2018), Hilda Chacón's *Online Activism in Latin America* (2018), Hojeong Lee and Joong-Hwan Oh's *Digital Media, Online Activism, and Social Movements in Korea* (2021) are some scholarly works considering the impact of digital activism on the political culture of particular regions. But how does digital literature contribute to the cultures of dissent and protest in digital environments? Moreover, what form must digital literary expressions take to effectively participate in social movements? Part III of *Global Perspectives* is concerned with these questions.

A prevailing understanding of resistant literary forms comes from the twentieth-century avant-gardes and their manifestos. Contemporary authors using experimental strategies of collage and erasure, among other techniques, successfully call attention to the ways in which conventionalized language and bureaucratic documents, among other commonplace objects, unjustly control the individual's relationship to the state. However, these radical literary experiments do not necessarily "go viral." Instead, easily quoted, easily shared pieces of image-text combinations—popular, ephemeral literary and cultural expressions—spread quickly over social media and mobilize people, raising social consciousness during contemporary protests. Indian writer Varun Grover's lyrical poem "Hum Kagaz Nahi Dikhayenge" ("We won't show the papers") and a video recording of him reciting it went viral during the 2019 Citizenship Amendment Act protests in India. Cartoons mobilized people to protest the Anti-Extradition Law Amendment Bill in Hong Kong, and digital posters and other word-image combinations, including Marjani Satrapi's artwork that shows a woman blended with the letter I in IRAN waving her chopped hair protesting the country's gender-based clothing mandates and other oppressive laws (posted online by Bangladesh-origin British author Leesa Gazi), were shared widely on social media.

Of course, virality is not the only way digital literature can intervene in social and political movements. Digital platforms also offer vital tools for archiving narratives that authoritarian governments seek to censor, though given the corporatization of major media platforms and the proliferating means of surveillance, these archives also face constant threat. Where actual archives are not available, artists create imagined and fictionalized archives to call attention to the absences. Cataloging all the major moments and movements in which digital literature contributed to the culture of resistance is beyond the scope of the present book. However, the following chapters by Seiça, Chu, Hosny, and Davis highlight certain flashpoints in that long, complex, and evolving history.

Using a variety of media theoretical approaches to politically charged digital literary practices and artefacts, Seiça, Chu, Hosny, and Davis offer a glimpse of how digital platforms are instrumentalized by different communities with distinct political goals. The scholars contributing to this section recognize how the innovative and creative uses of digital technologies for purposes of documentation and protest can be censored—this too is addressed in the chapters, countering any overly generalized understanding of digital platforms as democratic and inclusive spaces.

Apart from deepening our understanding of digital literary expressions within political contexts (of Hong Kong, Taiwan, Egypt, Chile, and other places), this section of *Global Perspectives* also consciously draws such expressions into a network of comparison. While the chapters maintain a sense of specificity when discussing aesthetic strategies, they also do not exclusively equate certain forms of expression with particular regional conditions or messages. For example, Seiça's study is transnational in its scope as it shows how artists across regional and cultural boundaries use erasure as a method of composition to protest censorship, surveillance, and other forms of political oppression. And while Seiça recognizes that the idea of political oppression carries different meanings in changing contexts, his chapter also argues that the explosion of erasure aesthetics on platforms like Instagram signals popularization of an artistic practice that was earlier associated with the avant-garde.

If erasure is used to generate resistant literary works today, so are cartoons. Kin Wai Chu discusses how digital manhua or cartoons function as a critical tool of political commentary in Hong Kong. Chu's chapter is focused on the collaborative activism and political participation engendered by digital cartoons in the last decade. She charts the role Internet has played in combatting the censorship of political cartoons in traditional media outlets. Her chapter also shows how same symbols accumulate different meanings in distinct political situations.

Hosny's study productively compares cinematic and digital texts representing the January 25th uprisings in Egypt. Her chapter explores how formal affordances of media interact and engender political messages.

In his chapter, Davis discusses an "archival turn" in digital literature that complements Seiça's observations about the documentary turn. The concerns of Davis's chapter include anxieties about production and circulation of information, potential for manipulation, possible responses to authoritarianism through decentralization and collaboration. What makes the cluster of chapters in Part III especially significant is that they show how literary strategies challenging oppression are both extremely contextual, situated within specific historical and geographical coordinates, but also equally fluid, transcending the borders of cultures, languages, and nation-states.

Bibliography

Barassi Veronica. 2015. *Activism on the Web: Everyday Struggles against Digital Capitalism*. New York: Routledge.

Chacón, Hilda. 2018. *Online Activism in Latin America*. London: Taylor & Francis.

Faris, David. 2013. *Dissent and Revolution in a Digital Age: Social Media, Blogging and Activism in Egypt*. London: Bloomsbury Publishing.

Hojeong Lee, and Joong-Hwan Oh. 2021. *Digital Media, Online Activism, and Social Movements in Korea*. Washington DC: Lexington Books.

Olabode, Shola A. 2018. *Digital Activism and Cyberconflicts in Nigeria: Occupy Nigeria, Boko Haram and MEND*. Bingley: Emerald Publishing Limited.

Schlogl, Lukas. 2022. *Digital Activism and the Global Middle Class: Generation Hashtag*. London: Taylor and Francis.

Vlavo, Fidèle A. 2017. *Performing Digital Activism: New Aesthetics and Discourses of Resistance*. London: Taylor and Francis.

7 The Erasing Impulse

Veiling and Unveiling the Poetic and the Political

Álvaro Seiça

Introduction

Erasure is a set of material, literary, and visual techniques that has gained global momentum in the past two decades. It is often used as an artistic composition method that employs appropriation, rewriting, reworking, or repurposing procedures, with either formalist or conceptual tendencies, as well as political concerns.

On a compositional and formal level, erasure often means appropriating and modifying found material in order to partially cover its content, while uncovering a new reading and meaning. Like other writers and artists before, who have emphasized the sculptural dimensions of erasure, American and Hong Kong-based artist Daniel C. Howe (2021, 02:08) highlights: "the history of erasure, broadly defined, goes farther back, perhaps originating, at least conceptually, in the practice of sculpture, where the removal of material is a fundamental task in the medium." A literary erasure is a textual, artistic, and aesthetic strategy that is constrained and often uses controlled vocabulary. By reworking literary and visual works, news pieces, or legal and political documents, authors may employ "erasure to create new works that both refer to, and go beyond, the source texts from which they are created" (Howe 2021, 02:32).

In this chapter, I will first go back to some of the antecedents that have been influencing contemporary literary and visual artworks, by debating what I would like to call "an erasing impulse" in the first two decades of the twenty-first century. Then, I will focus on affiliations, and propose three different types of constellations of practices. Finally, I will deal with images of veiling and unveiling, to highlight the poetic and the political in works by authors who use erasure to resist and to affirm their political stances. These works arise from the context of sources found on the Web or are programmed in the digital realm.

Erasure practices have had a higher implementation in two moments—the 1960–70s and the 2000–10s—, but the post-Web context has surely accelerated a globalized access and spread of specific techniques, as the form is popularized via social network sites. Despite the globalized aspect and the neoliberal conditions under which these authors work, their

DOI: 10.4324/9781003214915-11

political agendas shape this literary and artistic form in a flexible and heterogeneous manner. Yet the return of the documentary form shows shared ways of denouncing and protesting against social, gender, and political inequality, silenced individuals and minorities, censorship, as well as state and corporate surveillance and obfuscation. The works highlighted in this chapter are by non-Anglophone authors from Chile, Germany, Italy, Portugal, and Taiwan, and from Anglophone authors who have dual cultural background.

The Erasing Impulse

The practice of erasure is not new. Poets, writers, and artists will often cite common inspirational authors and sources. Some may reference Man Ray's untitled 1924 blackout poem published in the Dada journal *391*, Marcel Duchamp's modifications of artworks, Robert Rauschenberg's painting *Erased de Kooning Drawing* (1953), Tom Phillips's *A Humument* (1966–), Ronald Johnson's *Radi Os* (1977) or, more recently, Jen Bervin's *Nets* (2004), Jenny Holzer's *Redaction Paintings* (2006), and M. NourbeSe Philip's *Zong!* (2008).

Given the hegemony of American culture and English as lingua franca, these works have been influential for different generations of artists inside and outside the United States. Still, they seldom overshadow others, namely, from the non-Anglophone world:

- In Germany and Austria Heinrich Heine's *Reisebilder* (1827) or Gerhard Rühm's blackout over-paintings of newspapers and grammars, as in *L'Essentiel de la Grammaire* (1962).
- In Italy, Emilio Isgrò's ongoing and prolific *cancellaturas* with texts, encyclopaedias, paintings, and installations, which started with *Libro Cancellato* (1964).
- In Portugal, António Aragão's "Telegramando" (1965), an official telegram from the Portuguese Postal Service repurposed as a self-reflexive piece of literary art, which parodies, with cross-outs, the dictatorial New State regime's violation of private correspondence. Or Maria Velho da Costa's *Desescrita* (1973), a collection that proposes a new orthography by parodying the Censorship Commission's cuts as lipograms. While the author cuts or swaps beforehand the letters of the most relevant words, she self-censors her text, and as such the censor has no way to cut even further such a political literary work: "Ecidi escrever ortado; poupo assim o rabalho a quem me orta" [I ecided to ut out writing; this way I spare the ork of whom may ut me.] (Velho da Costa 1973, 55, translation mine)

The above works even overshadow some of those works from the Anglophone world that are now being rediscovered: Bob Brown's reading satire *GEMS: A Censored Anthology* (1931), Doris Cross's 1960s dictionary column erasures and over-paintings, such as the "Embassador," or Madeline Gins's intriguing, mind-blowing, and genre-bending *Word Rain or A Discursive Introduction to the Intimate Philosophical Investigations of G,R,E,T,A G,A,R,B,O, It Says* (1969).

These antecedents are important, since authors often follow them as affiliations that can be pinned down to the level of aesthetic decisions, material techniques, graphic output, or even which source texts to appropriate and erase. Visual and graphic marks of erasure in literary works can be traced to, among other cases, Laurence Sterne's *The Life and Opinions of Tristram Shandy, Gentleman* (1759–67), and to Heine's poetical narrative *Reisebilder* (1827), in which the author denounces state censorship by satirically mimicking the censor's cuts. In chapter 12, Heine's parody mocks the censors by erasing all words, except for: "Die deutschen Censoren — — — — (...) — — — — — Dummköpfe — —" [The German censors [...] idiots.] (Heine 1827, 228, translation mine).

If during the nineteenth and twentieth centuries we find sparse examples of erasure, then in the early twenty-first century we witness a boom of poems using erasing techniques. The increase of literary and artistic works that use erasure as a form of composition range from print to sound and digital media. Across media and fields, erasure makes its way through the graphic taste of an epoch, perhaps as a trend. When it comes to poetry, following Brian McHale (2005) and Travis Macdonald (2009), Andrew Epstein (2012: 319) speaks of a "mini-trend in 'erasure poetics.'" Mini or maxi, peripheral or mainstream, we can certainly speak of an impulse to erase. This erasing impulse may be part of a larger social, cultural, and technological context, where authors are adopting creative practices and methods that include appropriation, copying, and remixing—a phenomenon studied by, among others, Eduardo Navas (2012). Yet Epstein (2012, 310) is not shy from asserting: "the reproduction, sampling, and recycling of cultural materials (...) has become a dominant expressive mode, if not *the* dominant one. Today, the remix and the mash-up rule."

Erasure is staged in advertisement, such as Web ads or front shop windows. Moreover, it has been employed to mimic press censorship, like in the campaign in newspaper covers run by Australia's Right to Know coalition in 2019, when the media called for freedom of expression and transparency. Erasure is also staged as a graphic trope in generalist book covers, and even art catalogs that do not focus on erasure, yet graphic designers employ cross-outs in their titles (Hollein and Weinhart 2016). Other times, graphic design styling is not just meant as visual rhetoric but rather to underline a work's theme. Such is the case of Emil Kozole's interactive typeface "Project 'Seen,'" which live generates three modes of deletion based on the American National Security Agency's monitoring keyword list, and, according to the author, is "an experiment of evasive and reflexive techniques around the topic of online privacy" (Kozole 2015). Or Titus Kaphar and Reginald Dwayne Betts's "Redaction," a font that defaces its content in progressive stages, as part of a project that "seeks to highlight the abuses in the criminal justice system, in particular the way poor and marginalized people are imprisoned for failure to pay court fines and fees" (Betts, Kaphar et al. 2019).

Erasure is explored in different guises in the visual and literary arts around the globe. For instance, Adrian Piper's series of photocopied photographs *Everything* (2003) prevents any possibility of facial recognition by way of sanding and overprinting images with the sentence "Everything will be taken away." It is not solely a Western phenomenon, as can be inferred from a major Taiwanese exhibition and issue of the *Xianzai Shi* magazine. In 2008, poets and editors Hung Hung, Yung Man-Han, Tseng Shu-mei, and Hsia Yü created a participatory exhibition of erased material at Taipei's Contemporary Art Museum. Then, they turned this experience into a journal issue, using pencils, pens, markers, and collage to overdraw, blackout, whiteout, cross-out, and to recompose the images and characters of newspaper pages, glossy magazines, and literary anthologies (2012a). They produced a critical take on the poetic landscape of Taiwan, because, as one poem reads after being erased, they were "Fearing to Return to that Rather Obsolete Language" (2012b, 33). Hsia Yü had already self-published *Pink Noise* (2007), a book of English and Mandarin poetry partly generated from Weblog crawls and machine translation whose verses are printed on acrylic transparent pages and thus overprint, veil, and unveil each other. While Yü addresses love, Hung Hung has been concerned with politics and the erasures created in the wake of Taiwan's Martial Law imposed by the Chinese authorities, a line of inquiry and action that the poet and theatre director develops in "Those Vanished Sensitive Words" (2021).

Besides being global, yet predominantly American, the phenomenon of erasure is somehow polyhedral, or kaleidoscopic, in shape, form, and media. It has given rise to online poetry generators, such as Joshua Beckman and David Hirmes's *Erasures* for Wave Books (2006), or Katie Schaag's and team fog-inducing *The Infinite Woman* (2019). It has been popularized by Do-It-Yourself newspaper blackout books (Kleon 2010), self-help therapeutic blackout poetry (Carroll 2018)—according to its author, "communities of hope" on Instagram—and even *New York Times* blackout poetry contests directed at teenagers ("Winners…," 2019). Among others, this post-Web, social network site-spreadable and two-decade long wave of publications, as well as events and writing workshops have advanced the labels "erasure poetry" and "blackout poetry."

As of November 19, 2020, searching on Instagram for the tags "#erasurepoetry" and "#blackoutpoetry" shows some overlapping of techniques in the results of both tags. But it makes clear that while the former has ca. 27,000 posts, the later, "#blackoutpoetry," has ca. 170,000 (Seiça 2020a, 2020b). A numbing effect of hit results is also easy to reach by using a search engine and typing "erasure poem" (Seiça 2020c). This seems evidence enough that the techniques of erasing found material have become popular. Now, I want to suggest that these labels may obscure historical cases across media—where erasure, suppression, or censorship are dealt with in tandem (e.g., Rühm's 1969 sound poem "Zensurierte Rede" on censored speech)—that have reemerged with the documentary form in the 2000s.

A look at the intersection of erasure and the arts, at least since the 1960s experimental arts, has already galvanized revisions in thematic issues of journals, or exhibitions, such as the rich gathering *Under Erasure* at New York's Pierogi Gallery (2018a). Curators Heather and Raphael Rubinstein (2018b, n.p.) write that,

> For Derrida (as for Heidegger before him) to put a word under erasure (*sous rature*) is to signal the inadequacy of inherited language while also recognizing its inevitability. Since Derrida introduced the concept (…) this emphatically visual act of intervention has become an indispensable technique in diverse disciplines.

We are thus drawn to infer that from the late 1960s onwards—influenced by Jacques Derrida (despite the fact that *De la Grammatologie* only came out in English translation in 1976)—authors have increasingly pursued erasing techniques in their practice. Even though Derrida's philosophy of "trace" is most relevant to this discussion—as it has been argued, for instance, by John Nyman (2018)—I do not think we can assert that his work has been the source of erasure's proliferation. Below, I will back this claim with documentation.

Looking at the wider picture, which includes documenting as many works that use material erasure as possible, reveals a more complex scenario. I am approaching this scenario by not differentiating between labels (i.e., "erasure poetry" and "blackout poetry", Ramser 2020), because they both hide and reveal, they both remove and add, and they both delete and underline. On top, it is debatable whether such a distinction helps advancing or narrowing down the problems at stake. My approach is to find family resemblances or constellations of practices that start emerging once we see and read more works, and as common features or patterns become more evident.

Constellations of Practices: Documenting, Classifying, and Visualizing

I have now documented more than 400 works of erasure worldwide, between 1827 and 2021 (Seiça 2020d, 2). In order to describe them, I document different fields, such as author, title, country, year, language, publication type, source material and type, erasure type, software, and so on. Once this data is assembled, it is possible to filter its content in different ways. For example, we can look at the temporal progression of publication dates. Once we distribute works per decade of creation or publication, we see a slight increase from the early 1960s to the 1990s, but it is really in the 2000s and 2010s that there is an explosion, ending with more than the double of works in the 2010s in relation to the preceding decade (Seiça 2020d, 3).

Several reasons for this fact may have to do with the curation of my data and its documentation process, as bias is built into the way I search and find works. But from this sample it is still possible to extrapolate an impulse to erase, as described above. There is also a convergence of historical revisions with resistance and justice. Isobel O'Hare (2018, n.p.), who has been erasing public apologies of sexual assaulters, argues that

> We are living in a time when artists and writers are openly fighting with history and revealing its prejudices. So many people have been erased in the telling of history, so it makes sense to turn the tables and do some erasing right back.

Documenting so many works, while trying to classify their origin, materiality, content, and techniques, prompts a richer debate on erasure at a granular level. Categorizing these items into a typology is a rather complex and difficult task, because these cultural artifacts are created across several artistic areas that are analog and digital. In any case, I tried to blend different traditions that emerged from the way in which authors were naming their strategies and techniques, and as such the typology of erasure that emerged is a bottom-up model in which I progressively add other types as I document more works. The typology is made of five layers: the types of documents used as sources, the type of erasure, media, technique, and the reading effect (Seiça 2020d, 4). There are multiple ways to visualize this typology in trees or dendrograms (Seiça 2020d, 5–8), but here I would like to focus on how those visualizations can bring about an understating of affiliations, or constellations of practices.

Overall, what the documentation and classification make clear is that works that employ erasure are not homogeneous, but that they rather constitute a heterogeneous field of practices. This has to do with the themes staged by each author and work, but also the sources that they use to erase, the ways they erase them, and what media and techniques they use. So, if we start by filtering these works and by trying to aggregate those that share resemblances or direct influence, we can define, at least, three constellations (Seiça 2020e). It is revealing to juxtapose some of these works in dialogue, even though the way each work can be filtered, or associated with, is at times multiple. For now, I will propose three different types of constellations of practices:

- Constellation Blackout: Literary and Visual Documents, and Computational Scripts
- Constellation Covering: Overpainting, Overwriting, Sewing, and Collage
- Constellation Redaction: Public, Legal, and Secret Documents

The first constellation includes works with blackout techniques as a common denominator (Seiça 2020e, 2). For instance, we can cherry-pick works by Ray, Brown, Isgrò, Johnson, and, more recently, Howe, and Kathrin Passig, who work with computational scripts and media. The second constellation compiles works that use different types of source material—newspapers, dictionaries, and literary works—to cover their surfaces with the techniques of overpainting, overwriting, sewing, or collage (Seiça 2020e, 3). This constellation gathers works by Rühm, Cross, Phillips, Gins, and, more recently, Bervin and Mary Ruefle. Finally, in the third constellation, on redaction, authors use public, legal, or secret documents from archival sources (Seiça 2020e, 4). The constellation redaction gathers works by Holzer, Kristina Lee Podesva, Carlos Soto-Román, O'Hare, and Betts, but obviously we could also include here Kozole's, or Hsia Yü et al.'s. These constellations are meant to be basic organizers of information in relation to those fields of the typology: by type of document source, by mode of erasing, by media, by technique, or by effect: readable, unreadable, or partly readable. Another interesting constellation that could be organized is on works that employ fictional documentary erasures, in which authors fake documents to create literary or visual artworks: Heine, Gins, or Solmaz Sharif's work.

Veiling and Unveiling: Voices That Erase to Resist and to Affirm

The art of erasing is also the art of underlining. Ultimately, erasure deals with what is made visible and what is made invisible, with the act of veiling and unveiling. The act of erasing is a complex formation of negative and positive space. In bringing forward a study on the relations between poetics and erasure, my argument is that erasure is politically situated, not only in works that use public, legal, and secret documents, or that address social and political suppressions, but ultimately in all. Yet even if erasure cannot be thought of independently of its sociopolitical dimensions, it can aesthetically serve a creative work independently of its sociopolitical dimensions, or by minimizing them.

This critical perspective has been advanced by several writers and artists. For instance, Iranian-American poet Solmaz Sharif (2013, n.p.) stresses that

> the proliferation of erasure as a poetic tactic in the United States is happening alongside a proliferation of our awareness of it as a state tactic. And, it seems, many erasure projects today hold these things as unrelated. (...) Poetic erasure means the striking out of text. / Poetic erasure has yet to advance historically. / Historically, the striking out of text is the root of obliterating peoples.

Moving from prose to poetry, Sharif skillfully enacts her understanding of erasure as an aesthetic, poetic, and political signifier. In her poetry volume

Look, besides re-situating violence via the military dictionary, the poet exposes yet another type of brutality by fictionally staging the deletions made to the letters received by Salim, a Guantanamo prisoner. Instead of working with found material, Sharif reimagines state erasure as voids in the poem's lines. Likewise, Daniel C. Howe (2021, 02:49) points out that, "As a strategy, erasure directs our attention to important questions concerning voice, narrative and power in the present moment. Who is allowed to speak, and who is silenced?"

In a related guise, Hannah Dawn Henderson's book *Being, in a State of Erasure* (2017) explores the very notion that erasure is, first and foremost, what the body feels and what it is subjected to. "Let us not begin in the archive. Let us instead begin in my bedroom," (15) instigates the author. As a Scottish, with Jamaican ancestry, and based in the Netherlands, Henderson moves on to show how her Jamaican family and blackness are rendered invisible in the context of 1970s and contemporary United Kingdom. The work blends the deeply personal with rescued archival material. By doing so, Henderson stresses how racial prejudice erases identity:

> the violence of erasure when that stare assumes me to be white, or alternatively the violence of racial codification when it denotes me as black – yet still erasure, for the wealth of my Black cultural heritage is what they think of when they codify me.
>
> (20)

By addressing Frantz Fanon's critical work on racism and colonialism, as well as Édouard Glissant's *Poetics of Relation*, Henderson reinforces how racial prejudice erases the body as a site of violence. The geo-cultural and political dimensions of colonial heritage are felt in the body: "I am an occupied territory" (22). The topic of erasure as violence is already contained in her previous work, *From She Who the Water Cradled*, a blackout intervention on Virginia Woolf's *A Writer's Diary* that is "Contemplating the violence entailed in reducing an individual anonymous by means of obliterating their voice."

Race and erasure have been debated most notably by Robin Coste Lewis (2016), Raquel Lima (2021), and, before, by M. NourbeSe Philip. Her 2008 book *Zong!* is exemplary in this respect, because the material marks left by the erasure of the source text act in tandem with the obliterated human lives and their stories. The author uncovers them by deleting and isolating the legal text of the court record Gregory vs. Gilbert, the only account left from a brutal act of murder committed in 1781 by the ship captain of the slave boat Zong, who "ordered that some 150 Africans be murdered by drowning so that the ship's owners could collect insurance monies." As Cecily Parks (2020, n.p.) noted,

> Philip refers to the story as one that "might be told by not telling," a phrase that not only acknowledges the abject horror of a history that

no words will ever accurately account for but also justifies the erasure that allows Philip to excavate a rendition of it.

One could further argue that linearity and narrative coherence are all but the right approach to a literary retelling of Zong's slavery massacre.

In this light, as an act of intervention inscribed in societies immersed in social inequalities, erasure means stressing the silences, the acts of removal, the obliteration, and the deletion of those who have been left out. Thus, several authors use erasure tactics to think on how slavery and racial profiling occurs, how minorities are silenced, how populations, journalists, authors, or protesters are suppressed, how thinking and discourse is controlled, surveilled, and removed via several entangled physical and digital systems, but also on how privacy and the right to be forgotten are handled by the state or the corporation. A recent case that takes into consideration the "right to be forgotten," in relation to the General Data Protection Regulation, is the visual vignettes of Mascha Gugganig and Rachel Douglas-Jones (2021), where the latter erases parts of the Article 17 that is precisely concerned with data deletion.

The use of documents as found material, other than literary or visual works, form an essential basis for authorial, poetic, and political decision-making. The poet and the artist are already making a statement when they decide which sources to act upon. In *Redaction Paintings* (2006), Jenny Holzer appropriates United States confidential documentation declassified under the Freedom of Information Act. The artist then resizes, repurposes, and adds drawings or yet more redacted marks in large-scale installations. The result is often revelatory of the obfuscation, violence, abuse, and torture inflicted by the United States military interventions, a fact that is further highlighted in Holzer's subsequent series and exhibitions: *Secret* (2007), *TOP SECRET* (2010), *Dust Paintings* (2014), and *War Paintings* (2015). In *Dust Paintings*, oil progressively overshadows the declassified documents seemingly transferred into linen. By the time the viewer reaches the quasi-Suprematist paintings they could think of them as abstract art from the early twentieth century, only to find, at closer inspection, words veiled under the geometrical forms, such as "secret," "explosives," or "terrorist operation."

Soto-Román has also appropriated United States' declassified materials—which were nevertheless released partially redacted—and went to the extreme of intervention by leaving almost no recognizable text. The poet's tactics wish not to unveil the expurgated extracts, but to further veil the silences. These silences were left not only by the United States covert actions during the 1970s against the democratically elected president of Chile, Salvador Allende, but also the backing of Pinochet's coup, as well as the subsequent censorship of the materials documenting intelligence information and diplomatic cables. Soto-Román has followed this line of inquiry in books such as *Chile Project: [Re-Classified]* (2013, 2016) and *11* (2017). In *Chile Project*, the poet concentrates on the foreign interventions in Chile and the legacy of Pinochet's regime, by further redacting the Central Intelligence Agency's (CIA) redactions of declassified material. In doing so, his poetic and artistic gesture "reclassify" the partially declassified secret documents.

In the video poem *Borradura* (2021), the poet activates new tensions between negative and positive image, legibility and illegibility, by leaving only one word supposedly intact: "Pinochet." Juliana Spahr (2021) remarks:

> As Soto-Román whites out the words around it, words about time, worth, and human rights he talks about this practice where he puts into "questions the documents that describe violence." Then once all the remaining words from the CIA document have been erased except "Pinochet," he grabs a pen and crosses out this word with a ballpoint pen, making it illegible.

The poet crossed out the dictator with a pen that could be a scalpel. Bruno Ministro (2021) goes further on the issue of accumulating redactions to highlight their silences by pointing out that, "Where blackouts considered some information to be sensible, the further erasure made by Soto-Román considered almost all information to be sensible." Arguing that, "rather than being a contradiction this is an expressive radical gesture," Ministro stresses that the poet's aim is "to expose, to remember, to subvert." This act of rescuing memory from oblivion and hold truth to the testimony of the massacres committed by Pinochet's extreme-right wing dictatorial regime is also explored in *11*. In this hybrid book of poetry and short prose, Soto-Román uses archival material and government sources to unveil and veil, via obliteration and strikethrough, statistics on the numbers of forced disappeared Chilean citizens, or to question the regime's rhetoric of brutality and repression.

The connection between sociopolitical context and erasure is further made visible by works that address censorship and surveillance in contemporary societies, especially in authoritarian regimes. Examples of these approaches can be found in the digital artworks by Howe or Winnie Soon. Howe has been creating plug-ins as browser extensions that mimic the user's Web experience in Mainland China, such as *ChinaEye* (2016), which was banned from the Google Chrome store, and whose extreme example is *Redacto* (2016). With *Redacto*, all information on Web pages, including most text and images, becomes redacted via modified Cascading Style Sheets. This exploration of algorithmic redaction outputs censored blackouts when the user navigates any page, including newspaper sites or search engines, tied to a keyword list of sensitive words in China. In a different fashion, Soon's digital series *The Unerasable Characters* (2020–21) collects and repurposes censored micro messages posted on China's largest social network site Weibo—which is investigated by the project Weiboscope in Hong Kong—and recreate them via a new interface and visual display. As a platform, visual and literary artwork, the series algorithmically and aesthetically transcodes, while politically reframing and unveiling the archival data of censored output that could go otherwise unnoticed if one was unaware of Fu King-wa's Weiboscope research project.

Conclusion

The works discussed in this chapter put into question different aspects of globalization in the post-digital era, where artistic practices are computationally born, or spring from feedback between digital, print, and analog media. These works are born out of a context where globalization flattens differences across procedures and practices, especially via mobile applications and social network sites. Yet these works show idiosyncrasies in approaches, namely in the Global South. These idiosyncrasies might be cultural, aesthetic, material, or political.

Even though the phenomena are complex—as I have argued in relation to the strategy of artistic, literary, and computational modification (Seiça 2020f)—the incredible rise of erasure techniques and works in the 2000s and 2010s, in relation to the 1980s or 1990s, can be explained by different facts. This erasing impulse may well stem from the growing and then widespread access to the Internet in the rich and industrialized countries, how easily data can be reproduced and modified in digital media, the rapid and ubiquitous spread of images on the Web and in social network sites, the proliferation of databases and the concentration of social networks, the popularization of the form via influential works, publications, and events, as well as the netizen's overwhelming feeling that there is too much information. Too much information, too many documents, too many literary, visual, and sound works documented and available in archives. As a consequence, there is a huge pool of readily available documents that can be appropriated, reused, and remixed. Conceptual or not, for some authors working from scratch may seem too daring or unnecessary. Process-oriented techniques and literary figures are not anymore solely citation, collage, intertextuality, or pastiche. They are supplied with appropriation, repurposing, "re-reporting" (Leong 2020), and remixing. Once a technique like erasure is progressively known, it can be virtually and easily applied everywhere, to any document or file, physical, analog, or digital. These aspects may explain its popularity, especially when one searches in social network sites like Instagram.

The return of documentary art and literature seems to be widespread, as it can be seen as well in other artistic fields, such as documentary theatre. When comparing the output of works that use erasure, the two more active moments are the decades of 1960–70s and the 2000–10s. These two big waves of erasure techniques suggest a reemergence of experimental practices and documentary sources tied to global political turning points: the May 68, the Vietnam War; or the 9/11, the Iraq Invasion, the Arab Spring, the Occupy Movement, etc. Authors use erasure to denounce, resist, protest, and affirm progressive change, while taking advantage of varied media documents and archival material. Erasure has become a means for exposing covert state action and persecution, as well as gender, class, and racial inequality, and for reinventing what political art, literature, and poetry can be.

Acknowledgment

This project received funding from the European Union's Horizon 2020 research and innovation program under the Marie Skłodowska-Curie grant agreement no. 793147, ARTDEL. https://artdel.net

Bibliography

Aragão, António. 1965. "Telegramando." *Jornal do Fundão*, Supplement, January 24. https://po-ex.net/taxonomia/materialidades/planograficas/poesia-experimental-suplemento-do-jornal-do-fundao/
Beckman, Joshua, and David Hirmes. 2006. *Erasures*. Seattle, WA: Wave Books. http://erasures.wavepoetry.com
Bervin, Jen. 2004. *Nets*. New York: Ugly Duckling Presse.
Betts, Reginald D., Titus Kaphar, Forest Young, et al. 2019. "Redaction." www.redaction.us
Brown, Bob. 2014 [1931]. *GEMS: A Censored Anthology*, edited by Craig Saper. Baltimore, MD: Roving Eye Press.
Carroll, John. 2018. *Make Blackout Poetry*. New York: Abrams Noterie.
Cross, Doris. 2018 [ca. 1965]. "Embassador." In *Under Erasure*, edited by Heather and Raphael Rubinstein, 49. New York: Pierogi Gallery/NonprofessionalExperiments. www.under-erasure.com/artists-writers/cross_doris
Derrida, Jacques. 1976. *Of Grammatology*. Translated by Gayatri C. Spivak. Baltimore, MD: Johns Hopkins University Press.
Douglas-Jones, Rachel, and Mascha Gugganig. 2021. "Visual Vignettes." In *Sensing In/Security*, edited by Nina Klimburg-Witjes et al., 215–236. Manchester: Mattering Press. https://doi.org/10.28938/9781912729111
Epstein, Andrew. 2012. "Found Poetry, 'Uncreative Writing,' and the Art of Appropriation." In *The Routledge Companion to Experimental Literature*, edited by Joe Bray, Alison Gibbons, and Brian McHale, 310–322. Abingdon and New York: Routledge.
Gins, Madeline. 1969. *Word Rain or A Discursive Introduction to the Intimate Philosophical Investigations of G,R,E,T,A G,A,R,B,O, It Says*. New York: Grossman Publishers.
Glissant, Édouard. 2010. *Poetics of Relation*. Translated by Betsy Wing. Ann Arbor, MI: The University of Michigan Press.
Heine, Heinrich. 1923 [1826–7]. *Reisebilder. Die Nordsee, Ideen, Das Buch Le Grand*. Leipzig: Reclam.
Henderson, Hannah D. 2016. *From She Who the Water Cradled*. Object. www.hannahdawnhenderson.net/From-she-who-the-water-cradled
Henderson, Hannah D. 2017. *Being, in a State of Erasure*. London: Book Works.

Hollein, Max, and Martina Weinhart, eds. 2016. *Ich.* Cologne and Frankfurt: Walther König/Schirn Kunsthalle Frankfurt.
Holzer, Jenny. 2006. *Redaction Paintings.* New York: Cheim & Read. https://www.cheimread.com/publications/jenny-holzer-redaction-paintings
Holzer, Jenny. 2007. *Secret.* New York: Sprüth Magers.
Holzer, Jenny. 2010. *TOP SECRET.* New York: Yvon Lambert.
Holzer, Jenny. 2014. *Dust Paintings.* New York: Cheim & Read. https://www.cheimread.com/publications/jenny-holzer-dust-paintings
Holzer, Jenny. 2015. *War Paintings.* Venice: Museo Correr. https://correr.visitmuve.it/en/mostre-en/archivio-mostre-en/holzer-exhibition-correr/2015/03/11491/war-paintings-jenny-holzer
Howe, Daniel C. 2016. *ChinaEye.* Browser extension. https://rednoise.org/daniel/chinaeye
Howe, Daniel C. 2016. *Redacto.* Browser extension. https://rednoise.org/daniel/redacto
Howe, Daniel C. 2021. "Compressions." Presented at Erase!, *Vimeo*, September 21. https://erase.artdel.net/compressions/
Hung, Hung. 2021. "Those Vanished Sensitive Words." Presented at Erase!, *Vimeo*, September 24. https://erase.artdel.net/vanished-words/
Isgrò, Emilio. 1964. *Libro Cancellato.* Milan: Museo del Novecento.
Johnson, Ronald. 1977. *Radi Os.* Berkeley, CA: Sand Dollar. Rep. 2005. Chicago, IL: Flood Editions.
Kleon, Austin. 2010. *Newspaper Blackout.* New York: Harper Perennial.
Kozole, Emil. 2015. "Project 'Seen.'" https://projectseen.com
Leong, Michael. 2020. *Contested Records: The Turn to Documents in Contemporary North American Poetry.* Iowa City, IA: University of Iowa Press.
Lewis, Robin Coste. 2016. "The Race Within Erasure." Podcast, *The Archive Project*, Literary Arts, Portland, OR, February 25. Audio, 50:50. https://literary-arts.org/archive/robin-coste-lewis-2
Lima, Raquel. 2021. "Rasura: Performance, Oratura e Identidade." Presented at Erase!, *Vimeo*, September 20. https://erase.artdel.net/rasura/
Macdonald, Travis. 2009. "A Brief History of Erasure Poetics." *Jacket*, no. 38. http://jacketmagazine.com/38/macdonald-erasure.shtml
McHale, Brian. 2005. "Poetry under Erasure." In *Theory into Poetry: New Approaches to the Lyric*, edited by Eva Müller-Zettelmann and Margarete Rubik, 277–301. Amesterdam: Rodopi.
Ministro, Bruno. 2021. "On *Borradura.*" Presented at Erase!, September 23. https://erase.artdel.net/borradura/
Moure, Erín. 2009. "ErasU/re." *The Capilano Review* 3 (7): 122.
Navas, Eduardo. 2012. *Remix Theory: The Aesthetics of Sampling.* New York: Springer.
Nyman, John. 2018. "Double/Cross: Erasure in Theory and Poetry." PhD diss., The University of Western Ontario. https://ir.lib.uwo.ca/etd/5529
O'Hare, Isobel. 2018. "The Text Is My Enemy: Erasing the Patriarchy with Isobel O'Hare." Interview by Caitlin Cowan. *Luna Luna Magazine*, April 20. www.lunalunamagazine.com/blog/interview-with-isobel-ohare
Parks, Cecily. 2020. "On Erasure." *Kenyon Review Online.* https://kenyonreview.org/kr-online-issue/2020-julyaug/selections/cecily-parks-656342
Passig, Kathrin. 2018. "Poetry Blackout." *SYNC* 2 (28). http://sync.abue.io/issues/190712kp_sync2_28_blackout.pdf
Philip, M. NourbeSe. 2008. *Zong!* Middletown: Wesleyan University Press.

Phillips, Tom. 1966–. *A Humument*. London: Self-published. www.tomphillips.co.uk/humument
Piper, Adrian. 2018 [2003]. "Everything.". In *Concepts and Intuitions, 1965–2016*. Los Angeles: Hammer Museum at UCLA.
Ramser, Emily. 2020. "The Ocean of Texts: The History of Blackout Poetry." MA diss., Texas Woman's University. www.thehistoryofblackoutpoetry.org
Rauschenberg, Robert. 1953. *Erased de Kooning Drawing*. www.sfmoma.org/artwork/98.298/
Ray, Man. 1924. "Untitled." *391*, no. 17: 3. https://dada.lib.uiowa.edu/files/show/74
Rubinstein, Heather, and Raphael Rubinstein, eds. 2018a. *Under Erasure*. New York: Pierogi Gallery/NonprofessionalExperiments.
Rubinstein, Heather, and Raphael Rubinstein. 2018b. "Under Erasure." www.under-erasure.com
Rühm, Gerhard. 1962. *L'Essentiel de la Grammaire*. http://foundation.generali.at/de/sammlung.html#work=2534&artist=187
Rühm, Gerhard. 1969. "Zensurierte Rede." In *Phonetische Poesie*, edited by Franz Mon. Audio, 3: 43. Neuwied: Luchterhand Verlag, 1971.
Schaag, Katie, et al. 2019. *The Infinite Woman*. www.theinfinitewoman.com
Seiça, Álvaro. 2020a. "Instagram: #erasurepoetry query." *Zenodo*, November 19. https://doi.org/10.5281/zenodo.5500178
Seiça, Álvaro. 2020b. "Instagram: #blackoutpoetry query." *Zenodo*, November 19. https://doi.org/10.5281/zenodo.5500184
Seiça, Álvaro. 2020c. "DuckDuckGo: 'Erasure poem' query." *Zenodo*, November 18. https://doi.org/10.5281/zenodo.5500217
Seiça, Álvaro. 2020d. "The Erasing Impulse: Documenting, Classifying, and Visualizing." *Zenodo*, December 3. https://doi.org/10.5281/zenodo.5500277
Seiça, Álvaro. 2020e. "The Erasing Impulse: Constellations of Practices." *Zenodo*, December 3. https://doi.org/10.5281/zenodo.5500287
Seiça, Álvaro. 2020f. "Lit Mods." *Electronic Book Review* (September 6). https://doi.org/10.7273/hphy-bs66
Sharif, Solmaz. 2013. "The Near Transitive Properties of the Political and Poetical: Erasure," *The Volta: Evening Will Come*, no. 28. www.thevolta.org/ewc28-ssharif-p1.html
Sharif, Solmaz. 2016. *Look*. Minneapolis: Graywolf Press.
Soon, Winnie. 2020. "Unerasable Characters II." *Winnie Soon*, April 15. http://siusoon.net/unerasable-characters-ii
Soto-Román, Carlos. 2013. *Chile Project: [Re-Classified]*. San Francisco, CA: Gauss PDF. www.gauss-pdf.com/post/60951201700/gpdf082-carlos-soto-roman-chile-project
Soto-Román, Carlos. 2016. *Chile Project: [Re-Classified]*. Santiago de Chile: Libros del Pez Espiral. https://naranjavirtual.me/T0101_Chile-Project
Soto-Román, Carlos. 2017. *11*. Santiago de Chile: Self-published. www.naranjapublicaciones.com/producto/11-carlos-soto-roman
Soto-Román, Carlos. 2021. "Borradura." Presented at Erase!, *Vimeo*, September 23. https://erase.artdel.net/borradura/
Spahr, Juliana. 2021. "On *Borradura*." Presented at Erase!, September 23. https://erase.artdel.net/borradura/
Sterne, Laurence. 2013 [1759–67]. *The Life and Opinions of Tristram Shandy, Gentleman*. London: Vintage.

Velho da Costa, Maria. 1973. *Desescrita*. Porto: Afrontamento.
"Winners of Our Blackout Poetry Contest." *New York Times*, June 13, 2019. https://nytimes.com/2019/06/13/learning/winners-of-our-blackout-poetry-contest.html
Yü, Hsia. 2007. *Pink Noise*. Taipei: Self-published.
Yü, Hsia et al., eds. 2012a. *Xianzai Shi*, no. 9.
Yü, Hsia et al. 2012b. "Cross It Out, Cross It Out, Cross It Out: Erasurist Poetry from Taiwan's *Poetry Now*." *Asymptote*, no. 9. www.asymptotejournal.com/visual/hsia-yu-et-al-cross-it-out-cross-it-out-cross-it-outerasurist-poetry-from-taiwans-poetry-now

8 Digital Cartoons
Collaborative Activism in Hong Kong

Kin Wai Chu

Cartoons are often innately related to parody, satire, and humour (e.g., El Rafaie 2003; Morris 1993). Genealogically linked with political satire in print, political editorial cartoons can also be considered a synecdoche of cartoons (McDougall 1926, 304, cited in Campbell 2018, 16). Conventionally but not essentially, cartoons are always in single-panel form and distinguished from comics which stress more on sequential storytelling using multiple panels. In the early nineteenth century, comic strips were famously characterized by the works of the Francophone Swiss artist and teacher Rodolphe Töpffer whose texts emphasized "theatrical progressive actions" and "polygraphic humor" (Smolderen 2014, 37, 51). Apart from the formal differences, cartoons and comics were also traditionally separated by genres and publication formats. However, such boundaries have always been porous. This is especially the case for the all-inclusive definition of *manhua*, which is broadly known as the Chinese equivalent of comics, but the term encompasses both comics and cartoons, regardless of publication format.

Political cartoons are traditionally premised on the freedom of speech and press, and thereby act as barometers of the political climate, flourishing especially in times of turmoil (e.g., W. Wong 2018; Ng 2018, 110; Georges and Liew 2021, 9). Comic artist Chihoi (2014) astutely notes that political cartoons are one of the defining elements of Hong Kong manhua. After more than 150 years of British colonial rule, Hong Kong became part of China again in 1997. Due to People's Republic of China's drastically different approach to political commentary, Hong Kongers instigated media self-censorship in the pre-handover period, as evidenced by the dwindling of editorial cartoon columns since the 1990s (Lent 2015, 66; W. Wong 2018).

Even without traditional state censorship, there are more inconspicuous and effective forms of contemporary censorship, such as "proxy censorship" and "market censorship," which involve outsourcing the censorship functions to intermediaries and exerting financial pressure to non-compliant media outlets (George and Liew 2021, 24–25). This is especially the case in the transition period in Hong Kong, between 1990s and 2000s.

DOI: 10.4324/9781003214915-12

While editorial cartoons began to disappear in the 1990s, the rise of the internet provided a seemingly democratized publishing platform for digital cartoons by largely lifting the institutional threshold for getting one's works published. From the mid-2000s onward, the participatory affordances of Web 2.0 have continued to lower the threshold for amateur cartoonists (van Dijck 2013; Polak 2018). The digital culture also privileges fragmentation, oversimplification, and visualization of information, which has resulted in the popularity of infographics and bite-sized messages with soundbites (Castells 2012; Bennett et al. 2014; Howard and Hussan 2013; Salem 2015). Cartoons and short comic strips are well-suited to thrive in this evolving media ecology due to their innate brevity. Using Hong Kong cartoonists' creations from February to April 2019 as a case study in this chapter, I will explore how the interactive conditions of social media facilitate the production of digital cartoons or digital manhua. By closely examining a Facebook viral phenomenon known as "服藥者聯盟－黃手套之亂 (The League of the Medicated—The Chaos of the Yellow Gloves)," involving dozens of predominantly Hong Kong cartoonists, I will move on to discuss how digital cartoon-making can empower citizens and forge a form of collaborative cartoon activism.

To begin, I will introduce digital manhua from Hong Kong, followed by a close reading of important works that constitute the above-mentioned viral phenomenon in April 2019. These examples are representative of two trends associated with Hong Kong digital manhua. First, there is a tendency among artists and readers to create digital manhua by interacting with one another on social media. This mode of improvisational digital manhua production is contingent on the communicative process among cartoonists, resulting in the formation of a networked cartoonist community. Second, these works, as I will suggest in this chapter, can be read at various levels: individual, intertextual, and collective. In fact, they spearhead a new direction in cartoon making—traditionally a medium of individual creation, cartoon making is now a collaborative and communicative act as well. Around the time of the Anti-Extradition Bill protests in Hong Kong, many cartoonists diverted their energy to making political cartoons, both as a personal expression of their political views and as a form of activism. This newly established discursive practice of collaborative cartoon production became a form of collaborative activism.

Digital Cartoons in Hong Kong

Digital cartoons or manhua is bound by fewer geographical, material, economic, and editorial constraints than its print counterpart. Some digital cartoons have evidently revolutionized the relatively sterile medium from production to reception by adapting to the evolving digital media ecology and integrating with other multimedia expressions. While not yet a major trend, the recent development of augmented reality comics further blurs the media's boundaries. However, the digital cartoons discussed in this chapter are closer to the digitized version of traditional print cartoons.

Globally, the low production threshold and social media hype have attracted illustrators and amateur artists to publish digital cartoons and comics. Nowadays, there is a thin line between amateur and professional digital cartoonists because of complex digital media business models. Social media platforms also birth new cultural practices of self-exhibition (Hogan 2010), so many cartoonists in Hong Kong display their personal life and sociopolitical commentary in a variety of posts featuring their alter-ego cartoon characters, blending the personal and the social as well as fiction and non-fiction.

Each social media platform has its own algorithm to mediate user engagement, their overall interactivity and immediacy ensures a global reach and instant feedback loops that partially shape the structure and form of digital cartoons. Nevertheless, the digital cartoons that Hong Kong cartoonists produce are still mainly consumed by the local and diasporic digital community, due to the culturally specific humour, references to local current affairs, and the use of culturally and regionally specific Cantonese text.

An Undercapitalized Cultural Production

In Hong Kong, most digital cartoons are free content on social media. Popular digital cartoonists can get sponsorship from advertisers or from a social media platform if they reach key opinion leader (KOL) status. Some creators also publish their comic collections in print and sell their own comic character spin-off products. Due to their brevity, non-serialization, and sociopolitical or personal themes, these digital cartoons do not always fit the requirements of commercial online comic platforms, such as South Korea's Webtoons (which has developed its own genre) and Mainland China's Tencent Animation & Comics. Both these websites also offer a mobile phone application featuring popular topical cartoons and comic series well-adapted to be read on both the computer and the smartphone. On these digital comic platforms, auto-fictional stories are usually categorized under the "slice-of-life" genre while sociopolitical commentary cartoons are usually absent.

One of the most popular contemporary digital cartoonists in Hong Kong is Cuson Lo, who has made his name making political cartoons and autobiographical cartoons shared via Facebook since 2010. His cartoon stories about his wife were so popular that they were later published as a comic book series, but the average sale of each comic volume is fewer than 2000 copies.[1] In other words, publishing comic books is not really a financially viable venture, although the city's highly consumerist culture leaves open a market for transmedia character franchising and adaptation. Indeed, transmedia comic character franchising is an age-old practice. For example, the *kibyōshi*[2] characters were printed in the package of merchandises in Japan way back in the eighteenth century (Kern 2019, 109). When mass-entertainment industries began to thrive in the nineteenth century, the British comic character Ally Sloper became the first-recorded comic character who was present in a complex circuit of mass entertainment (Sabin 2003). Similar trends could be seen in the *Yellow Kid* and *Little Nemo* in America. Throughout the twentieth century, comic character franchising only became increasingly visible in synergistic advertising, media products, and merchandising. Strongly affected by the cute or *kawaii* culture in Japan, many contemporary Hong Kong digital cartoonists have created cute auto-fictional comic characters as their avatars on social media. Benefiting from the digital marketing trend, these cartoonists attract advertisers' interest in commissioning them for cartoon adverting productions.

Digital Cartoons in the 2010s

The 2010s was a watershed era—different parts of world witnessed an unprecedented wave of social activism. Hong Kong was no exception. Some sociopolitical events of the decade triggered public outcry and large-scale protests, such as the controversial introduction of Moral and National Education that led to mass sit-in and hunger strikes in 2011–12; the decision of the Standing Committee of the National People's Congress on electoral reform that triggered the Umbrella Movement in 2014; and the Anti-Extradition Bill protests in 2019–20. Anthony Dapiran (2017) asserts that protests are an "embodiment of [Hong Kong's] identity, embracing as it does the freedoms of speech, expression and assembly" (5).

Contemporary social activism relies on "informal networks operating as trans-movement free spaces," and this network activism combines users' everyday digital network presence with technological affordances (Ting 2019, 3264; also see Diani 2000). The convergence of virtual and physical social activist spaces has also contributed to the proliferation of protest artworks. Among various protest art forms, political cartoons have bloomed online and offline in Hong Kong since the 2010s (Lui 2012; J. Wong 2018).

Theoretically, digital platforms operate outside geographical and regional constraints. In practice though, digital cartoons are bound by language and contextual constraints that undermine their global reach. This is particularly true for the political cartoon, which is innately highly contextualized, requiring readers with prior knowledge to digest the message.

The Anti-Extradition Bill protests marked the pinnacle of the Hong Kong protest arts owing to their quantity, poignancy, and reach. Some cartoons were translated into multiple languages to expand their target reader groups. Apart from the cartoonists' artistic contribution, the protesters' acts of sharing, creating, appropriating, meshing, and parodying visual iconography to signify their collective identity or voice their stance gave rise to different forms of collaborative visual activism (Kwok 2020). Nowadays, it is easy for lay people to create their own cartoons without the need to draw—they can simply use photographs and/or a variety of digital graphic/photographic applications with text editing functions. George and Liew (2021, 199) believe that memes with political messages are "the most prevalent genre of political cartooning these days." The power of memes is illustrated in the mass appropriation of known comic characters, such as LIHKG Pig and Pepe the Frog, in the 2019–20 protests in Hong Kong.

LIHK Pig was created in 2019 on the Hong Kong LIHKG[3] online discussion forum as a comic character to celebrate the Year of Pig. Some netizens adopted it as a symbol that they used to mock politically apathetic Hong Kongers, jokingly referred to as "Kong pig." There was a contrasting twist in the evolution of the symbol which later became an avatar of protestors. Pepe the Frog was originally a character in American artist Matt Furie's comic series *Boy's Club*—alt-right American groups later appropriated it as a hate symbol. Drastically different from the supremacist connotation in the United States, Pepe was adapted as an anonymous face that masked Hong Kong protesters during the faceless protests in 2019–20, much like another globally known protestor symbol—the Guy Fawkes' mask in Alan Moore and David Lloyd's *V for Vendetta* (Victor 2019; Munt and Richards 2020; Pang 2021; Peters and Allan 2022).

Apart from commenting on journalist Ryan Broderick's (2020) observation of Pepe's apolitical connotation in Mainland China as "the sad frog" to satirize "one frog meme, two meanings" echoing "One Country, Two Systems,"[4] media scholars Chris Peters and Stuart Allan (2022, 225–226) warn of the tendency of "mimetic weaponization" in transforming the digital news ecology by drifting political cartoons further away from their traditional and rational functions of editorial journalism. Exemplifying such a tendency, Pepe and LIHKG Pig memes served sensational and populist functions rather than prompting public discussions in Hong Kong. Protestors modified the cartoon characters' images according to the various news events arising during the protests. For instance, both cartoon characters were drawn with an eye patch to show solidarity and raise awareness about a first aider whose eye was injured by a beanbag round. In the research project, "The Rise of New Political Cartoon Movement in Hong Kong since 2012,"[5] political cartoonist and academic Justin Wong (2018, 31–41) claims that Hong Kong digital political cartoons are characterized by: (1) new cartoonist-reader power; (2) changing role of political cartoonists from artists to activists and KOLs; (3) formal and content breakthroughs that social media-specificity conditions; and (4) a tendency to depoliticize under economic constraints. The first two features are related to the impact of social media that blurs the line between cartoonists' personal life and professional work. The cartoonists usually publish a mishmash of posts featuring their works and snippets of their personal lives on the same social media page. The activist messages embedded in digital cartoons would then be perceived as the cartoonists' personal voice. The third feature about creative breakthrough is usually related to media-specific communication.

The fourth feature seems to be counter-intuitive since digital cartoonists post free content on social media without economic reward. But it makes sense when we begin to consider how digital cartoonists earn from making commercial illustrations for companies that usually avoid being seen politically incorrect. This market-induced depoliticization increases as sycophantic corporations acquire more and more media outlets (Ma 2007). Worse still, the depoliticization is not solely instigated by market forces. On the one hand, the Hong Kong government continues to reaffirm that the freedoms of Hong Kong's press and local people are being upheld. On the other hand, the World Press Freedom Index, established in 2002 by Reporters Without Borders, ranked Hong Kong in 18th place—the highest in Asia in 2002—followed by 34th place in 2010, 80th in 2020, and 148th in 2022 out of 180 countries and regions (www.rsf.org).

The enactment of the National Security Law (NSL) in Hong Kong by the top legislature of the PRC on 30 June 2020 as a reaction to the city's territory-wide protests has further depoliticized political cartoons. According to Xinhua News Agency (2021), the NSL has been effective in restoring peace in the city by targeting terrorism, subversion, sedition, and collusion with foreign forces. The arrest of the senior management of the local newspaper *Apple Daily* in August 2020 and online news website *The Stand News* in December 2021 under the NSL alarmed the cartoonist community in the city and beyond.[6] In mid-2021, Malone, the editorial cartoonist of *Apple Daily*, announced that he was ending his almost four-decade career; Justin Wong also announced the temporary closure of his political cartoon Facebook page.[7] The mass deletion of political cartoons and incognito cartoon-making out of fear of repercussion are not isolated cases. Meanwhile, given the popularity of visual storytelling, the Hong Kong government-owned Hong Kong Education City Limited created an animated video to introduce students to the NSL. Journalist Chris Madden (2021) describes it as a "worthy first attempt" but the lengthy children-unfriendly legal explanations without concrete examples of what acts lead to national security crimes is "tautological."

Under the current political climate, Hong Kong political cartoonists have no choice but to find alternate and apolitical ways of interjecting their commentaries into the public sphere. In retrospect, a collaborative phenomenon that took place in 2019, known as "the Chaos of the Yellow Gloves," involving digital cartoons created by artists who identified themselves as members of "The League of the Medicated", is an interesting case demonstrating many of the budding trends in digital cartoon-making among Hong Kong cartoonists. The funny digital cartoons produced in the process seemed apolitical—avoiding commentary on current local policies—but they intermittently contained heterogeneous observations on wider sociopolitical topics. The participatory production of loosely connected cartoons also engendered a new poetics of cartoon production, leading to the formation of an informal artist collective and spearheading a new form of collaborative cartoon activism during the Anti-Extradition Bill protests. This revived the genre of political cartoons after the Umbrella Movement in 2014, though such a revival was short-lived.

"The League of the Medicated" and "The Chaos of the Yellow Gloves"

"The League of the Medicated" ("the League" hereafter) and "The Chaos of the Yellow Gloves" ("the Yellow Gloves" hereafter) are two Facebook hashtags linked to a collection of cartoons that more than a hundred digital cartoonists contributed to between February and April 2019. The combined hashtags were used as a Facebook fan page title, and the page documented all the cartoons using these hashtags along with the background and timeline of their appearances.

The viral phenomenon began when Chao Yat (pen name of Leung Chung-kin) published a comic strip (Figure 8.1) in his newspaper column and on his Facebook page in response to fellow cartoonist Cuson Lo's post showing his girlfriend's painting of the couple holding hands.[8] Chao Yat's autofictional comic character is known as Ah Sam, while Lo uses Cuson as both his pen name and his autobiographical comic character's name. In Figure 8.1, Ah Sam mentions Cuson's romantic post with envy, followed by a parody of the painting, which depicts Ah Sam holding another hand gloved in yellow. The last panel reveals that he is holding an unworn glove that his wife Yan Yan offered to him, asking him to tidy up the table with an implied additional request to do the dishes; it is customary to wear rubber gloves to wash the dishes in Hong Kong. Intertextually, Ah Sam wearing yellow rubber gloves unwillingly to do the dishes is a narrative trope in Chao Yat's long-running newspaper comic strip.

After that, Chao Yat and Cuson posted three-panel comic strips on their own Facebook pages and tagged each other. The narratives in these oscillate between their rivalry as a romantic lover and popular cartoonist, but the punchlines always center on the yellow rubber gloves. At one point, Cuson uploaded a cartoon and tagged Chao Yat with an extradiegetic text on his Facebook post: "Is it the end? … [Do you] want to make Marigold (a British rubber glove brand) sponsor us?" (@怪叔叔の散步道24 February 2019, author's translation). In general, drawing cartoon advertisements has also been a marked trend among Hong Kong illustrators and cartoonists over the past decade, propelled by the influencer marketing trend. The glove brand did not react, but the comic strips successfully attracted media coverage and active participation of local cartoonists that bolstered the cartoon/comic phenomenon.[9]

The manhua collection gradually established a link between the yellow gloves and the zaniness. Ah Sam and Cuson also exaggerated their zaniness by displaying themselves as patients with mental illness. Their rivalry gradually turned into mutual attraction. In April 2019, Chao Yat posted

Figure 8.1 Chao Yat. "Meow Meow Mi Mi Mo". *Ming Pao*, 19 February 2019 and *Facebook*, 20 February 2019. © 2019 Chao Yat. Used with permission from Chao Yat and Ming Pao (Hong Kong).

a comic strip showing Cuson and Ah Sam wearing hospital patient attire in a cushioned room. In Figure 8.2, Ah Sam claims that the netizens want to see more cartoonists joining this cartoon crossover; this saying incorporates the reality in the diegesis. What follows further blurs the boundary between fact (online interaction) and fiction. They tagged a few cartoonists as an invitation for a manhua contribution. Instead of turning this into a comic relay, there was active participation of both the invited cartoonists and their peers. They all inserted the hashtags "The League of the Medicated" and "The Chaos of the Yellow Gloves" in their comic posts. The former polysemous hashtag refers to a translation of a Cantonese metaphor about a group of mentally ill patients, and it is also a parody of the American superhero comics *The Justice League*. The latter hashtag is a self-deprecating joke about the menace that these cartoonists and their cartoon spree was creating. By late April 2019, dozens of cartoonists, public organizations such as the Hong Kong Observatory, and some commercial brands had contributed their works to "the Yellow Gloves" theme.

Connectivity, Interactivity, and Collectivity

"The Yellow Gloves" phenomenon engendered new tactics of digital manhua production and consumption, facilitated by social media's connectivity and interactivity. The works were created communicatively right from the start through comic dialogue, social media challenges, comic relays, and the use of hashtags. "The Yellow Gloves" storyworld was spontaneously co-constructed with loosely connected narratives that could be viewed collectively as an instance of impromptu artistic collaboration. Since every Facebook user could contribute to the cartoon constellations by producing their own cartoons and commenting on the works, "the Yellow Gloves" universe remained relatively fluid and chaotic.

On the reception side, the loosely connected narratives allowed different levels of reading after the readers grasped some basic background information, namely, a group of comic characters with the self-proclaimed collective identity of mental health patients who jocularly wear yellow gloves and create havoc. Three-panel comic strips and single-panel cartoons are common comic forms in "the Yellow Gloves." Each manhua can be read individually, intertextually, and collectively. There are multiple points of entry into the storyworld because the cartoons are scattered across the individual artists' Facebook pages. Simultaneously, the works are linked together through tags and hashtags that create a summative reading of the tagged artists' cartoon collection or the whole collection of works. Virality is guaranteed due to the cartoonists' large fan base and participating organizations as well as the algorithmic aggregation pushing this trending topic forward.

I discuss a comic relay here to further stress how "the Yellow Gloves" manhua constellations were communicatively and collaboratively produced for multiple levels of reading. In Figure 8.2, Ah Sam's straitjacket, the white patient uniform, and the cushioned room in the first panel imply Ah Sam and Cuson's mental illness. This becomes clear in the second panel, after Cuson invites another cartoonist, Lobintan, to join but she refuses by saying that she does not want to mingle with "the silly guys."[10] However, the last panel depicts Lobintan laughing uncontrollably, and her daughter yells, "Mama, you are so crazy!" Chao Yat's depiction of Lobintan as their fellow patient sets the unwritten rule that the participating cartoonists should also have common characterization.

Cuson shared this post, tagged Lobintan, and uploaded a sequel illustrated in Figure 8.3. It continues with the last panel of Figure 8.2, showing Cuson protecting Lobintan and her daughter from Ah Sam and warning him not to bother other fellow cartoonists. Like Figure 8.2, a narrative twist is shown when Ah Sam and Cuson are about to kiss each other right after their dispute in the last panel. Meanwhile, Cuson is holding a torch, setting two new characters—Mandycat and Primary School Chick—on fire. The torch and fire constitute a Chinese metaphor referring to someone causing trouble by starting a fire in different spots. Within the same day, Lobintan and Mandycat joined the relay. Mandycat posted two episodes: the first is a dirty joke complaining about Ah Sam and Cuson's "sword fighting" (gay relationship) being none of her business because she does not possess a "sword," but only "two oranges" as the metaphor that she is a female. The second episode is illustrated in Figure 8.4, showing Mandycat putting one orange in a yellow glove and one in a fishnet stocking to use as weapons. Her yellow glove identifies her as a member of "the League" while the stocking is a metaphor of her female identity. Her bloodshot eyes indicate her sudden loss of sanity. She is randomly attacking Ah Sam, Cuson, and another comic character, Jie Jie, who swiftly took the comic relay baton.

Likewise, Ah To, the creator of Primary School Chick, responded to Cuson's comic post. In Figure 8.5, Primary School Chick, with burning tailfeathers as a continuation to the last panel of Figure 8.3, also moans that the human beings' affair is none of his business. While his tailfeathers are still ablaze, he has already been placed on a plate held by a waiter played by Lobintan's husband Ah Zan. In the last panel, Ah Sam asks Cuson: "Cu-BB, did you order a roasted spring chicken?" While Ah Zan the waiter is delivering the delicacy—roasted spring Primary School Chick—Mandycat the waitress is approaching with two oranges. Narrative sequence and cohesion are established intertextually.

Each comic strip in this comic relay can be seen as an individual vignette because its three-panel structure is a self-contained jest with a simple opening, climax, and ending. Additionally, they obviously offer a serial reading because of their loosely connected narrative. Figures 8.4 and 8.5 are sequels of Figure 8.3 and they simultaneously suggest a parallel and episodic reading because of separately featured characters. Figure 8.5 has also established a nuanced linear temporal flow from Figure 8.4 based on the intertextual link of Mandycat's two oranges in the last panel. This

Figure 8.2 Chao Yat. (No title). *Facebook*, 9 April 2019. © Chao Yat. Used with permission.

comic relay is an example of concocted stories communicatively and collaboratively created with a high degree of spontaneity. These cartoons lent momentum to weeks-long prolific cartoon creations by dozens of professional and amateur digital cartoonists and illustrators.

Figure 8.3 Lo, Cuson. (No title). *Facebook*, 9 April 2019. © 2019 Cuson Lo. Used with permission.

Another prominent feature among the works of "the Yellow Gloves" is the frequent visual parodies of famous comic characters and scenes. For example, Cuson created one cartoon featuring him and Ah Sam parodying Goten and Trunks of *Dragon Ball Z* (Figure 8.6). There are also a rich body of works involving local comic characters mimicking or parodying comic characters in internationally known comics, such as the Japanese manga series *One Piece* and the American superhero series *The Justice League* and *The Avengers*, that both cartoonists and fans created. Though such adapted or appropriated cartoons have created strong visual parallels that may extend their transcultural reach for readers, the use of Cantonese

Figure 8.4 Mandycat. (No title). *Facebook*, 10 April 2019. © 2019 Mandycat. Used with permission.

and cultural references in such works have simultaneously narrowed down the participants and readers to those with a shared collective identity and knowledge.

As mentioned, "the Yellow Gloves" manhua is more interested in broader sociopolitical commentaries rather than local, topical criticism. Its overarching theme about comic characters with mental issues in "the League" when possessing a pair of yellow gloves is satirical towards the superheroes from *The Justice League* who wear special attire to fight for justice with underlining ideological promotion of "capitalism, patriarchy, heterosexuality and white supremacy" (Curtis 2019, 9). With participants from diverse backgrounds in "the League", some slapstick cartoon humour is embedded with the creator's sociopolitical commentaries. For example, Jasmine Tse's alter-ego cartoon character Tse Sai Pei is known for her disapproval of the prevailing pursuit of wealth and fame as well as stereotypical gender role expectations. In her "the Yellow Gloves" cartoon, Tse Sai Pei's

Figure 8.5 Ah To. (No title). *Facebook*, 10 April 2019. © 2019 Ah To. Used with permission.

unglamourous send-up of the scantily clad Sailor Moon (an iconic character in Japanese *shōjo* manga) during her transformation sequence reflects her concerns about the over-sexualized costume design of comic heroines. Only showing her bare back, Tse Sai Pei is topless after her heroine transformation, donning merely white knickers and a pair of yellow gloves, leaving her solid grey coloured skin and hairy legs exposed.[11]

This phenomenon is significant because it has reconfigured the digital cartoon/comic scene in Hong Kong. Co-production of serial comics is a common industrial practice while cartoons and editorial comic strips are usually solely cartoonists' creations. Occasional collaboration between Hong Kong cartoonists can be seen in the character strip crossover between Alfonso Wong's *Old Master Q* and Sze-ma Wong's *Ngau Chai* in

Figure 8.6 Lo, Cuson. (No title). *Facebook*, 10 April 2019. © 2019 Cuson Lo. Used with permission.

the 1970s, and between Hok-tak Yeung and Siuhak in the 2000s. "The Yellow Gloves" cartoons, nonetheless, differ from the above examples in their inclusive contributions from Facebook users in an instant and spontaneous manner.

The virality of "the Yellow Gloves" cartoons has empowered the cartoonists in four aspects. Socially, the artistic exchanges among the cartoonists unexpectedly engendered a sense of solidarity and collective identity among the participants. Politically, this sense of collectivity galvanized into a form of collaborative production of digital political cartoons as a form of collaborative activism in the Anti-Extradition Bill protests that broke out two months after the phenomenon. Economically, some advertisers invited those cartoonists to produce cartoon advertisements in similar veins as "the Yellow Gloves." The advertisements, posted on the cartoonists' Facebook page, are released one by one through the interactions among the cartoonists and are interlinked with each other using tags and hashtags. This has become a new popular form of digital advertisement in Hong Kong.

Culturally, this phenomenon has transformed the Hong Kong digital cartoon/comic culture by further expanding character franchises across the fictional and realistic boundaries. Since most cartoonists use their autofictional cartoon characters across fictional gag strips, sociopolitical commentaries, and personal life stories, the comic characters exist in transnarrative storyworlds. A good example is the local cartoonists drawing cartoons covering the news of Hong Kong athletes at the 2020 Tokyo Olympics. This is a quasi-reportage because the cartoons mixed factual reporting with fictional character strips in which the athlete cartoon characters were interacting with the cartoonists' autofictional characters. These funny cartoons brought a gust of long-lost joy to many people in the aftermath of the 2019 protest and lingering COVID-19 pandemic.

Collaborative Activism through Cartoon/comic Production

The word "activism" is chosen over "resistance or rebellion," following sociologist Jeffrey Goldfarb's (2006) idea that activism is decentralized, lying in the everyday life struggle of the powerless. In addition, political sociologists Kees Biekart and Alan Fowler (2013, 532) propose that activism since the 2010s is characterized by: (1) a paradigm shift from organized collective actions with a united political goal to bottom-up and dispersed actions with heterogeneous goals for broader universal values and justice, and (2) distinctive technological preconditions spanning new forms of "mobilisation, manifestations, movements, networks, organised virtualities, campaigns, etc."

"The Yellow Gloves" ushered in an era of collaborative cartoon/comic activism. The practice of communicative production of cartoon/comics galvanized as a collective voice was seen in the city-wide protests that broke out weeks after "the Yellow Gloves" phenomenon (J. Wong 2019 and 2020; Dynel and Poppi 2020; Ng 2021). The digital political cartoons that cartoonists and netizens individually created can also be aggregately viewed as collaborative works and a form of collaborative activism if they are created through networked communication.

An example of collaborative cartoon activism can be seen in the *pro bono* cartoon advertisements that some Hong Kong cartoonists drew to show support for the Japanese sports drink, Pocari Sweat, in July 2019 after a retaliatory mass boycott was called upon in the social media against Pocari Sweat's decision to withdraw its commercials from a Hong Kong television station that allegedly reported news in a fashion favourable to the authority (for the incidents, see Hui 2019; Chen and Song 2019; Sum 2019). The way that these cartoon advertisements were individually made but intertextually linked to each other mirrored the dynamics of "the Yellow Gloves." Comic character endorsement and product placement in comics had already been practiced with occasional collaboration among digital cartoonists, but seldom did those comic advertisements involve narratively connected cartoons that were released as cartoon dialogue among cartoonists. This new form of guerrilla digital advertisement has strengthened cartoonists' collective bargaining power.

During the following few months, some cartoonists, known and unknown, actively created cartoons in response to certain protests and events. One typical example is a derivative of a widely circulated manga panel in *One Piece*. The original version is a farewell scene between the major characters and their friend. To avoid exposing the sadness of their separation, these characters turn their back to their friend, but raise their arms to expose an "X" mark on their wrists, which they previously added to distinguish them from the infiltrators who can transform into any of them. This scene thus becomes a metaphor of friendship and solidarity. A large group of local cartoonists parodied this scene by drawing their own cartoon character donning protest gear (black tee-shirt and yellow helmet) and posing like these *One Piece* characters. This was an unplanned and loose collaboration in which some followed this trend by producing their own version of cartoon parody, and some collected different individual cartoonists' works and made one composite image before sharing it on the social media as a collective voice. Similar individual cartoon making, as a personal political expression and a collective voice, can be viewed as a form of digital activism which thrived during the protests. It is important to point out that the media impact of such cartoons was limited, considering the overload of multimedia activist arts and information about the protests such as street art, song and social media memes from all directions and channels. Not long after the enactment of National Security Law on 30 June 2020, all forms of protests subsided and were rendered powerless. There was a wave of self-imposed mass deletion of activist cartoons and social media posts on the social media. Some political cartoonists, such as Ah To, Justin Wong, Lau Kwong Shing, left Hong Kong because they felt themselves at a precarious position.

According to Cuson and Chao Yat, the Hong Kong digital cartoonists have built up an unspoken discursive practice of using cartoons or comic strips as conversation. They also sometimes compete with one another in publishing cartoon news on hot issues as a friendship race.[12] With the current social pressure to adjust to the post-NSL-induced Hong Kong political reality, the local digital cartoonists, despite having to retreat from drawing political cartoons out of fear of unintentionally trespassing on "the red lines," have collectively found a new way to create digital cartoons that speak to the current cultural moment.

Conclusion

The digital cartoon phenomenon, "The Chaos of the Yellow Gloves," shows how networked communication on social media has contributed to the emergence of new practices in digital cartoon production, circulation, and consumption. The digital cartoons of "the Yellow Gloves" can be read both individually and collectively because structurally they contain a standalone gag, but they are also dialogically, intertextually, and narratively connected with one another.

The "Yellow Gloves" phenomenon was conducive to the creation of a collective identity among the cartoonists as well as the formation of a new cultural practice that forged conditions for collaborative activism. The autofictional comic characters that the cartoonists used on their social media pages appear as a combination of personal life stories, fictional humour, and sociopolitical commentary. Consequently, the characters transnarratively oscillate between fiction and reality, thus blurring the boundary between the two realms. These practices are aptly significant under the rampant political climate in Hong Kong where writers and artists have had to find new, interactive ways to communicate with one another, build critical solidarities, and circumvent the possibilities of treading on "the red lines."

Notes

1 Lo, Cuson. 2021. Interview by the author, Hong Kong, 18 August 2021.
2 Japanogist Adam Kern (2019, 104) suggests that the first comic book as a mass-print booklet of 10–20 pages for younger readers that "told sequential stories without being picture books" appeared in Japan as woodblock-print books called kusazōshi from 1700 to 1750s, more than a century before the appearance of the European and American counterparts. Their popularity was soon expanded by the introduction of kibyōshi (yellow books) for adults in which thousands of copies could be sold per print run during the heyday from 1775 to1806 (ibid.).
3 LIHKG is an online discussion forum on sociopolitical and popular cultural topics about Hong Kong. Established in 2016, its members are predominantly from Hong Kong and written Cantonese in traditional Chinese characters is often used in the forum.
4 "One country, two systems" is a constitutional principle governing Hong Kong after its sovereignty was returned from the United Kingdom to the PRC. It means that Hong Kong, as a special administrative region of the PRC, retains its judicial and legislative systems and capitalist practices under the PRC (one country) which adopts a socialist system with Chinese characteristics.
5 The University Grants Committee in Hong Kong funded this research from January 2019 to June 2021. However, it is unknown if the final research report has been released because it is not searchable at the time of writing of this chapter.
6 After the arrest of the top management and editorial staff of *Apple Daily* and *The Stand News*, both news outlets decided to cease their operations and permanently delete their digital content. Concomitantly, there has been an avalanche of closures and dissolution of some other media outlets, civic groups, and professional unions such as *Citizen News* and the Hong Kong Professional Teachers' Union (HKPTU) since mid-2021.
7 These two pieces of news were covered by the now shut *The Stand News* on 29 June and 27 July 2021. The relevant contents were permanently deleted from the internet.

8 Cuson Lo's Facebook page is known as "Uncle Strange's wandering route" and his comic character is known as Cuson, so "Cuson" is used to address both him and his auto-fictional character in this chapter. Chao Yat is the pen name of Leung Chung-kin and Ah Sam is the name of his autofictional comic character. The title of Chao Yat's first comic strip illustrated in this chapter is "Meow Meow Mi Mi Mo," which is Chao Yat's newspaper comic column title in *Ming Pao*. This comic strip was also posted on Chao Yat's Facebook page "Chao Yat Manhua."
9 Examples include B (2019) and multiple articles in *Metropop* Magazine on 1 April, 3 April, and 2 May 2019.
10 All English translation of the cartoons and comic strips are the author's unless otherwise stated.
11 The concerned comic strip is no longer available on Tse Sai Pei's Facebook page.
12 Chao Yat, 2021. Interview by the author, Hong Kong, 20 August 2021.

Acknowledgements

My sincerest thanks go to Ah To, Cuson Lo, Chao Yat, Mandycat, and Ming Pao (Media Chinese International) for giving me the permission to reproduce the images in the chapter. My extended gratitude goes to Cuson and Chao Yat who spared their time for an interview. Credit is also due to Jan Baetens and editor of this book Torsa Ghosal for their support and valuable advice on the draft.

Bibliography

B. 2019. "不斷更新：本土插畫家組成「服藥者聯盟」引爆「黃手套之亂」", 新假期, 15 April. www.weekendhk.com/weekspecial/黃手套之亂-服藥者聯盟-cusonlo-草日-插畫家-923678/

Bennett, W. Lance, Alexandra Segerberg, and Shawn Walker. 2014. "Organization in the Crowd: Peer production in large-scale networked protests." *Information, Communication & Society*, 17, no. 2: 232–260.

Broderick, R. 2020. "How a Pepe the Frog Pop-Up Store Fractured a Divided Hong Kong." *BuzzFeed News*. 25 January. www.buzzfeednews.com/article/ryanhatesthis/hong-kongpepe-the-frog-lihkg-copyright

Biekart, Kees, and Alan Fowler. 2013. "Transforming activisms 2010+: Exploring ways and waves." *Development and Change*, no. 443: 527–546.

Campbell, Eddie. 2018. *The Goat Getters: Jack Johnson, the Fight of the Century, and How a Bunch of Raucous Cartoonists Reinvented Comics*. Ohio State University Press, IDW and the Library of American Comics.

Castells, Manuels. 2012. *Networks of Outrage and Hope: Social Movements in the Internet Age*. Cambridge and Malden, MA: Polity.

Chao Yat. 2019. "Meow Meow Mi Mi Mo." *Ming Pao*, 19 February and *Facebook*, 20 February. www.facebook.com/permalink.php?story_fbid=2327814650576608&id=179143265443768

Chen, Qingqing, and Song Lin. 2019. "Pocari Sweat urged not to take wrong stance on Hong Kong." *Global Times*, 10 July. www.globaltimes.cn/content/1157441.shtml

Chihoi. 2014. "Please remember the lesson for Hong Kong: Zunzi's Zunzi Manhua Hong China-Britan" [In Chinese] 緊記香港教訓 -- 尊子《尊子漫畫「港」中英》 *Chihoi Books* (blog). 14 August. http://chihoibooks.blogspot.com/2014/08/blog-post.html

Curtis, Neal. 2019. "Superheroes and the mythic imagination: Order, agency and politics." *Journal of Graphic Novels and Comics*, 12, no. 5: 360–374. https://doi.org/10.1080/21504857.2019.1690015

Dapiran, A. 2017. *City of Protest: A Recent History of Dissent in Hong Kong: Penguin Specials*. New York: Penguin Random House.

Diani, Mario. 2000. "Social movement networks virtual and real." *Information, Communication & Society*, 3, no. 3: 386–401. https://doi.org/10.1080/136911 80051033333

Dynel, Marta, and Fabio Indio Massimo Poppi. 2020. "Caveat emptor: Boycott through digital humour on the wave of the 2019 Hong Kong protests." *Information, Communication & Society*, 24, no. 15: 2323–2341. https://doi.org/10.1080/1369118X.2020.1757134

El Rafaie, Elizabeth. 2003. "Understanding visual metaphor: The example of newspaper cartoons." *Visual Communication*, 2, no. 1: 75–95.

George, Cherian, and Sonny Liew. 2021. *Red Lines: Political Cartoons and the Struggle against Censorship*. Cambridge, Massachusetts: MIT Press.

Goldfarb, Jeffrey. 2006. *The Politics of Small Things: The Power of the Powerless in Dark Times*. Chicago, Illinois: University of Chicago Press.

Hogan, Bernie. 2010. "The presentation of self in the age of social media: Distinguishing performances and exhibitions online." *Bulletin of Science, Technology & Society*, 30(6): 377–86. https://doi.org/10.1177/027046761 0385893

Howard, Philip. N., and Muzammil. M. Hussain. 2013. *Democracy's Fourth Wave?* New York, New York: Oxford University Press.

Hui, Mary. 2019. "A sports drink called Pocari Sweat is caught in the middle of a Hong Kong-China spat." *Quartz*, 11 July. https://qz.com/1663759/pocari-sweat-drink-embroiled-in-hong-kong-extradition-law-spat/

Kern, Adam L. 2019. "The Power of Manga マンガ Comparative Historical Perspective." In *The Citi Exhibition: Manga マンガ*, edited by Nicole C. Rousmaniere and Matsuba Ryoko. London: Thames & Hudson and The British Museum, 103–113.

Kwok, Evelyn. 2020. "Women to the front: Women's participation and visual activism in Hong Kong's protest movement 2019." In *Feminist Visual Activism and the Body*, edited by Basia Sliwinska, 165–181. London: Routledge.

Lent, John A. 2015. *Asian Comics*. Mississippi University Press.

Lui, Man Shan. 2012. "Hong Kong Independent Comics and Social Movements." Paper presented at the *Annual Conference of the Cultural Studies Association of Taiwan*, Taipei, January 7–8. www.csat.org.tw/Years.aspx?ID=96&ek=44&pg=1&d=

Ma, Ngok. 2997. State-Press Relationship in Post-1997 Hong Kong: Constant Negotiation amidst Self-Restraint." *China Quarterly*, 192, 949–970.

Madden, Chris. 2021. "Who are they kidding? You can't make a cartoon out of Hong Kong's security law." *Hong Kong Free Press*, 12 February 2021. https://hongkongfp.com/2021/02/12/who-are-they-kidding-you-cant-make-a-cartoon-out-of-the-national-security-law/

Metropop. 2019a. "Writing *Ossan's Love* with Chao Yat—featuring Cuson." [In Chinese] "與草日共譜「大叔的愛」—Cuson篇." *Metropop*, 3 April 2019. www.metropop.com.hk/草日-Cuson-首度回應-香港插畫界大叔的愛-怪叔叔-草日漫畫

———. 2019b. "Chao Yat crossover Cuson (vol. 1)" [In Chinese] "草日CUSON聯事件簿 (上篇)." *Metropop*, 1 April. www.metropop.com.hk/草日Cuson另類聯乘事件簿

———. 2019c. "Chao Yat crossover Cuson (vol. 2)." [In Chinese] 草日CUSON聯事件簿(下篇)." *Metropop*, 3 April. www.metropop.com.hk/草日CUSON聯乘事件你要知下篇

———. 2019d. "Writing *Ossan's Love* with Cuson.—featuring Chao Yat." [In Chinese] "與草日共譜「大叔的愛」—草日篇." *Metropop*, 2 May. www.metropop.com.hk/與Cuson共譜大叔的愛草日篇

Morris, Ray. 1993. "Visual rhetoric in political cartoons: A structuralist approach." *Metaphor and Symbolic Activity*, 8, no. 3: 195–210. https://doi.org/10.1207/s15327868ms0803_5

Munt, Sally R., and Rose Richards. 2020. "Feminist comics in an international frame." *Feminist Encounters: A Journal of Critical Studies in Culture and Politics*, 4, no. 1: 01.

Ng, Benjamin. 2018. "Drawing Chinese political cartoons in Japan: Blessing in disguise or trade-off?" *International Journal of Comic Art*, 20(Fall/Winter): 110–127.

Ng, Terrie. 2021. "Protesting with text and image: Four publications on the 2019 pro-democracy movement from Hong Kong civil society." *China Perspectives*, no. 1: 55–60. https://doi.org/10.4000/chinaperspectives.11459

Pang, Laikwan. 2021. "Mask as identity? The political subject in the 2019 Hong Kong's social unrest." *Cultural Studies*. https://doi.org/10.1080/09502386.2021.1882522

Peters, Chris, and Stuart Allan. 2022. "Weaponizing memes: The journalistic mediation of visual politicization." *Digital Journalism*, 10, no. 2: 217–229. https://doi.org/10.1080/21670811.2021.1903958

Polak, Sara A. 2018. "Posting the presidency: Cartoon politics in a social media landscape." *Media and Arts Law Review*, 22, no. 4: 403–419.

Sabin, Roger. 2003. "Ally Sloper: The First Comics Superstar?" *Image&Narrative*, 7, www.imageandnarrative.be/inarchive/graphicnovel/graphicnovel.htm

Salem, Sara. 2015. "Creating spaces for dissent: The role of social media in the 2011 Egyptian revolution." In *Social Media, Politics, and the State*, edited by Daniel Trottier and Christian Fuchs, 171–188. London: Routledge.

Smolderen, Thierry. 2014. *The Origins of Comics: from William Hogarth to Winsor McCay*, translated by Bart Beaty and Nick Nguyen. Mississippi University Press.

Sum, Lok-hei. 2019. "Pocari Sweat among big brand advertisers ditching Hong Kong broadcaster TVB over claims its extradition bill protest coverage was biased." *South China Morning Post*, 10 July. www.scmp.com/news/hong-kong/politics/article/3018074/pocari-sweat-among-big-brand-advertisers-reportedly-fleeing

Ting, Tin-Yuet. 2019. "Everyday networked activism in Hong Kong's Umbrella Movement expanding on contemporary practice theory to understand activist digital media usages." *International Journal of Communication*, 13: 3250–3269.

van Dijck, José. 2013. *The Culture of Connectivity: A Critical History of Social Media*. Oxford University Press.

Victor, Daniel. 2019. "Hong Kong protesters love Pepe the Frog. No, they're not Alt-Right." *New York Times*. 19 August. www.nytimes.com/2019/08/19/world/asia/hong-kong-protest-pepefrog.htm

Wong, Justin C. T. 2018. "New comics movement: Exploring the internet political Cartoons in Hong Kong." *Hong Kong Visual Arts Yearbook*, 18–45.

———. 2019. "An initial investigation of political cartoons and illustrations in the anti-extradition bill protest in Hong Kong." *International Journal of Comic Art*, 21, no. 2: 47–73.

———. 2020. "Be water - An investigation of political cartoons in the Anti-Extradition Bill protest in Hong Kong." Paper presented at International Graphic Novel and Comics Conference, London College of Communication (online), 2 July. https://figshare.arts.ac.uk/articles/presentation/Justin_Wong_-_Be_Water_-_An_investigation_of_Political_Cartoons_in_the_AntiExtradition_Bill_Protest_in_Hong_Kong/12578243?backTo=/collections/Friday_3_July_Session_2/5043617

Wong, Wendy S. 2018. *The Disappearance of Hong Kong in Comics, Advertising and Graphic Design*. London: Palgrave Macillan.

Xinhua News Agency. 2021. "National security law effective in restoring peace in Hong Kong: security chief." *XinhuaNet*, 16 June. www.xinhuanet.com/english/2021-06/16/c_1310011248.htm

9 Between Two Screens

The January 25th Revolution in Egypt

Reham Hosny

The two screens referred to in the title of this chapter are the screen of cinema, which presents images changing over time and its developed mutation, and the screen of the computer. The media technology of cinema has its precursors in previous cultural forms such as "theater, magic lantern shows, and other nineteenth century forms of public entertainment," and after that, "cinema's aesthetic strategies have become basic organizational principles of computer software" (Manovich 2002, 88–92). The development and spread of television in the 1950s and 1960s highlighted the role played by TV as a medium and opened the door for analyzing the multiplicity of media engagements. Then, Marshall McLuhan's writings brought media under the spotlight of scholarship (Murray 2003, 7).

In this chapter, the two media technologies of computer and cinema will be investigated as distinct media types that open new horizons for materializing meaning. This study adopts a two-pronged comparative approach. The affordances and constraints of media to be used as creative frameworks are scrutinized. This chapter also reflects on the sociocultural and political contexts surrounding the use of these media. The two-pillar methodology helps create a clear idea of how the January 25th revolution as a political activist practice was channeled through different media, providing a capacious purview of sociocultural and cross-cultural aspects of the landscape in which the artists under study operate.

For Aristotle, mode, manner, and medium of imitation are the criteria of differentiating among works of art. By medium of imitation, Aristotle meant rhythm, language, and melody to be three types of mediating art (Aristotle and Butcher 1922, 1). With the technological progress of art production new media of imitation is added. Computer and cinema are two new media forms made possible by technological advances. The mechanism of producing meaning by these new media is the focus of various emerging disciplines such as new media studies. The computational and cinematic poetics are the two driving forces behind the 2011 Egyptian revolution's narrative as told by the common people and the revolutionaries in two artistic works *A Dictionary of the Revolution* (2017) and *The Square*

DOI: 10.4324/9781003214915-13

(2013). "Computational poetics" is defined as "an approach to *making* literary artworks (*poeisis*) that consciously draws on the computer's distinctive capacities for processing and displaying words" (Zuern 2013, 258, emphasis original). How the January 25th revolution's different narratives use the distinctive capacities of computer and cinema is the focus of this chapter. Reflecting on *A Dictionary of the Revolution* and *The Square* from a comparative media standpoint is important to detect how both works make the fullest use of their media to materialize the political and activist aspects of the environment in which they appear.

The Background

The Arab Spring was initiated in December 2010 by the Tunisian Mohammed Bouazizi's self-immolation as an act of protest against the country's oppressive conditions, including unemployment and extensive police brutality. Protests quickly erupted across Tunisia and expanded to other areas of the region. After Tunisia, Egypt witnessed protests based on causes similar to those of the Tunisian revolution in addition to the corrupted elections and politicians. The 2011 Egyptian revolution triggered another creative revolution on the artistic and literary front. *A Dictionary of the Revolution* is an Arabic electronic literature (e-lit) piece, which is also available in the English language. This piece revolves around the idea of the January 25th revolution in Egypt, which is a special event to all Egyptians. Weaving different voices into one text and visualizing it in a wheel-shaped dictionary is the main technique behind this piece. *A Dictionary of the Revolution* is the winner of various international prizes, such as the 2019 Public Library Prize for Electronic Literature, the 2018 New Media Writing Prize, and the 2017 Artraker Award for Changing the Narrative.

Amira Hanafi is an Egyptian-American poet and digital artist, whose work has been shown in various exhibitions around the world such as Aarhus, Chicago, Vilnius, Montréal, New York City, and Lisbon. For her work *A Dictionary of the Revolution*, she interviewed 200 persons from six Egyptian governorates: Alexandria, Aswan, Cairo, Mansoura, Sinai, and Suez in the time period from March to August 2014. Those people were asked to choose a card from a keywords box of 160 Egyptian colloquial words commonly used in public political discourse between 2011 and 2013. The terms are divided into four categories: characters, objects, concepts, and places and events. People were required to contemplate the word written on the card they chose and to speak about it; namely, its definition as they perceived it, its related stories and events, and how since the revolution their meanings had mutated. The aim was to test how the language had changed before and after the January 25th revolution in Egypt and to create a narrative world documenting the original stories and realities perceived by common Egyptians about the 2011 revolution. Hanafi revised and edited the people's conversations and preserved them into an audio archive including mp3 clips for each term. After that, she transcribed these recordings to be able to edit and weave them into multivoiced storytelling on the Egyptian revolution. Finally, Hanafi translated the texts from the Egyptian Arabic into English after digitally releasing the project in 2017 (Hanafi 2018).

Jehane Noujaim is an Egyptian-American director, who directed important works such as *Mokattam* (1996), *Control Room* (2004), and her Oscar-nominated documentary *The Square*, which won three Emmy Awards and was nominated for the Academy Award for Best Documentary Feature at the 86th Academy Awards. In contrast to *A Dictionary of the Revolution*, which compiles the memories and impressions of ordinary people, *The Square* tries to provide an alternative or a counternarrative of the revolution from the viewpoint of a number of real revolutionaries, who participated in the 2011 Egyptian revolution and believed in its fair demands: Bread, Freedom, and Social Justice. This documentary reflects on a number of important dates in the journey of the Egyptian revolution since its start in January 2011 till August 2013. Ahmed Hassan, "a born storyteller and street revolutionary"[1] and the first protagonist to appear on the screen, takes over the responsibility of narrating the events of the revolution from its start in January 2011 until August 2013, in collaboration with other revolutionaries, who have first-hand experiences. Ahmed starts the narration in a symbolic scene of a power cut: "The lights are out all over Egypt. Many things are like this, it is not just the electricity" (Noujaim 2013b). The narration goes back to report the status of Egypt under the Mubarak regime when "Egypt was living without dignity, Injustice existed everywhere … there was no hope for a better future in this country. We were tied down by an unjust regime and its dictator" (Noujaim 2013b).

After this very short and condensed reflection on Egypt under Mubarak's regime, calls for the January 25th revolution spread among people until it was declared that "we have taken Tahrir Square!" It is a cheerful moment when Egyptians speak out loud: "The people demand the fall of the regime," one of the most famous slogans and demands of the revolution. At this moment, the title *Square* appears on the screen in Arabic and English as a declaration of the real start of the incidents that this movie is focusing on. After that, the rest of the protagonists, the Muslim Brotherhood member Magdy Ashour,[2] the actor Khaled Abdallah, the young filmmaker Aida El Kashef, and the singer of the revolution Ramy Essam are introduced.

After glorious 18 days in the square, the Supreme Council of the Armed Forces declares that Mubarak steps down from authority on February 11, 2011. The next point of time that *The Square* spots is Spring 2011, "two months after the start of the revolution, Egypt remains under Emergency Law with Mubarak's regime still in power." (Noujaim 2013b). Many revolutionaries undergo military trials and incidents accelerate to reach the next point of time signposted in the movie: Summer 2011, "6 months after the start of the revolution, with thousands arrested and put on military trials, protestors take back the square to demand civilian rule." Ten months pass after the revolution and revolutionaries find themselves opposed by the Military Council, the Muslim Brotherhood, and the state-sponsored media, as Ahmed declares, and this situation sparks protests against the military regime. The next period signposted is Winter 2011–12, which is one year "after the start of the revolution, when parliamentary elections are held and the Muslim Brotherhood win and begin the race for the presidency."

Presidential elections on May 24, 2012, bring the Muslim Brotherhood's candidate Mohamed Morsi to power, but Morsi does not meet the revolutionaries' aspirations after 150 days of his rule. During Winter 2012–13, two years after the revolution, tensions are on the rise between President Morsi, who makes constitutional amendments, and revolutionaries, who believe that the President gives himself "unchecked powers." The chronicle reaches Summer 2013, when "protests increase across Egypt against President Morsi" until June 30, 2013, when large numbers of protesters take to streets raising the old slogan: "The people demand the fall of the regime." A dramatic acceleration of events leads to the ousting of President Morsi on July 3, 2013, by the army. *The Square* ends updating the viewer about the situation in August 2013, when hundreds of Morsi supporters are killed by the military forces in the pro-Morsi sit-in.

In discussing aesthetic political resistance, Maria Alina Asavei differentiates between political art and propaganda art. Political art is defined as

> art which criticizes and opposes the status quo of the moment and gives a voice to those who are marginal, forgotten, and excluded ... political art is not merely a container of political messages (as propaganda is), but it is politically polyvalent in its criticality.
>
> (2018, 2)

Propaganda art, by contrast, is "about politics and concerned with that type of politics it aims to impose on art's spectators/viewers" (2). As a counternarrative to the propaganda art adopted by the authority, political art is a tool of resistance that opposes the dominant authority. Both Hanafi and Noujaim start from this concept of political art to spotlight common people's opinions of and personal accounts on the revolution and the new human relations created as a result of participating in this special event. As they do so, they expose the propaganda media in Egypt that propagates the state's narrative and deforms the revolutionaries' narrative.

To defy the state's account of the 2011 Egyptian revolution, both works give voice to the unvoiced real revolutionaries and common people who lived and experienced these events, and with whom both artists share hopes of change. Both works want to provide firsthand accounts of Egyptians who suffer and fight for reform and political freedom. There were precursors to this struggle in a number of activist movements, such as the Kifaya movement (2004), which occurred a few years before the 2011 revolution.

Computational and Cinematic Poetics Against State-Run Media

Common Egyptian people used their digital devices to capture and disseminate events of the revolution, especially documenting the security forces' brutality in dispersing protesters, to constitute a civic media as a substitute for the state-run media, which was biased against the revolution and the revolutionaries in its coverings. Under a thread titled "The Media" in *A Dictionary of the Revolution*, the bias of the state-run media is captured eloquently:

> Obviously, the media is on one side and the public is completely on the other ... TV media hasn't changed at all. It's exactly the same because it just goes along with the regime. If they thought the regime was leftist, then the TV would be leftist. Islamist, and they'd be Islamist. The media will go along with any regime.

In this milieu, social media became a prominent political tool. As Christopher Wilson and Alexandra Dunn observe, during the months and years leading up to the protests, and even during the demonstrations themselves, social media, specifically Facebook and Twitter, were crucial for coordination and vital resources for disseminating information to the outside world, reinforcing the impression that the whole world was watching (2011, 1251–2).

The need for a free and honest media to convey the bare truth about what is happening on the ground is stressed by Khalid, one of *The Square's* heroes. He says:

> The battle is not just the rocks and stones, the battle is in the images, the battle is in the stories ... We decided to create a space, which supports those fighting for the revolution through videos and various types of media. It's what's called "popular media."

In the following scene, Ahmed says, "if people are being fooled about what is really happening here, we must film everything and show them the truth. As long as there is a camera, the revolution will continue." The role of media is upgraded to an artistic level to play the role of "political art" when Khalid and his revolutionary friends create *Tahrir Cinema*[3] "to remind us why we are here ... Because only we can tell our stories." This faith in the power of media led to the development of an archive in 2018 that collected and is still collecting all the available videos on the 2011 revolution. This archive is named *858: An Archive of Resistance*[4] and is licensed under the Creative Commons. It is conspicuous that the communicative function of digital media played a vital role in directing and accelerating the incidents of the January revolution and this was extended into an archival function after that to continue to impact how the revolution is and will be remembered, contesting state censorship and erasure.

Both artists, Hanafi and Noujaim, believe that the individuals have the right to document their own stories of the revolution and to tell the events from their points of view. The act of decentralization—that is, moving from the center, powered by the authority, to the margin, powered by revolutionaries and common people—was made possible by the capabilities of the computer and cinema media, which played the most important role in constituting the collective memory of this revolution as perceived by its own people. Additionally, *The Square*, as Lucia Sorbera (2017) notes, gives "names and faces to what are generally conceived as abstract categories, such as secular, leftists and Islamists" (par. 29). *A Dictionary of the Revolution* similarly particularizes collective experiences.

Artistic collaboration with media affordances produces a new kind of rhetoric. As Janet H Murray (2003) clarifies,

> we do something with the computer—whether it is shooting at a fantasy enemy or manipulating words or images or moving from one Web site to another—and it processes our input and responds in a way that makes sense to us.
>
> (6)

Combining the semantic units of shots, in the case of *The Square*, and words, in the case of *A Dictionary* with the help of media functionalities, culminates in the dissemination of a distinct message about the power of collectives. Additionally, the specific media used bring broad audiences to both works. By rendering the texts in both the Arabic and English languages, Hanafi and Noujaim document the Egyptian revolution, not just for Egyptians, but for the whole world. In the following sections of this chapter, I look closely at key media affordances and constraints constituting the two texts and their ethical implications. As my analysis will show the ethical import of finished text—its structure—may sometimes remain at odds with the ethics of textual production.

Hypertexting as Preserving the Collective Conscience

In the 1960s, Ted Nelson introduced the term hypertext to mean "nonsequential writing—text that branches and allows choices to the reader, best read at an interactive screen. As popularly conceived, this is a series of text chunks connected by links which offer the reader different pathways" (Nelson 1992, 0/2). Nonlinearity is the most important aspect of the hypertextual form. Thus, in the present chapter, by hypertexting, I mean the branching structure both artists use to shape their works.

152 *Reham Hosny*

The process of making *A Dictionary of the Revolution* is based on what Hanafi calls "Revolutionary vocabulary cards." As mentioned above, there are 160 cards, and each card contains an Egyptian colloquial word circulating in the political discourse between 2011 and 2013. Practically, during conducting the interviews with 200 Egyptians from 6 governorates, each card worked as a trigger/hyperlink that harnessed the thought of those people to narrate their stories and perceptions related to the word on the chosen card. They "talked about what the words meant to them, who they heard using them, and how their meanings had changed since the uprising" (Hanafi, n.p.). The recorded interviews[5] were transcribed and reproduced in a wheel-shaped, hypertext dictionary as shown in Figure 9.1. The work's website says that ultimately 125 texts were woven into a multivoiced story "to define the evolving language of the Egyptian revolution." Clicking on any term in the wheel leads to a new page that contains a related narrative woven out of people's stories around this term. The new page also contains another wheel, smaller than that of the main page. The small wheel features other terms related to the clicked term.

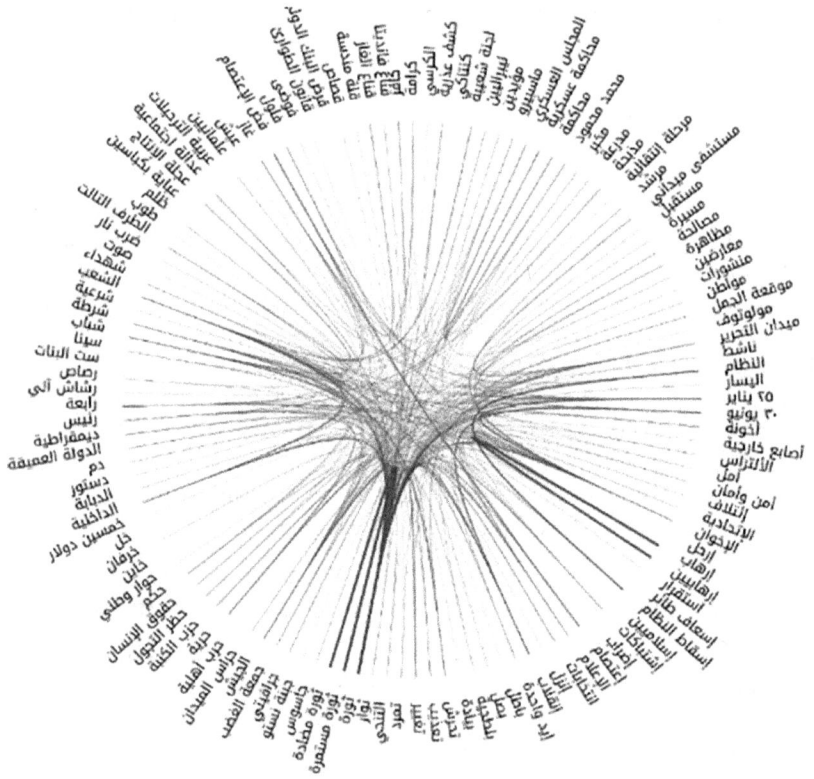

Figure 9.1 Screenshot of the Arabic version's main page of *A Dictionary of the Revolution* by Amira Hanafi.

The relations between the main term and its related terms are represented either using thick threads, indicating the strong relationships between the terms, or thin threads, indicating weaker relationships. According to Hanafi, the diagrams were created after analyzing the complete text (Hanafi 2017a).

Cinema, as opposed to a digital hypertextual text, combines units of meaning (shots and footage) in a much more sequential form. Accordingly, in *The Square*, events are featured in the order of their occurrence, however, they are connected and edited associatively. The text is also divided into a number of time intervals, each of which starts with a certain date appearing on the screen and is followed by the incidents that happened in the specified period of time. The first screen of *The Square* is a black screen with "January 2011, Cairo, Egypt." The date works as an unclickable hyperlink waiting to be activated by the capabilities of the cinematic medium.

The two media of computer and cinema thus materialize the Egyptian revolution in distinctive hypertextual forms. The branching structure common to both works results in a nonlinear exploration of the revolution's incidents and this technique further upholds multiple points of view as real revolutionaries and common people narrate the various events from their points of view. Decentralizing narration by hypertexting helps develop a counternarrative to the monolithic state account of the revolution.

Nonetheless, it is worth noting that the decentralization of narration is more explicit in *A Dictionary*, due to in part its production in a digital environment that easily enables hyperlinking and combinatorial storytelling. Hanafi puts the terms of her *Dictionary* in no particular order to shape a circle around a thread-tangled center in a reference to the equal position that all Egyptians and revolutionaries with different affiliations occupy at the margin against the center/authority that holds all the ropes of the game in its hands. The form of the text does not privilege one account over the other: this has saved Hanafi from the accusations leveled at Noujaim and the rest members of her team. For example, one of the criticisms of *The Square* was that the incident of "Rabʿa Massacre" was poorly and briefly depicted, signaling the biased perspective of the documentary producers. Max Fisher observes,

> the film spends so little time on Egyptian security forces' August 2013 crackdown on the peaceful pro-Morsi protest camp at Rabʿa al-Adawiya mosque, where hundreds of civilians were killed—practically the only major protest event of the past three years that we do not see firsthand. That crackdown, often called the Rabʿa massacre, contradicts the film's view of the liberal/secular protesters as the sole champions of freedom fighting against a Mubarak-military-Brotherhood continuum.
>
> (2014, 24)

The Rabʿa massacre was referred to at the end of the documentary with a very brief sentence on a black screen: "In early August 2013 Magdy was violently removed from the pro-Morsi sit-in where hundreds were killed by security forces" (Noujaim 2013b). Magdy, the Brotherhood member who has shared the revolutionaries the dream of social justice and participated in this documentary, took part in the pro-Morsi sit-in, which was violently dispersed and resulted in many deaths. The updated version of *The Square*, which was initiated to include the incidents of the 30th of June's demonstrations and the 3rd of July's military coup, and the dispersal of Morsi supporters' sit-in in August, doesn't pay enough attention to one of the bloodiest massacres in Egypt's modern history. In an article entitled "Egypt: no Justice for Rabʿa Victims 5 Years on," Human Rights Watch reported that on one day, the 14th of August, 2013, at least 817 "largely peaceful protesters" were killed by the security forces. They gathered in the two squares of Rabʿa and Nahda calling for the reinstatement of Egypt's first elected civilian president Mohamed Morsy, whom the armed forces toppled and detained on July 3, 2013 (2018, par. 2).

The same incident was represented differently by Hanafi. The large number of participants and the vast space provided by the digital environment helped Hanafi convey the event in a more objective way. Under a thread named "Rabʿa," we can follow a long narrative woven from different accounts of different people:

> I saw Christians at Rabʿa, and not a small number. I saw people who don't even know anything about religion, not Muslim Brothers or Salafis or anything like that at all. There were people who had never once worn hijab, but were still Muslims. People who couldn't find anything to eat would go to Rabʿa to eat. They were the people, the rich and the poor … everybody was there at Rabʿa … What happened to them was too much … Someone I know told me that because of the number of dead bodies, we were stepping on people's brains as they were coming out of their heads. We were standing in blood … I mean, we were standing in blood. From my perspective, it was literally a massacre.
>
> (Hanafi, 2017b)

The counter to this account is also given similar space. On the opposite part of the page, there is a small wheel representing the term "Rabʿa" and its relations, whether strong or weak, to other terms such as the Brotherhood, January 25, sit-in, and so on. These terms are represented in a column, which can be scrolled down, under the wheel as clarified in Figure 9.2. There are other features, in the same interface, which help expand the wheel or go to the "homepage," "archive," "previous term," or "about" pages.

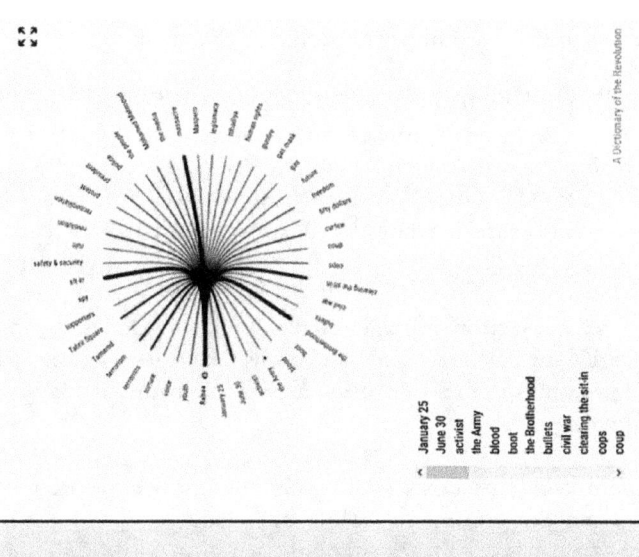

Figure 9.2 Screenshot of the thread "Rabʿa" of the English version of *A Dictionary of the Revolution* by Amira Hanafi.

Media Constraints and Social-Political Constraints

The mechanism of shooting a documentary with a camera in turbulent circumstances presents a number of problems. Noujaim

> repeatedly put herself at risk while making *The Square*, even spending several days as an unacknowledged prisoner of the Egyptian government before she was accidentally discovered by a lawyer who managed to get her freed ... many sequences filmed by running and ducking camera operators and is echoed by the film's principal on-screen figures.
> (Jenkins, 2013)

However, the live-action footage of real incidents and shooting from different angles such as street level and above the square creates a feeling of intimacy and puts the viewer inside events. Noujaim (2013a) has noted that her film

> is made in a cinéma vérité style, giving us an up-close view of revolution from the ground ... While our characters put their lives on the line to battle the largest standing army in the Middle East with nothing but stones, we as filmmakers were right behind them with our cameras.

The experience of watching *The Square* is immersive and the live footage of real incidents makes the documentary a part of every Egyptian's memory.

Hanafi adopts a different style in recording the conversations for her *Dictionary*. In an interview, she says,

> I wasn't present for all, or even most, of the conversations that took place. There's a way that I'm read in Egypt—as foreign [she is an Egyptian-American]—that has a strong effect on how people speak to me. So, I worked with people who interviewed others, often with whom they already had relationships and established trust.
> (Heisler, n.d.)

Using the technique of recording interviews with the help of others provided a more secure channel of access to the makers of *A Dictionary of the Revolution* than the makers of *The Square*. Using a recorder in places away from surveillance is easier than using a filming camera in open and under-surveillance places such as the Tahrir Square or the other important places, where vital revolutionary events happened such as Mohamed Mahmoud Street. In a sense, then, the decentralized presentation of *A Dictionary* is predicating on its makers circumventing the challenges faced by the documentary filmmaker on the ground who acts as much as a witness as the common people and the revolutionaries. This complicates the perceived ethical import of the two texts.

The technique of recording common people's accounts about the 2011 revolution makes verbal modality the main concern of Hanafi's work. She depends on 125 texts to develop imagined dialogues among a large number of common people. Two hundred people are involved in the dialogue, whose names, characters, and political affiliations are not exposed to the readers. The dialogues are developed and enhanced by using a web-based storage website via interserver.net. The website's design uses JavaScript, HTML, CSS, WebGL to visually render the verbal. Although other media formats such as png, jpg, mp3, and pdf can be found in *A Dictionary*, they are represented in the background of the work and gain less focus than words. In spite of the various capacities of computer as an artistic expressive medium, Hanafi focused on using computer as a powerful kind of "textual media," which are, as N Katherine Hayles observes,

> more powerful as historical resources than visual and aural media, they provide primary access to the thoughts, beliefs, discoveries, arguments, developments, and events that have preceded us; they hold the key to understanding the past, analyzing the present, and preparing for the future.
> (2013, ix)

The visual and aural modalities peculiar to the cinematic technique of *The Square* help personalize events following the perspectives of a fixed number of real revolutionaries. It takes a more traditional approach to what and who are presented on the cinema screen. For example, after the army viciously evacuated a sit-in and arrested a number of revolutionaries with the help of "paid thugs," one scene shows the singer Ramy Essam with signs of torture and electrocution on his back. He gives a testimony on March 10, 2011, narrating the brutal torture:

> My name is Ramy Essam. On Wednesday 9th March in Tahrir Square, the army suddenly attacked with a huge number of thugs in tow. They had agreed with each other that they would come in and clear the sit-in. They arrested lots of people, and I was one of them. They took me to the Egyptian Museum. As soon as we got inside the grounds, they started beating us violently without listening to anything we said, or asking what we were doing. They threw me to the ground and took my clothes off and they cut my hair. They beat me in lots of different ways.
> (Noujaim 2013b)

During the same day, an incident concerning a group of Egyptian revolutionary girls remains unspoken of in *The Square*. This incident was given the name "virginity tests." Under a thread entitled "virginity tests," *A Dictionary* provides a verbal account woven from the accounts of various Egyptians:

> They were one of the really difficult things I found in Tahrir Square—the worst thing after the January 25th Revolution. Worse than death.

> In death, a person's life is lost, but with virginity tests, girls lose their feminine human dignity ... That someone decides to see if she's a virgin or not, even if they're doing it so that no one can come out later and say that something was done to her inside ... The idea was that they stood them up facing each other, and there were people and soldiers passing by while the door was open, and people were taking video ... Using things like that is very serious, in that you break someone, because you don't know how to break them any other way.
>
> (Hanafi 2017c)

The verbal modality and the weaving technique adopted by Hanafi make it easy for her to give details of this critical event without disclosing the real personalities of the speakers and making them vulnerable to any threats. Such incidents could not be covered in *The Square* that is based on the visual and aural modalities, for social and political considerations as I believe. This context gives the impression that the narrative viewpoint is neutral in the case of *A Dictionary* as opposed to mainly masculine in *The Square*; focusing on males' rather than females' suffering due to the sociocultural context that prefers silence when it comes to discussing females' problems. While anticipating that *The Square* would refer to the "virginity tests" in the subsequent scenes, the viewer is disappointed with a later scene, in the 2011–12 Winter section, where a girl exchanges a friendly talk with the army spokesman, describing how she was beaten "with boots and sticks" all over her body by the army forces and the army spokesman denies that the army could have done such practices.

A close watching of *The Square*, however, reveals another important information in this context. After the evacuation of the March 2011 sit-in, a shot on the 00:34:19 minutes shows a street graffiti visualizing a female face. In fact, it's a graffiti for Samira Ibrahim, one of the girls who underwent "virginity tests," and the one who sued the army for it. The same face appears in the following three shots.[6] While the film does not miss any chance to criticize Muslim Brotherhood and blame them for many of the revolution's failures, it makes use of the visual modality of the cinematic medium to make a symbolic reference to this important happening – "virginity tests" – rather than openly investigate it.

Conclusion

With hindsight, it took a long time for the truth behind the 2013 political situation in Egypt to be realized by common people; the matter which had affected the narration viewpoint of incidents in artistic works. While the digital text is performatively neutral, this neutrality also allows its makers to avoid authoritarian scrutiny, while the filmmakers or the revolutionaries the filmmakers focus on cannot avoid this scrutiny like what happened with Magdy Ashour.

The nature of any medium affects the form and content of the creative message and the way of delivering it. As it has been discussed in this chapter, the media of computer and cinema materialize the January 25th revolution differently according to the peculiar capabilities and limitations of each medium. Investigating *A Dictionary of the Revolution* by Amira Hanafi and *The Square* by Jehane Noujaim from a comparative media standpoint reveals distinctive kinds of media rhetoric. Cultural and sociopolitical factors participate in constructing this rhetoric. By exploiting the media capabilities to document the Egyptian revolution's events, Hanafi and Noujaim keep the revolution alive.

Notes

1 A full description of the protagonists' characters can be found on *The Square's* website archived at: https://web.archive.org/web/20220808164822/http://thesquarefilm.com/about, accessed on March 25, 2023.
2 It was reported on *The Square*'s Facebook page on June 10, 2015, that Magdy Ashour was arrested: www.facebook.com/TheSquareFilm/posts/it-has-been-reported-that-magdy-ashour-a-character-in-the-film-has-been-arrested/697638400358542/
3 Video footage and clip screenings of incidents, collected from the 25 January revolution, were scheduled to be run every night at 10:30 pm, with the aim of countering the propaganda of official media and helping people to imagine how their own story was narrated.
4 This archive was designed and launched by a volunteer media activist collective named Mosireen, which appeared at the beginning of the 2011 revolution: www.mosireen.com/
5 These recordings were edited into an audio archive that could be accessed via this link (accessed on March 24, 2023): http://archive.qamosalthawra.com/#%D8%A3%D8%B1%D8%B4%D9%8A%D9%81%2F%D8%A3%D8%B5%D9%88%D8%A7%D8%AA
6 A graffiti for Samira Ibrahim is available from https://commons.wikimedia.org/wiki/File:Samira_Ibrahim_-_%D8%B3%D9%85%D9%8A%D8%B1%D8%A9_%D8%A7%D8%A8%D8%B1%D8%A7%D9%87%D9%8A%D9%85.jpg

Bibliography

Aristotle, and Samuel Henry Butcher. 1922. *The Poetics of Aristotle / Edited with Critical Notes and a Translation by S.H. Butcher*. Fourth edition. London: Macmillan.
Asavei, Maria Alina. 2018. *Aesthetics, Disinterestedness, and Effectiveness in Political Art*. Lanham, MD: Lexington Books.
Danesi, Marcel. 2009. "Hypertext." In *Dictionary of Media and Communications*. New York: ME Sharpe.
"Egypt: no Justice for Rab'a Victims 5 Years on." 2018. *Human Rights Watch*, accessed on March 25, 2023. http://webcache.googleusercontent.com/search?q=cache:6eGEI6j9YP4J:https://www.hrw.org/news/2018/08/13/egypt-no-justice-raba-victims-5-years&client=firefox-b-d&hl=en&gl=eg&strip=1&vwsrc=0

Fisher, Max. 2014. "'The Square' is a beautiful documentary. But its politics are dangerous." *The Washington Post*, January 17, 2014.

Hanafi, Amira. n.d. "A dictionary of the revolution (2014–2017)." *Amira Hanafi*. Accessed on November 11, 2021, https://amirahanafi.com/tagged/qat

———. 2017a. "About." *A Dictionary of the Revolution*. Accessed on March 25, 2023, http://qamosalthawra.com/en#

———. 2017b. "Rabʻa." *A Dictionary of the Revolution*. Accessed on March 25, 2023, http://qamosalthawra.com/en#84

———. 2017c. "Virginity Test." *A Dictionary of the Revolution*. Accessed on March 25, 2023, http://qamosalthawra.com/en#119

———. 2018. "Trauma and Translating 'A Dictionary of the Revolution'." Accessed on November 11, 2021, www.4cs-conflict-conviviality.eu/post/trauma-and-translating-a-dictionary-of-the-revolution?fbclid=IwAR3vFIC7mRRWQ5Kv0CSJ6nj80Rxk5x_7Qjj0GpL7LR9mQtwI2dzGTQpH_QQ

Hayles, N. Katherine, and Jessica Pressman. 2013. "Making, Critique: A Media Framework." *Comparative Textual Media: Transforming the Humanities in the Postprint Era*. Minneapolis: University of Minnesota Press.

Heisler, Eva. n.d. "Amira Hanafi, Cities and Dictionaries." *ASYMPTOTE*. Accessed on November 11, 2021, www.asymptotejournal.com/visual/eva-heisler-amira-hanafi-cities-and-dictionaries/

Jenkins, Mark. 2013. "'The Square': Egypt in Crisis, and Its People in Focus." *Npr*, October 24. Accessed on March 25, 2023, www.npr.org/2013/10/24/239075021/the-square-egypt-in-crisis-and-its-people-in-focus

Manovich, Lev. 2002. *The Language of New Media*. Cambridge, MA: MIT Press.

"Mosireen," 2018. Accessed on November 11, 2021, www.mosireen.com/what-is-858

Murray, Janet H. 2003. "Inventing the Medium." In *The New Media Reader* edited by Noah Wardrip-Fruin and Nick Montfort. Cambridge, MA: MIT Press.

Nelson, Theodor Holm. 1992. *Literary Machines: The Report On, and of, Project Xanadu, Concerning Word Processing, Electronic Publishing, Hypertext, Thinkertoys, Tomorrow's Intellectual Revolution, and Certain Other Topics Including Knowledge, Education and Freedom*. Sausalito: Mindful Press.

Noujaim, Jehane. 2013a. "About The Square." *The Square*. Archived at: https://web.archive.org/web/20220808164822/http://thesquarefilm.com/about, accessed on March 25, 2023.

———, dir. 2013b. *The Square*. Sundance: GathrFilms. Accessed on March 25, 2023, www.youtube.com/watch?v=2a6SLuVtiVU&ab_channel=RealStories

Scott, Anthony Oliver. 2013. "Brave Optimism of Tahrir Square Meets Other Fierce Forces." *The New York Times*, October 24, 2013. Accessed on March 25, 2023, www.nytimes.com/2013/10/25/movies/the-square-jehane-noujaims-documentary-on-egypts-unrest.html

Sorbera, Lucia. 2017. "Review – The Square." Accessed on November 11, 2021, www.e-ir.info/2017/05/05/review-the-square/

Wilson, Christopher, and Alexandra Dunn. 2011. "Digital Media in the Egyptian Revolution: Descriptive Analysis from the Tahrir Data Sets." *International Journal of Communication (19328036)* 5.

Zuern, John David. 2013. "Reading Screens: Comparative Perspectives on Computational Poetics." *Comparative Textual Media: Transforming the Humanities in the Postprint Era*. Minneapolis: University of Minnesota Press.

10 "If this document is authentic"
On Bill Bly's Archival Fiction

Brian Davis

In the Bill Bly Collection of Electronic Literature housed in Maryland Institute for Technology in the Humanities (MITH) at the University of Maryland, USA, there is a xerox of a handwritten document inscribed with the phrase "If this document is authentic, then a complete reappraisal will be necessary."[1] Originally written in a leather-bound journal in 1984, this apocryphal statement would become the animating force behind hypertext author Bill Bly's multivolume web-epic *We Descend: Writings from Archives Pertaining to Egderus Scriptor*. Began in Storyspace, the hypertext software developed by Jay David Bolter and Michael Joyce in the late 1980s, the first volume of *We Descend* was published on floppy disk in 1997 by Eastgate Systems. Between 1997 and 2021, Bly revised and migrated volume one to HTML as well as completed two additional volumes using Storyspace's successor program, Tinderbox. *We Descend* is less of a trilogy, however, than an ever-growing living archive (as is the Bill Bly Collection at MITH). Arguably the most underappreciated among the canonical Storyspace hypertexts, *We Descend* came to be one of the longest running hypertext sagas in electronic literature history, eventually earning Bly the Media Ecology Association's 2020 Mary Shelley Award for Outstanding Fictional Work.

We Descend is a fictional archive set in the distant future long after an unspecified global cataclysm has occurred. Written, compiled, and transmitted by many different characters over the course of two millennia, the writings preserved in *We Descend* do not always directly relate to one another and sometimes their only commonality is that they belong to the same archive. As readers make their way through the messy detritus that is *We Descend*, however, they come to realize that this archive tells a story, or rather multiple *competing* stories, concerning the history and veracity of the archive itself. Readers are introduced to a large cast of characters, from scholars, historians, scribes, and archivists to kings, bishops, soldiers, and vagabonds, most of whom never meet one another because they belong to different historical periods. Each generation of writings reflects the writing culture and sociopolitical institutions of its age and at some point is drawn into *We Descend*'s primary concern of authenticating (or disauthenticating) the archive's ever-growing body of writings. Converging into a network

DOI: 10.4324/9781003214915-14

of eternal conflicts between a long succession of despots whose tyrannical reign depends on maintaining a Big Lie and an opposing secret society (The Fellowship) committed to preserving The Truth about the origins of the global cataclysm, Bly's hypertext is a Manichean allegory of epic proportions that anticipates America's post-digital legitimation crisis. The social decline in the confidence of traditional institutions, leadership, and expertise, no doubt brought on by increased partisanship, lobbying, and the preponderance of "fake news," has increased social and political polarization and helped to usher in our so-called "post truth" era.[2] While the style and mood of *We Descend* veer heavily toward medieval gothic romance, Bly's hypertext is inflected by contemporary fears and anxieties having largely emerged in response to digital technology and culture.

Complete with critical commentary, glosses, and annotated cross-references, and in ways that are similar to Armand Schwerner's *The Tablets* (1968–1999) and Mark Z. Danielewski's *House of Leaves* (2000), *We Descend* masquerades as a scholarly edition of a rare and mysterious archive. Each volume presents newly discovered writings that complicate and in some cases vindicate the reader's reconstruction of an incomplete and speculative history/future. *We Descend* takes a deep dive into the epistemological problems posed by the archive's ownership and interpretation in an historical moment inflected by cold war politics, neoliberalism, fears over environmental collapse, increasing distrust of the fourth estate, postmodernist incredulity, and the utopian/dystopian promises of the World Wide Web. As a fictional archive, *We Descend* interrogates how archives are curated and maintained over time, how they index the link between a document and the original context of its production and use, how they can be used either as a tool for democracy or a tool to legitimize power, and perhaps most importantly how documents are *authenticated*—that is, how, when, by whom and for what purpose any document or collection of documents can be said to be authentic, original, or true (see Figure 10.1 for a Screen Grab of "this work" from *WDv3*).

Digital Literature's Archival Turn

Bly's hypertext is what I have elsewhere called *archival fiction*, and as such is an early exemplar of the "archival turn" within the *literary* arts.[3] This mode of fiction has become increasingly prevalent among writers of multimodal literature over the past two decades, but it has its roots in the electronic hypertexts of the early 1990s.[4] In practicing an archival poetics—a poetics of documentation and preservation, of curation and transmission—writers of archival fiction draw attention to how subjectivity, knowledge, history, and memory are increasingly configured through distributed networks of people and artifacts in different social and institutional spaces. Early hypertext authors, such as Deena Larsen (*Marble Springs*, 1993), John McDaid (*Uncle Buddy's Phantom Funhouse*, 1993), Adrienne Swortzell (*Electronic Chronicles of the Casaba Melon Institute*, 1994), Rob Wittig (*Blue Company*,

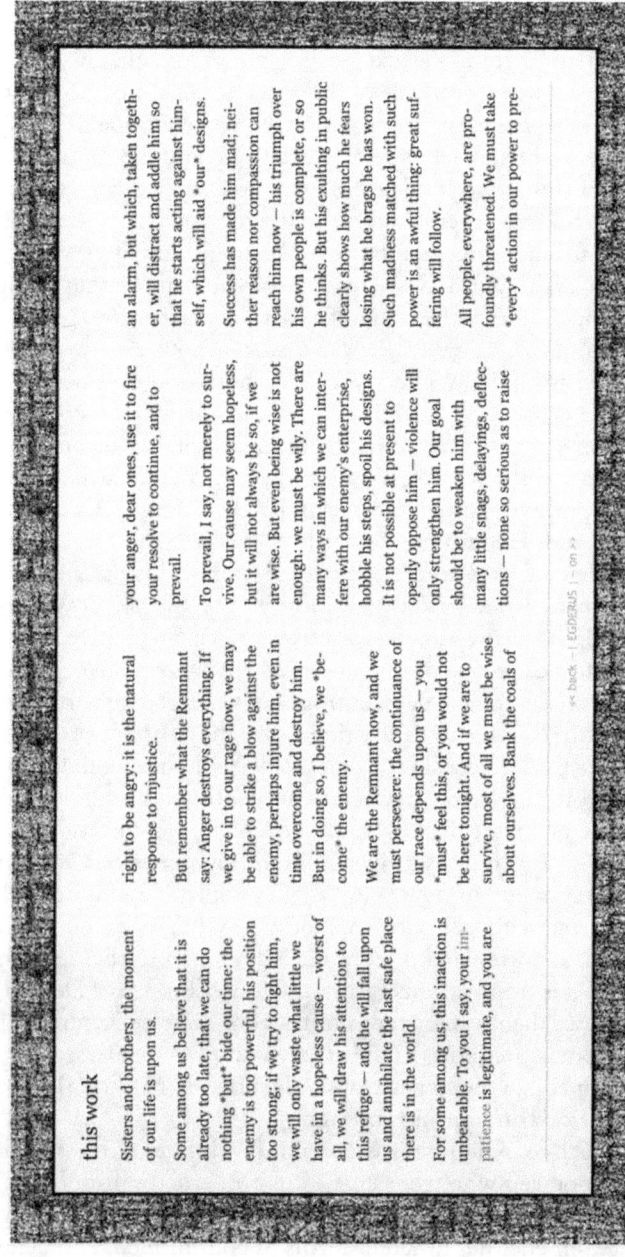

Figure 10.1 Screen Grab of "this work" from *WDv3*.

2001), and of course Bill Bly, were conscious of how archives, just like the hypertext programs they were writing in, were essentially *networks* of nodes or lexia connected by a linking mechanism. Indeed, the basic organizing principle of any archive is a general network of relational ties—material, social, institutional—that brings together documents and other kinds of artifacts. Early hypertext writing programs like Storyspace and Hypercard were always amenable to the processes of annotation and cross-referencing. That so many archives have been and continue to be digitized demonstrates how beneficial hypertext programs and the tools of digitization have been to the work of professional archivists and preservationists worldwide. While not every hypertext is necessarily an archival fiction, their linking mechanisms facilitate the kinds of activities we typically associate with archiving and archival research, namely the collocation, cross-referencing, and synthesizing of textual artifacts.

What is unique and makes *We Descend* stand out as a work of *digital* archival fiction is how Bly effectively incorporates the principles, topoi, and textual heterogeneity of the archive into virtually every nook and cranny of his hypertext. After some traversing, readers will come to realize that the older a specific writing is within the archive the deeper it is buried within the hypertext's nested and hierarchical structure. Bly's application of Storyspace and Tinderbox effectively formalizes the hierarchical data structure of the software into the fictional world's historical and spatiotemporal thematics. The older a writing is, the further down we must go into the depths of the archive to retrieve it. As an archive of disparate documents stacked on top of one another, *We Descend* incorporates into its formal and technological devices tropes of vertical depth. But *descension* is not only figured in terms of digging through the strata of earth or the lexia of a hypertext. Descension also has to do with the search for truth and authenticity, going inward or down into the depths of the self; it symbolizes the conditions of moral depravity, the leveling of civilization, of going underground, as it were, to survive and transmit secrets in a world run by authoritarian regimes. Survival, a topos of dystopian fiction, in *We Descend* is also bound up with genealogical notions, with the need to transmit artifacts, ideas, and knowledge from one generation to the next, in order to save the species from various forms of demise. From *We Descend*'s deep time to its most salient topics and motifs, from how it encourages readers to become amateur archivists to the different hypertextual apparatuses that organize and mediate the hypertext's collection of artifacts, *We Descend* is an archival fiction through and through.

Bly's approach to hypertext is also strikingly different from that of many of his contemporaries who were steeped in poststructuralism.[5] *We Descend* is more committed to a project of *reconstruction* than of deconstruction; it is more invested in eliciting different forms of commitment and belief from its readers than it is to the earlier, more prevailing postmodernist forms of irony and incredulity. With *We Descend*, Bly is genuinely trying to put the pieces of a broken world back together, a task that he asks his readers to partake in as well. In this context, *We Descend* practices "the aesthetics of reconstruction" that takes comfort in the "protocols of mourning" and that believes in "the power of sign systems to actually convey experience rather than reflect the workings of the sign system themselves" (Funk 2015, 3–5). In cultivating what Lee Konstantinou calls an "ethos of belief," *We Descend* tries to turn its readers into "postironic believers" so that they might have the courage to stand by their convictions and circumvent the destruction of the world (Konstantinou 2016, 174, 166). To this end Bly's reconstructivist project attempts to foster readers' ethical commitment and to steer their beliefs toward an interpretation of his archive that favor's the underdog.

Archival Form of *We Descend*

A plot summary of *We Descend* might go something like this. An unnamed Scholar discovers the previously unknown work of a scribe named Egderus who lived many generations before, approximately a thousand years according to one estimate (*WDv1* "Scholar's Diary" and "Scholar's Draft"). Egderus' writings lead to even older writings dating back approximately another thousand years that consist of a fragmentary archive that somehow survived the global cataclysm that destroyed the civilization of an ancient people (*WDv1* "Egderus and 'The Historian', Part 2"). A survivor of this cataclysm known as Last One supposedly creates the first collection of writings that eventually form the archives put together by Egderus (*WDv3* "return"). These writings are subsequently discovered by the Scholar many generations later. Among the collection of writings there are a "handful" of what the Scholar calls "ante-cataclysmic hyper-texts," that is, hypertexts that pre-date the global cataclysm and that may point to the real "causes and events and ideas that have long been lost" (*WDv1* "Of the demise…"). The Scholar believes by authenticating the archive he can not only verify the existence of this ancient civilization he can prove that they invented "the computer" (*WDv1* "Of the demise…") and that this technology likely played a significant role in the global cataclysm (*WDv1* "Scholar's Address"). This belief, however, is not well received. When the Scholar argues for the archive's authenticity at a conference he is not only reprimanded, someone tries to poison him (*WDv2* "The Locust Grove") and he is forced to hand over the writings and told to never to speak of the archive again (*WDv1* "Scholar's Farewell"; *WDv2* "Scholar's Confessio").

In both Egderus' and the Scholar's age, the public is led to believe that the Ancients were "deities" and that they were the ones who destroyed human civilization in the name of divine retribution. In Egderus' age this myth is enforced by the characters known as the Good Doctor and the Missionary, agents of the Inquirer General, "whose charge it was to ensure the proper reverence for the deities, by whose authority the Golias was said to rule" (*WDv2* "Writings of [The] M[issionary]" and "M Part Two"). In the Scholar's age this narrative is strictly enforced by a shadow group known only as the "Council" (*WDv2* "Scholar's Confessio"), the same group that confiscates the Scholar's "treasure" and declare the "whole thing a silly hoax" (*WDv2* "The Retreat House"). Positioned on the other side of this Manichean conflict is a secret society known as the Fellowship. The Fellowship is led, generation after generation, by lowly scribes and archivists (*WDv1* "The First Sermon of Egderus"). As Egderus puts it, "the Ancients…were not gods at all, but rather plain human beings like us…who had somehow mysteriously destroyed themselves… .[O]ur puny towns and fortresses are built upon—indeed, fashioned from—the residuum of their unimaginably glorious but wholly mortal civilization" (*WDv1* "Egderus' Last writings"). Egderus, the Scholar, as well as the other members of the Fellowship believe the archive is evidence for this claim, a claim that contradicts what the powers-at-be have been claiming for thousands of years to legitimize their authority. The centuries-long mission of the Fellowship is to pass down the archive to future generations, securing it from the Council and other authorities and thereby preserving True History. This mission is most succinctly stated in one of Egderus' speeches to the Fellowship on the brink of war: "we must persevere: the continuance of our race depends upon us—you *must* feel this, or you would not be here tonight… .Together we *will* prevail, if not in our own persons, then in the persons of those who come after us, for whom we do our work" (*WDv3* "this work").

Although there are additional characters and writings from each historical age, *We Descend* can be divided into three general types of writings: primary, secondary, and tertiary (see Figure 10.2 for my visualization of *WD*'s narrative layers and historical periods). Primary writings are the foundational writings of the archive and index at least five distinct historical ages. These writings include poems, meditations, sermons, testimonies, anecdotes, longer narratives, interview transcripts, textual scholarship, speculations, and conspiracies. For the most part, the plot of *We Descend* is to be found in and across these disparate and often fragmented writings. However, *We Descend* is less a traditional novel than it is a collection of disparate artifacts whose veracity and relationship with one another is often put into stark relief and whose contentiousness is part of the hypertext's intrigue. The plot of *We Descend*, in other words, is very *gappy*, and there is often very little narrativity in the writings themselves. As Dene Grigar puts it, "to read *We Descend* as a novel is to assume it will deliver something it is not intended to" because it is less "a nonsequential work of fiction" than a "compilation of interconnected archives relaying bits of information as incompletely as one would expect of an ancient text" (Grigar 2017, 205). Consequently, many of *We Descend*'s characters come across less as narrators than as readers arguing over the meaning and authenticity of documents in the archive. Secondary writings are called Scholia and Legomena. The Scholia cross-reference all the writings in the archive as well as offer commentary on many primary writings. The Legomena, writings produced by the archive's diplomatists (experts in the study of

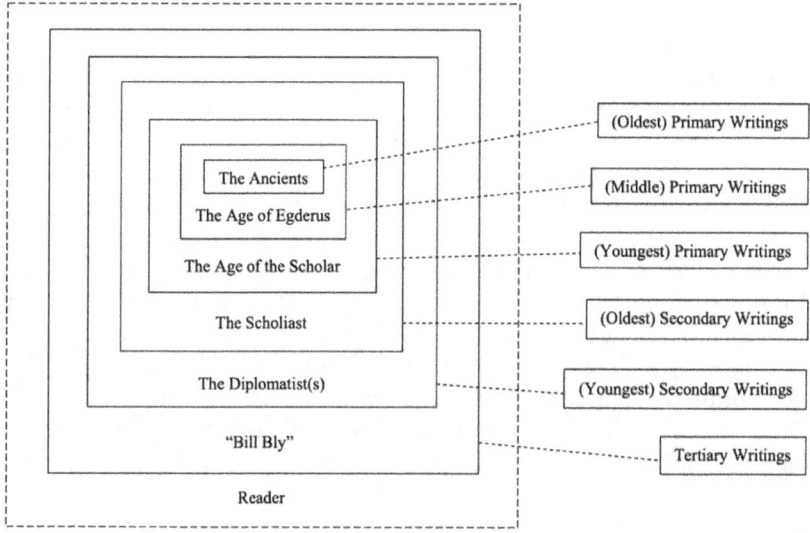

Figure 10.2 Narrative layers and historical periods, including readerly figured layer.

documentary evidence), are an updated and more sophisticated version of the Scholia and focus primarily on questions of authenticity and attribution. Tertiary writings include prefaces, forewords, and directions for navigating the hypertexts. These writings reveal that the present curator of the archive is a man named Bill Bly—Bill Bly's fictional doppelgänger—who is also responsible for rendering the archive into hypertext form.[6]

Bly's heavy use of a premodern Latin and Greek lexicon (e.g., Goliards, Eparchs, Scholia, Legomenon) encourages readers to initially map *We Descend*'s "futuristic" timeline onto an "historical" timeline beginning from roughly the rise of the Roman Empire to the early twenty-first century. Indeed, it will likely take readers some time to realize that the timeline is not from classical antiquity to the present, but from the present to approximately 4000 AD. Bly intentionally steers his readers into misreading *We Descend*'s chronology in order to invite parallels between a modern global catastrophe and the fall of the Roman Empire. What follows the global cataclysm resembles the West's descent into the Dark Age. The world that Egderus lives in resembles the conditions of Feudalism and anticipates the coming Protestant Reformation (and Counter Reformation). Naturally, given this every-1000-years cycle, readers are invited to locate the age of the Scholar at the turn of the millennium. But in truth, *we* are the Ancients, not the Scholar, and like Classical Antiquity, the modern world remains mostly unknowable to those in the distant future. The authentication of the archive is thus Bly's way of resolving this historical travesty, and by interpolating his readers into this historical process as the archive's next handler and interpreter, Bly prompts his readers to become amateur archivists and textual scholars in order to right the wrongs of history, if ultimately only symbolically.

In R. Phillip Brown's account of the European Middle Ages, "the ultimate justification for all conduct was not reason, but authority of divine scriptures and institutions" (Brown 1996, 36). Ideas that circulated in the public sphere "were shaped by Roman concepts and Christian doctrines" and "law was given to, not made by the individual" who was guided by a church that "was itself governed by a monarchical, descending, theocratic theme of government and law according to which original power was located in one supreme authority" (Brown 1996, 39). But things began to change around the time of Martin Luther, whose doctrine "undermined the whole hierarchical system of the church and legitimized a universal priesthood of believers.... The authority of the bible, as interpreted by every individual, substituted for the authority of the church" (Brown 1996, 47). *We Descend* allegorizes the historical shift from a premodern Catholic consciousness, where the individual is dominated by tradition and authority, to a more modern Protestant consciousness founded on the assumption of the autonomous individual as the sole source of meaning and truth.

At the same time, because *We Descend* projects a future world, not a counterfactual medieval history, this more modern understanding of the individual and the world is actually a repetition of an early order that likely leads to the world's demise in the first place. Therefore, *We Descend* would not argue for a societal return to some modern, premodern, or forgotten ancient past. That no character in *We Descend* is ever given a real or full name, except for the hypertext renderer "Bill Bly," suggests a rejection of the modern notion of the sovereign individual, at least figuratively, in favor of collective anonymous experience where subjects have been replaced by generic denominations (e.g., the Scholar, the Historian). Formal fragmentation, juxtaposition, anonymity, the mystical, the unrepresentable—topoi of postmodernism—are foci of Bly's hypertext as well. Perhaps most importantly, we see the dissolution of distinctions and boundaries, such as those between document and hoax, truth and falsehood, subject and object, self and other. If postmodernism is the triumph of the artificial, signifying the end of the natural, the original, and the authentic, then *We Descend* would seem to be simply parodying medieval and enlightenment tropes within a postmodernist framework. However, Bly actually shores up (pre)modern notions of authenticity in order to explore their contemporary relevance.

The Problem of Authentication

When it comes to how characters authenticate documents in *We Descend*, because modern procedures such as microscopic, microchemical, radiographic, and spectroscopic tests are no longer possible in *We Descend*'s deindustrialized, post-apocalyptic future, procedures for authenticating documents tend to resemble those of the pre-Enlightenment period (Nickell 2009, 11, 15–38). Here, we must take a brief detour into the field of diplomatics, the systematic study of documentary evidence. According to Bonnie Mak, the type of authenticity that has informed most discussions of archival sources since the sixteenth-century and that has become "a fixture in discussions about the creation, maintenance, use, and preservation of digital records," is what is known as "diplomatic authenticity" (Mak 2012, 3). Diplomatic authenticity is concerned with "examining documents of purportedly common origins with a view to compiling a list of their common characteristics—including material, physical, structure, style of script, system of dating, and orthography" (Mak 2012, 4). Designating a document as "diplomatically authentic indicates only that a particular record *appears* to meet a measure of consistency with other similar documents" (Mak 2012, 4–5).

Although diplomatic authenticity has become the most revered type of authenticity in recent years, it has not always been the most regularly applied method since the development of the discipline in the sixteenth century. Documents can also be designated "legally authentic" or "historically authentic," and in both cases the evidence for their "diplomatic authenticity" may be quite limited and/or of little significance. For a document to be legally authentic it must be "demonstrated to be authentic according to legal code," which is to say, "accompanied by the attestation of a competent authority…established and recognized as such by the legal system" (Mak 2012, 6). Documents designated as legally authentic carry "limited significance and usefulness outside the context in which the status was conferred" (Mak 2012, 6). Documents designated historically authentic must demonstrate a "relatively accurate representation of an event, entity, or sentiment," including another "object, image, text… or attitude" (Mak 2012, 7). A historically authentic document can also indicate "faithfulness to authorial and artistic intent, to a moment or circumstance now lost, or even a particular passage of time" (Mak 2012, 7). The authentication plot of *We Descend* that spans nearly two thousand years is a Manichean struggle between legal and historical authenticity, between those who create law and defend the powerful and those who preserve history and fight oppression.

The value and usefulness assigned to archival sources are essentially context-dependent and can change according to the social and institutional standards by which sources are appraised. Mak's discussion of these different types of authenticity occurs within the context of disputes among hagiographers in France during the seventeenth century when "emerging communities" used "different notions of authenticity to reframe sources in order to create a place for themselves in the social order" (Mak 2012, 15). Challenges brought forth by various scholars toward the authenticity of archival sources "was an accepted means of challenging the status quo, used to stimulate change even if it did not guarantee a positive outcome" (Mak 2012, 16). Like in *We Descend*, these early debates over textual authenticity were "about power, privilege, and prestige" and not "limited to trustworthiness of documentary sources" (Mak 2012, 16). Indeed, *We Descend* dramatizes the competition between different types of authenticating to emphasize how there are no absolute criteria for authenticating documents and how questions of reliability that people have today regarding digital materials are not at all new. Furthermore, and as Mak points out, disputes over the authenticity of archival sources have historically tended to emphasize less what authenticity *is* than what authenticity *does* within the larger social context of a given authenticity dispute (Mak 2012, 2). In *We Descend*, what tends to matter most is how authenticity functions at the sociopolitical level, how it challenges or legitimizes social norms, and how it affects the integrity and authority of institutions. When interpretive disputes over textual authenticity fall into matters of jurisdiction, there is always the possibility that "might makes right," as the common saying goes. However, Bly avoids endorsing this form of absolute relativism by enlisting his readers to follow the path of his post-ironic believing archivists in questioning who it is that benefits from such a dispute, what motivates one's attempt to authenticate a particular document (the search for truth or maintaining absolute authority, for instance), and what the social and legal consequences are that follow (do they increase or curtail democracy).

In *We Descend*, the authoritarian institutions led by Goliards (kings) and Eparchs (bishops) are stand-ins for the principles of *legal authenticity*. The doctrine that posits the Ancients as deities, which "was universally believed" during Egderus' era (*WDv2* "Legomenon for Egderus"), doubles as the law of the land, making civic law identical to religious law, as was the case in most premodern European societies. Because the writings contained in Egderus' archive are believed to pose a direct threat to the metaphysical presuppositions of these laws, challenging them publicly would likely lead to both his execution and the confiscation of the archive, thus Egderus never attempts to authenticate the archive in any capacity beyond his Fellowship of *believers*. While Edgerus and the Fellowship continue to compile, study, and copy the archival sources, a war erupts and what happens to the archive and to Egderus is unknown (*WDv3* "this work"). Generations later "a copy" (*WDv1* "Scholar's Diary") of Egderus' archive falls into the hands of the Scholar, but his attempt at *historical authenticity* results in his "We Descend Heresy" conviction by the Council (*WDv2* "Legomenon for the Scholar"). As Grigar observes, "heresy" in *We Descend* "is specifically *historical* heresy," for Egderus and others were "expected to write the past as it should have been" according to the wishes of the powerful, "not as it was" (Grigar 2017, 210). The tragic irony of course is that those who persecute the members of the Fellowship for heresy are actually the ones committed to maintaining the Big Lie. During both ages, *legal authenticity* is imposed on the archive by an authority who is not interested in either its historical or diplomatic authenticity. When the Council declares the archive "a silly hoax," it becomes useless within the context of the society's legal/religious system, as well as inaccurate in its representation of or attitude toward historical events.

The Fellowship, those who believe in the historical authenticity of the archive, stands in direct opposition to powerful authorities who enforce legal authenticity. Needless to say, there is no room for negotiation between the two groups. However, since *We Descend* is an archive *pertaining to Egderus Scriptor*, readers are presented with far more information in support of the archive's historical authenticity than for its legal authenticity. That the archive's materials are written, compiled, copied, and preserved by ordinary men, minority figures cast into the margins of society instead of bishops, hagiographers, or new age *euangelikos*, is not incidental. *We Descend* privileges outcasts, exiles, and alienated idealists, which makes them authentic, for they not only show commitment to their beliefs, they possess the courage to challenge the status quo. As such, characters like Egderus and the Scholar resemble what Konstantinou terms "postironic believers." Bly invites his readers to believe that the sincerity of these characters lays the foundation for opposing powerful, undemocratic institutions, but that this strategy can only work if alternative institutions are set up to replace them. This is arguably one of the highest objectives of the Fellowship, to supplant current institutions and their obfuscation of history with more communal acts of preservation, remembering, and truth telling. In this context, Grigar reminds that "Truth, or *alethe* in Greek, literally means 'not forgetting' and carries with it the idea that things that are true are really just those things we need to remember" (Grigar 2017, 208–09). If "truth," Grigar writes, "is indeed those things we remember, then truth is personal" and "contingent upon our willingness to share it with others" (Grigar 2017, 216). In an age when Big Lies have captured great swaths of the public, *We Descend* asks its readers to return to the primary sources of history, to become archivists of the truth, and to question the motivations of the powerful institutions.

Truth telling, however, is not only a personal and social act of remembering in *We Descend*. Rather, like Foucault's concept of *parrhesia*, truth telling seems only "possible from an exposed and vulnerable position," where someone speaks their truth "to power... from an unprivileged position" (Funk 2015, 33). As such, Bly not only asks his readers to sympathize with his humble archivists, he asks them to yield any doubts they might have toward what the archivists believe to be true because their belief originates from a place of historical oppression.

Bly does test our belief, however, through the character of the Scholiast. The Scholiast stresses the necessity of critique, practicing a "hermeneutics of suspicion" in his interpretation of the archive. Rather than asserting positive statements about the archive or fully committing himself to its historical authenticity, the Scholiast grapples with "oversights, omissions, contradictions, insufficiencies, [and] evasions" (Felski 2012), aspects of the archive that readers are meant to downplay in their alignment with the archivists. Bly does not fully discredit the value of critique, however, nor does he champion the aims of so-called surface reading. Rather, it seems that the Scholiast has been commissioned by the Council to challenge any claim that undermines its authority, therefore his motivations are compromised and he should thus not be trusted. In response to the writing known as "Scholar's Address," one of the two surviving documents from the Scholar's speech at the Conference, the Scholiast poses two concerns. He asks readers to be "skeptical about the author of the [speech]," for he claims that it is uncertain "whether [it was] made by the Scholar," and he questions the historical authenticity of the Scholar's "portrait" of the Ancients because it purportedly "diverges rather widely—in spirit if in nothing else—from the various references to be found elsewhere in the archives" (*WDv1* "Note for the Ancients"). While some readers may find these and other challenges compelling in their skepticism, they are red herrings. Moreover, since the Scholiast sides with the Council in many instances, he acts primarily as a loyal adversary; his function is to test our belief in the authenticity of the archive.

If there is one "lesson to be drawn from the *transmission* of these tales" (*WDv2* "Legomenon for Egderus"), it is for us to rediscover a sense of historical authenticity lamented by the The Last One in the aftermath of the global cataclysm:

> History used to be a question of finding out, not remembering. You read books, you studied with a teacher, you watched performances with actors in costumes. Occasionally, after slogging through lists of names and dates and places, you entered the realm of the historian's delight: you got the feel of a time and place long ago and far away, you came to *know* at least one man or woman who lived there and then. That's all over. Every time is over now, every place infinitely remote. With no past, what's the present? In a shapeless present, what future can there be?
>
> (*WDv1* "New Ecclesiastes")

The Last One's lament over the demise of history echoes criticisms concerning the "weakening of historicity" during postmodernity (Jameson 1991, 6, 10), but it also participates in the end-times rhetoric that characterizes much political and artistic thought since the Second World War. While *We Descend* does not offer a global solution to any of the global problems of the twenty-first century, Bly's hypertext does try to cultivate in its readers a historical consciousness aware of both the necessity and fragility of cultural traditions and democratic institutions, as well as the distance (and depth) that must often be traveled in order to preserve them.

Conclusion

Reflecting on the consequences of digital technology for generating and transmitting knowledge, Grigar suggests that *We Descend* provokes us to consider how we could ever possibly "make sense of our past when the information comprising our present is nearly impossible to sift" (Grigar 2017, 214). Bly's response to such concerns, I would venture to argue, is reflected in the Superius Frater's advice to Egderus regarding how he should interpret the archive: "Believe what seems to your heart to be true, but be prepared to abandon that truth the instant it plays you false" (*WDv1* "Egderus at Mountain House"). Like the British Romantics, *We Descend* is emphatic in its belief in the power of subjective *intuition*, which Bly wishes to distinguish from the power of *dogmatism* (emblematized by the tyrannical Council). Being able to "abandon" a truth that "plays you false" requires enduring a painful process of defamiliarization, a constant questioning of assumptions and negotiating with oneself and one's social reality. Bly's archivists, like Andrew Keen's "noble amateur," are figures who rise above the chatter of "the crowd" to become symbols of knowledge and truth (Keen 2007, 92). But while there is much to admire in this personage, cultivating an ethos of belief and doing your homework are truly insufficient solutions to the modern world's many global challenges and threats (e.g., global pandemics, ecological collapse, cyberwarfare, nuclear war). In the end, *We Descend* provides an ethical solution to a political problem and thus tends to fall into the trappings of neoliberalism's master trope of individual responsibility.

We Descend remains remarkable for its ability to integrate the procedures and idioms of archiving into its hypertext structure and for how it incorporates different modes and genres of writing to produce a text that not only resembles the heterogeneity of a living archive, but interpolates the reader into the messy and often frustrating archival research process itself. Bly's archival poetics, which again have their roots in first generation Storyspace hypertexts and have become the increasing foci of many multimodal literature writers, can also be found in many works of interactive fiction and video games of the past decade or so, further highlighting the lager cultural significance of the archival turn in recent decades. Notable examples include Zach Barr's *Gone Home* (2013), Aaron Reed and Jacob Garbe's *Ice-Bound Concordance* (and its accompanying AR book *Ice-Bound Compendium*, 2014/2016), Sam Barlow's *Her Story* (2015), Will Luers, Hazel Smith, and Roger Dean's *Novelling* (2016), Jason Nelson's *Nine Billion Branches* (2017), and Amira Hanafi's *A Dictionary of the Revolution* (2017). Moreover, social media itself has developed into a globally networked archive of public writing and media that encourages the kinds of activities associated with archival poetics: the documentation of ordinary life through text and image, including the curation, transmission, and authentication of such artifacts. Whether social media users are conscious of it or not, they are producing personal digital archives with their devices. Though, one suspects social media companies have very little incentive to ever turn their users into amateur archivists or textual scholars. For that we must turn to the instruction of experts and to archival fictionists like Bill Bly.

Notes

1 The Bill Bly Collection of Electronic Literature is located at the Maryland Institute for Technology in the Humanities (MITH), a center within the College of Arts and Humanities at the University of Maryland, College Park.
2 Timothy Snyder's January 2021 *New York Times*' article "The American Abyss" reintroduced the term "Big Lie" to the American public. For discussions of "post-truth" politics and authenticity in pop culture and literature, see Sam Browse (2017) and Marjorie Worthington (2017).
3 Cheryl Simon (2002) appears to be the first scholar to refer to an "archival turn" in the human and social sciences. However, Jacques Derrida's *Archive Fever* (1996) is arguably the single most influential text to inspire this turn. For scholarship specifically on archival principles in contemporary art and literature, see Hal Foster (2004), Ernst van Alphen (2015), Alexander Starre (2015), Sara Tanderup Linkis (2019), and Brian Davis (2021, 2019).
4 Notable examples of print-bound multimodal book-archives would include Mark Z. Danielewski's *House of Leaves* (2000), Leanne Shapton's *Important Artifacts and Personal Property* (2009), Anne Carson's *Nox* (2010), Warren Lehrer's *A Life in Books* (2013), Matthew McIntosh's *theMystery.doc* (2017), and Rian Hughes's *XX* (2020).
5 Early theories of hypertext were highly influenced by poststructuralist thought (e.g., see Bolter 1991, Delany and Landow 1991, Moulthrop 1991, and Landow 2006).
6 Though Bly interpolates himself into his fictional world as the editor and digital curator of the archives, I do not consider *We Descend* a work of autofiction.

Bibliography

Bly, Bill. 1997. *We Descend: Writings from Archives Pertaining to Egderus Scriptor, Volume One*. Eastgate Systems.
Bly, Bill. n.d. *We Descend, Writings from Archives Pertaining to Egderus, Volume One*, Second Internet Edition (unpublished).
Bly, Bill. 2017. *We Descend: New Selected Writings from Archives Pertaining to Egderus Scriptor, Volume Two*. The New River.
Bly, Bill. 2019. *We Descend: A Preliminary View of Further Selected Writings from Archives Pertaining to Egderus Scriptor, Volume Three*. The New River.
Bly, Bill. 2021. *We Descend: A Final Selection of Writings from Archives Pertaining to Egderus Scriptor, Volume Three* (unpublished).
Bolter, Jay David. 1991. "Topographic Writing: Hypertext and Electronic Writing Space." In *Hypermedia and Literary Studies*, edited by Paul Delany and George P. Landow. Cambridge: MIT Press. 105–118.
Brown, R. Phillip. 1996. *Authentic Individualism*. Maryland: University Press of America.
Browse, Sam. 2017. "Between Truth, Sincerity and Satire: Post-Truth Politics and the Rhetoric of Authenticity." In *Metamodernism: Historicity, Affect and Depth After Postmodernism*, edited by Van Den Ackker, Alison Gibbons, and Timotheus Vermeulen. London: Roman & Littlefield. 167–181.
Davis, Brian. 2021. "Instrumentalizing the Book: Anne Carson's *Nox* and Books as Archives." *Frontiers of Narrative Studies* 7, no. 1: 84–109.

Davis, Brian and Bill Bly. 2019. "Descending into the Archives: An Interview with Hypertext Author Bill Bly", *Electronic Book Review*, March 3, 2019, https://doi.org/10/7273/6e1x-8581.
Delany, Paul and Landow, George P. 1991. "Hypertext, Hypermedia, and Literary Studies: The State of the Art." In *Hypermedia and Literary Studies*, edited by Paul Delany and George P. Landow. Cambridge: MIT Press. 3–50.
Derrida, Jacques. 1996. *Archive Fever: A Freudian Impression*. Trans. Eric Prenowitz. Chicago: University of Chicago Press.
Felski, Rita. 2012. "Critique and the Hermeneutics of Suspicion." *M/C Journal*, 15 no. 1.
Foster, Hal. 2004. "An Archival Impulse." *OCTOBER*, 110: 3–22.
Funk, Wolfgang. 2015. *The Literature of Reconstruction: Authentic Fiction in the New Millennium*. New York: Bloomsbury Academic.
Grigar, Dene. 2017. "The Archives Pertaining to Bill Bly, Curator and Translator." In *Traversals: The Use of Preservation for Early Electronic Writing*, edited by Stuart Moulthrop and Dene Grigar. Cambridge: The MIT Press. 203–225.
Jameson, Fredric. 1991. *Postmodernism, Or, The Cultural Logic of Late Capitalism*. Durham: Duke University Press.
Keen, Andrew. 2007. *The Cult of the Amateur*. New York: Doubleday.
Konstantinou, Lee. 2016. *Cool Characters: Irony and American Fiction*. Cambridge: Harvard University Press.
Landow, George P. 2006. *Hypertext 3.0: Critical Theory and New Media in the Era of Globalization*. Baltimore: Johns Hopkins University Press.
Linkis, Sara Tanderup. 2019. *Memory, Intermediality, and Literature*. London: Routledge.
Mak, Bonnie. 2012. "On the Uses of Authenticity." *Archivaria*, 73: 1–17.
Moulthrop, Stuart. 1991. "Reading from the Map: Metonymy and Metaphor in the Fiction of 'Forking Paths.'" In *Hypermedia and Literary Studies*, edited by Paul Delany and George P. Landow. Cambridge: MIT Press. 119–132.
Nickell, Joe. 2009. *Real or Fake: Studies in Authentication*. Lexington: The University of Kentucky Press.
Simon, Cheryl. 2002. "Introduction: Following the Archival Turn." *Visual Resources*, 18, no. 2: 101–107.
Starre, Alexander. 2015. *Metamedia: American Book Fictions and Literary Print Culture after Digitization*. Des Moines: University of Iowa Press.
van Alphen, Ernst. 2015. *Staging the Archive: Art and Photography in the Age of New Media*. Reakton Books.
Worthington, Marjorie. 2017. "Fiction in the 'Post-Truth' Era: The Ironic Effects of Autofiction." *Critique*, 58, no.5: 471–483.

Part IV
Medial and Cultural Crossings

Distribution and circulation of digital literature across the world occur through different modalities (visual, auditory, tactile). However, in literary criticism the remediation and transfer of texts from one medium and modality (say, written and printed text) to another (say, audiobooks) is rarely studied as a creative process in its own right. Yet, as Klaus Kaindl notes

> the transfer from a medium that is read into a medium that is heard and seen already requires change, not to mention constraints such as commercial factors, is static aspects, censorship specifications, which have a decisive influence on the final product.
>
> (250)

In other words, medial transfers grapple with not only affordances and constraints of multiple media, but also infrastructural restrictions placed on particular media. The process entails several layers of negotiation and mediation.

The transfer of a text across media and modes, especially when such transfer also involves multiple languages and cultural or historical contexts, reconfigures the text significantly while also opening them up to new audiences and new interpretations. Today, medial and modal transfers are integral to distribution practices by which literature reaches beyond national and cultural boundaries. Thus, chapters in this part of *Global Perspectives* explore how medial transfers of literary texts lead to a series of creative decisions and are, in fact, analogous to processes of linguistic translation.

Connecting medial changes with practices of translation, Rebecca Walkowitz (2015) observes that "translation saturates our everyday culture of reading, writing and viewing" (1). Even traditional books are released in various formats and languages at once: "they appear simultaneously or near simultaneously in multiple languages. They start as world literature" (1–2). Walkowitz calls a group of contemporary novels "born translated" drawing upon the term "born digital." Approaching medial crossings as translation, Madeleine Campbell and Ricarda Vidal repurpose Roman Jakobson's phrase "intersemiotic translation" to mean a transactional process different from adaptation, illustration, or interpretation in the deep engagement and immersive reading of source artifacts by the translating artist, while also taking into account different approaches to loyalty or duty to an artifact's prior instantiation.

(2)

This sort of deep engagement and immersive reading characterizes the many instances of modal and medial transfers discussed in the following chapters. For example, Amissah-Arthur and Opoku-Agyemang focus on the presentation of Akan folktales in YouTube videos and the interpretations and transactions integral to such adaptation. They also comment on the challenges involved in studying and writing about African symbols and creative expressions in a language like English, since English came to Africa through the process of colonization. Amissah-Arthur and Opoku-Agyemang then take on the role of translators and gloss meanings of Adinkra symbols for new audiences. Translation is thus a scholarly method permeating the chapter, informing both linguistic and medial transfers. In her chapter, Hazel Smith offers various examples of what she calls "musico-literary miscegenation" and traces the reciprocal relation of words with sound, originating in different cultural contexts, across print and digital arts. A case in point is the incorporation of different translations of the Persian text "The Rubáiyát of Omar Khayyám" in Jeneen Naji's "The Rubayaat" (2014), a poem that incorporates singing.

Toikkanen and Hatavara come to the topic of medial and cultural crossings from a different direction. They focus on two contemporary renditions of the American author HP Lovecraft's fiction and chart the changes that come about in the transfer of affect in these renditions. Modal and medial transfers happening in the audiobook and the podcast, like linguistic translations, can result in differing interpretations of the text, as Toikkanen and Hatavara discuss. That Lovecraft is the author whose work is being rendered in this way is noteworthy. In American literature, his figure is often overshadowed by the more canonical Edgar Allan Poe. And yet Lovecraft is also read widely in Anglophone cultures, and his work has been translated to languages like French and Italian as well as adapted into movies. Timothy S Murphy (2016) considers Lovecraft's weird fiction a part of "world literature" since they offer insights into "the intensifying revolt against the constraints of normative subjectivity, its molar forms, stabilizing ideologies, and comfortably recognizable cognitive maps …" (178). Lovecraft's appeal to producers of digital audiobooks and podcasts today might be partly explained with reference to Murphy's understanding of his fiction.

The chapters in Part IV adopt comparativist methods wherein texts are not identified first and foremost as national but as part of broader networks of connections and transactions. There is a sustained focus on orality and sound across the chapters. Smith and Toikkanen and Hatavara in particular show how sound is a channel of meaning-making that can both work in tandem with language and independent of it in digital literary works. While discussing translation, Valeria Henitiuk (2012) observes that

> Texts become successfully worlded only through interpretive acts of mediation profoundly bound up in aspects of culture; countless acts of rewriting and repackaging must be performed before a given work of literature can enter and have a chance to influence the global informational flow.
>
> (31)

The studies constituting Part IV of *Global Perspectives* are interested in the "worlding" of texts and considering the possibilities inaugurated by medial and cultural encounters.

Bibliography

Campbell, Madeleine, and Ricarda Vidal. 2018. "The Translator's Gaze: Intersemiotic Translation as Transactional Process." In *Translating Across Sensory and Linguistic Borders: Intersemiotic Journeys Between Media*, edited by Madeleine Campbell and Ricarda Vidal. New York: Springer International Publishing. 1–36.

Henitiuk, Valerie. 2012. "The Single, Shared Text? Translation and World Literature." *World Literature Today* 86, no. 1: 30–34. https://doi.org/10.7588/worllitetoda.86.1.0030

Kaindl, Klaus. 2018. "Comics, the Graphic Novel and Fan Fiction." In *The Routledge Handbook of Literary Translation*, edited by Ben Van Wyke and Kelly Washbourne. London: Taylor & Francis. 240–254.

Murphy, Timothy S. 2016. "Supremely Monstrous Thought: H. P. Lovecraft and the Weirding of World Literature." *Genre* 49, no. 2: 159–179. doi:https://doi-org.proxy.lib.csus.edu/10.1215/00166928-3512309

Walkowitz, Rebecca L. 2015. *Born Translated: The Contemporary Novel in an Age of World Literature/Rebecca L. Walkowitz*. New York: Columbia University Press.

11 From Oral to Digital and Back

Adinkra Symbols and Kweku Ananse on YouTube

J.B. Amissah-Arthur and Kwabena Opoku-Agyemang

How can we understand the evolution of African creative expression in the digital age, a time when modes of creation, engagement, and dissemination across the continent are radically affected by new media technology? This is an admittedly broad question that cannot be answered within the space afforded by this chapter, not least because African digital creative expression is multifold and multifaceted. This limitation notwithstanding, we propose an approach to appreciating African digital creative expression in a manner that is informed by an interplay of two philosophical concepts: Sankofa and Ananse Ntontan. These two concepts are part of a larger family of philosophical symbols known as the Adinkra, and are sacred to the Akan, an ethnic group who are found along the coast of West Africa – specifically present-day Ghana and parts of la Cote d'Ivoire. Commonly known as Adinkra symbols, they have been part of the Akan identity for centuries and are intimately intertwined with traditional creative processes. This feature forms the platform for the connection with digital creative forms in African contexts.

The identity of African creative expression is commonly connected to oral tradition – of which the Adinkra are a part. The current pervasiveness of digital technology means that African creative expression inevitably evolves (from oral tradition through print-based forms) to incorporate new genres, including YouTube videos. These modes of creative expression can be seen as having roots in oral tradition through a variety of ways. In this chapter we employ Sankofa and Ananse Ntontan as a framework for processing this relationship between oral tradition and digital technology – specifically in this instance, the internet. Using a YouTube series that stars the renowned Akan trickster Kweku Ananse, we argue that the identity and usage of these two Adinkra concepts are crucial to understanding the evolution of African digital literature.

The YouTube series we discuss is known as *Ananse Tales* and was created by Parables Animation Studios, a content-creating company based in Accra, Ghana. They are one of a handful of similarly small companies in Ghana that craft narratives around folktales or contemporary incidents. According to the Parables Facebook page, they are a "a full service cartoon illustration/animation studio" that is interested in moving "images to

Figure 11.1 Screenshot from an Ananse Tale.

animate for commercials, shorts, features, not to forget ANANSEmations for all the folkish fun tales." They have built their brand around digital renditions of Akan folktales, which are fully animated short episodes that run for about five minutes each. These episodes are characterized by different narrative styles and are interspersed with music and sound effects for the purposes of suspense and comedy. These stylistic and creative choices signal departures from and approaches to oral tradition, underlining the resurgence of oral tradition in digital contexts. The identity of African digital creative expression is thus informed by the nature of oral tradition, and in this case, oral tradition is represented by examples of the Adinkra (Figure 11.1).

Adinkra: A History and Evolution

While the Adinkra are commonly known as Adinkra symbols in mainstream Ghanaian contexts, there are alternative proposals as to appropriate nomenclature. Christel Temple, for instance, opines that they should be known as "communicators" and not symbols, finding that the choice of symbols serves as yet another "European-inspired oversimplification of African culture" (130). Her point is that traditional African thought cannot be captured by foreign diction that lacks the required range to understand and appreciate the depth of an aspect of African culture. While her suggested word can also be criticized as not being adequate, the larger issue remains, that approaching certain aspects of African culture in a non-African language requires nuance and an acknowledgment of potential shortfalls.

Understanding African digital creative expression, in this light, can also benefit from a more Africanized framework that affords cultural understandings that are not as far removed as western thought. Such a mode of thinking is not intended to place African and western conceptions in diametrically opposite positions – a more productive way of reflecting on this situation is to think of relevance in terms of approaches and methodologies that have cultural commonalities, making for a smoother engagement with texts. For the purposes of our chapter, therefore, we interchange between the terms Adinkra, Adinkra concepts, and Adinkra symbols.

As noted previously, the Adinkra are traced to an Akan origin: while some scholars claim that the symbols were created in the 19th century (Owusu-Sampah), other researchers suggest the early 18th century (Quarcoo). Such disagreements are common to origins in oral tradition and do not diminish the importance of the concepts. Adinkra symbols refer to different ideas, messages, and concepts, and Alfred Quarcoo notes that in Akan culture, symbols play a powerful role in communication. They are used mainly on cloth and traditionally they are worn for specific occasions such as funerals, festivals, and ceremonies. They can represent proverbs and folktales; they can also send messages related to death, birth, marriage, conflict resolution, and belief in a supernatural power. In contemporary times, they are used in more banal contexts and are not always connected to their meanings. They are increasingly seen on commercial vehicles and are used by companies, institutions, and governmental organizations as symbols and logos.

Examples of Adinkra include Nkyinkyim (translated to mean "twists," representing creativity and versatility), Nyame Ye Ohene (translated as "God is King" and representing the supremacy of God), Bi Nka Bi (meaning "no one bites the other," representing peace and harmony), Denkyem (translated as "crocodile," representing adaptability), Sankofa (translated as "go back for it" and representing the concept of the return), and Ananse Ntontan (translated as "the spider's web" and representing creativity and intelligence).[1] In this chapter, we are interested in how the latter two concepts help formulate approaches to creativity, since we find them inherently linked to the creative process in digital contexts. While neither Sankofa nor Ananse Ntotan is specifically referenced in the episodes, Nkyinkyim and Gye Nyame (translated as "except God" and representing the omnipotence of God) are present, leading to an even more direct connection between Adinkra and the YouTube Series. This connection is contextualized within a larger framework of African philosophical thought systems that reject restrictive foreign modes of being (Figure 11.2).

The Socio-Politics of Adinkra and African "Writing"

It is imperative to digress here and provide a brief insight into the politics of ideas that have governed scholarship on African thought and writing systems. As Lansana Keita observes in a recent study, "There has been

Figure 11.2 Examples of Adinkra symbols.

an arbitrary Eurocentric creation and reification of theories and terms founded on whimsical and unsupported claims concerning the evolutionary status of Homo sapiens Africanus" (2020, 17). In connection with Keita's observation, Adebayo Olukoshi worries about the phenomenon where "external Africanists" appropriate the role of interpreting Africa to the international community (2006). There are also countless instances where mainly western voices are tagged as experts despite lacking the grounding to present themselves in that capacity. One such example occurred in February 2014 when the American actor Ben Affleck testified before the American congress as an "African expert" (Rwemwa). Such instances form part of a longer history where scholarship often projected African culture as illiterate, and Africans as a people without writing traditions. Nothing can be farther from the truth. Indeed, such suspicious anthropology betrays a lack of knowledge about the nuances of traditional education in precolonial Africa. It behooves the present writers to try to put African writing traditions in its proper perspective, in spite of the limited space afforded by the present publication.

To begin with, ancient Egypt or Kemet, which established a lasting writing system around about 3000 BC – and influenced the North African and Nubian writing systems – was not the only literate tradition in Africa (Gregersen 1977, 176). Indeed, long before the European incursion to Africa, the Arabic language and script had inspired writing systems in many African cultures (Mumin and Versteegh 2014). Other indigenous African writing systems also evolved teleologically without Arabic influence.[2] The brief historical sketch on African traditional literacy provided above contextualizes our discussion of the Akan Adinkra symbology, of which the subject of our enquiry, the Sankofa motif, is an integral part.

Prior to the British conquest of the Asante Empire in the early 20th century, Adinkra was a writing system under development in the Akan culture and reflected the philosophical sayings, proverbs, ethics, moral edicts as well as the social, economic and political beliefs and cosmological views of the Akan people. A highly valued writing and educational system, Adinkra was used by precolonial Akan goldsmiths, wood carvers, boat-makers, architects, and cloth-weavers to make ethical, political, religious, and economic statements on their structures and artifacts. The development of the Adinkra as a system of writing was prematurely halted by colonization when Kumasi, the capital of the Asante Empire and the epicentre Adinkra literacy, fell to British aggression in 1902 and was incorporated into the Gold Coast colony.

Subsequently, the introduction of Euro-Christian education in the colony stopped the evolution of the Adinkra writing system. The system has since become fossilized as an ideographic art form, although it still carries huge relevance in traditional and national affairs as it embodies ancestral wisdom. The Akan word Sankofa means "going back to retrieve it." Graphically, the Sankofa concept is depicted by a bird that is moving forward while looking backward to see how far it has come. In other renditions of the concept, the bird turns backward, while still moving forward, to retrieve the golden egg it has left behind. Sankofa is a powerful ideographic representation of African self-recovery, a return to African selfhood and value systems while still forging ahead into the future. Sankofa provides an authentic Akan/African conceptual framework that recognizes and validates the aboriginal Akan/African storytelling tradition in the context of digital modernity. This temporal relationship is universal, as illustrated by the example below.

Sankofa and Ananse Ntontan as Frames

In his classic essay, "Tradition and the Individual Talent," T.S. Eliot speaks about the fluid, indeterminate interrelations between the past and the present in literary productions. In his view, "tradition" does not represent an archaic body of knowledge and cultural phenomena fossilized and waiting to be exhumed for inspection. Rather, what constitutes tradition is the recurring conversation between the past and the present: the influence the past wields on the present, and the potency of the present to shape the past. Tradition, in other words, is not a static and monolithic body; it is an evolving process that adapts to suit ever-changing conditions.

In this sense, tradition "involves a perception, not only of the pastness of the past, but of its presence;" a situation which

> compels a [writer] to write not merely with his [or her] own generation in his [or her] bones, but with a feeling that the whole of the literature of Europe from Homer and within it the whole of the literature of his [or her] own country has a simultaneous existence and composes a simultaneous order. This historical sense, which is a sense of the timeless as well as of the temporal and of the timeless and of the temporal together, is what makes a writer traditional.
>
> ([1921], 1982, 37)

It is within the context of interpenetration between the past and the present and its simultaneous relationship with time and timelessness, that the evolution and contemporary relevance of ancient Akan cultural symbols seek justification.

As mentioned previously, Sankofa is transliterated as Return (San) Go (Ko) Take (Fa), meaning return to go and take it. It is related to the Akan proverb – "se wo were fi na wo san kofa a, yennkyi," which is translated as "if you forget something and you return for it, no one has a problem with that." The proverb is not to imply that everything in the past is worth returning to, however. It is important to sift through the past in order to filter out the unnecessary aspects and retain what is important. The proverb thus disregards the pitfalls associated with nostalgia by acknowledging that the past need not be unnecessarily valorized. Sankofa is represented by a symbol that looks like the popular rendition of the heart, with a series of uniform curves (see Figure 11.3). There is also the Sankofa bird which has various contemporary representations but is usually a bird trying to pick an egg from its back (see Figure 11.4). There is an attached folktale that admonishes people to remember their roots and community.

Ananse Ntontan on the other hand is a circular object with seven lines reaching outward (see Figure 11.5). The concept recalls Kweku Ananse, the trickster figure (usually either a human or a spider) who uses his intelligence to overcome tricky situations. His greed and love for mischief, however, sometimes get him into trouble. There are a multitude of stories starring the spider both in Africa and in the diaspora, where the figure is rendered differently. For example, it is known as Nancy in Jamaica and Brer Rabbit in North America. The diasporic renditions of Ananse, coupled with his shapeshifting nature, echo the alterations of Sankofa and reveal a sense of versatility attached to both symbols. Accordingly, their flexibility and adaptability open the door for their use in ways that can be far removed from their original intentions.

Figure 11.3 Sankofa as an Adinkra Symbol.

Figure 11.4 The Sankofa Bird.

Figure 11.5 Ananse Ntontan Adinkra Symbol.

Ananse's involvement with the emergence of the universe is the subject of a sacred Akan creation myth – *odomankomasem*. He is held responsible for the emergence of all cultural phenomena, such as language, light, technology, stories, diseases, wisdom, and so on. Thus, the Akan regard him as a cultural hero. Evidently, Ananse and all associated cultural symbols, such as Ananse Ntontan, emerge from an aboriginal, Akan cognition. In tandem with his time transcending nature, his relevance in the contemporary world allows for our argument that Ananse and his web, Ananse Ntontan, represent the conceptual framework for the World Wide Web or the internet. In other words, the structure of the World Wide Web lends itself to the prodigious mind of Ananse and of his all-embracing Ananse Ntontan. We shall elaborate on and offer justification for our argument presently.

First, as a demiurge, the Akan trickster-God of creation, Ananse's web represents the intricate hypermodal configuration of reality, of meaning and of the phenomenal universe. To the Akan, he and his web represent the superordinate consciousness that covers all the phenomenal and noumenal worlds. In the Akan tradition, there are two related Ananses: Kweku Ananse the trickster and Ananse Kokuroko the Great Spider (the Supreme God). In his philosophical essay, "Akan Theory of Mind: Negotiating the Divine Middle Ground in the Akan Folktale Tradition" (2022), Joseph Brookman Amissah-Arthur provides a complex interpretation of the Akan trickster and the sacred. According to Amissah-Arthur, Kweku Ananse and Ananse Kokuroko are not merely uterine brothers, but Ananse is simultaneously the earthly bound intelligence of Ananse Kokuroko and cosmic-bound intelligence of humankind, making Kweku Ananse the embodied consciousness of God in its downward descent and of humanity in its upward ascent. Amissah-Arthur's complex perspective of Ananse and Ananse Kokuroko provides a metaphor for own interpretation of Ananse and his web in the present study. In other words, we recognize in Ananse and his web the symbolic manifestation of the boundless, complex universal consciousness that is the World Wide Web. From the perspective of the Akan tradition, therefore, the World Wide Web signifies the super intelligence which Ananse represents.

Second, Ananse is the archetypal figure of the limen straddling thresholds and moving in and out of the three worlds of the Akan: *esor* (cosmic/spiritual world), *asaase* (mundane world), and *samanadze* (underworld). His liminality and ubiquity provide the quintessential trope for epistemological indeterminacy which, again, represents a fundamental characteristic of the internet. The World Wide Web encapsulates phenomenal myriads of knowledge packaged in hypermedial formats leading to indeterminacy: of the limits of knowledge and how these knowledges can be accessed, processed, and disseminated. The internet behaves exactly like Ananse in its ubiquitous, crossworld, relativistic operability. If the World Wide Web defies any rigid characterization in terms of what the internet is, where it can reach, and what is contained in its "consciousness," it is precisely because it is the metamorphosis of the elusive trickster-spider-human-god whose essence is inapprehensible.

Third, it is important to note that Ananse is "online," for his web consists of multitudinous lines of fine silk that have been carefully woven into an intricate matrix of thought. Ananse's web serves multiple purposes as a home, trap, protection, and vehicle all of which symbolically translate into the comprehensive uses to which humanity puts the internet. But Ananse is not merely online, Ananse is also the line itself; he spews the silk out of his body to construct the web. Similarly, humans create the internet and feed it with the material. The superconsciousness of the World Wide Web emanates from self-produced knowledge. The reflexive logic of the internet is, therefore, another characteristic inspired by Ananse.

From our argument so far, it is quite evident that the digital phenomenon – the World Wide Web – that we have come to depend on in countless ways can be processed as a representation of the archetypal Akan trickster-hero-god, Ananse and his Ntonton (web). The internet in our view is merely another of Ananse's numerous tricks. Our argument reinforces Eliot's seminal perspective on the timelessness of tradition: the fact that the past, as remote as the trickster, is still significant for the present, and that the present also provides a richer understanding of the potency and dynamism of the past. Processing the internet as another trick of Ananse's alludes to the genesis of Ananse stories, where Ananse overcomes a series of challenges to ensure that storytelling is named after him. Another implication of this processing allows us to associate Ananse with the internet in ways that detract from stereotypes that place Africa in an opposition to digital technology. Making Ananse synonymous with the web, then, leads to an analysis of an aspect of the web as presented in the YouTube videos to see how they reflect the concepts of Sankofa and Ananse Ntontan.

Analysis

The episodes chosen for the study form the story for *Ananse and the Sticky Gum/Grave Mischief*, a three-part series. The narrative is a rendition of a well-known Akan oral folktale that explains how Ananse faked his death to avoid working on his farm, but was eventually caught due to greed. As with oral folktales, there is a source template from which multiple varieties of the same story are imagined by whoever is telling the story. Characters, setting, plot, and other literary aspects can change because of the performative nature of oral tradition.[3] In this particular story, Ananse creates a customized grave and promptly "dies" three days later, instructing his family on how to bury him: they are not allowed to drive nails into the coffin, neither should they put soil on the coffin. He is therefore able to escape from the coffin and engages in mischief. His mourning wife and children realize that produce on their farm is being consistently pilfered, and hatch a plan to apprehend the thief. After a series of mishaps one fateful night, Ananse is caught after he fights with a sticky gum figure that is placed on the farm as a trap (Figure 11.6).

The narrative starts with an old man welcoming his audience, similar to how narrators introduce themselves and their performance in oral

Figure 11.6 Screenshot of "Ananse and the sticky gum (grave mischief) pt_1."

Figure 11.7 Screenshot of "Ananse and the Sticky Gum/The Grave Mischief pt_2."

tradition. The use of the old man again hints at the seriousness of the story – old people in traditional African settings are usually revered.[4] The story incorporates contemporary aspects of society into the plot, giving it a modern feel. Ananse's funeral poster for instance is entitled "What a Shock," which is a title that is typically reserved for the death of someone who dies unexpectedly. Joseph Oduro-Frimpong takes this idea of disbelief further by theorizing on the ability of funeral posters to remediate and materialize unique Ghanaian cultural narratives about achievement situated within traditional views concerning social norms (2020, 26). Ananse is positioned as the traditional breadwinner of the family, even though it is noted that after his death, the family still has generated enough food from their farm; enough for him to steal (Figure 11.7).

Ananse is also called "George," and the use of the English name underscores the influence of the British colonial experience, as what Ghanaians call "Christian names" are sometimes seen as prestigious and important to have and are sometimes the "official" name.[5] The name again recalls the playwright Efua Sutherland-Addy, who used the same English name for Ananse in her play *The Marriage of Anansewa* (1975). This play is an earlier example of how oral tradition is transposed into a modern setting. Sutherland-Addy's work is more intricate and extensive than this YouTube series, and the reimagination of Ananse is done in a way as to exploit oral tradition in ways to pursue socioeconomic and political peace (Affiah and Osuagwu 2012: 12). This exploitation is again done in ways that both overlap and depart in this digital version through a nod to intertextuality (Figure 11.8).

Figure 11.8 Screenshot of "Ananse and the Sticky Gum/ The Grave Mischief pt_3."

As mentioned earlier, there is an explicit nod to Adinkra in the series, as there are scenes that have Adinkra symbols as motifs. For example, Ananse's grave has the Nkyinkyim symbol, while a cross in the church to mark the burial of Ananse has both Nkyinkyim and Gye Nyame. The two concepts have obvious connections to the themes in the story – the former underlines Ananse's creative impulses while the latter foregrounds God. They perhaps more crucially highlight explicit connections to traditional African concepts, thereby providing identity to the text by grounding them in African thought.

There are less direct connections to oral tradition that can also be interpreted as influenced by the nature of digital technology. For instance, YouTube affords users the ability to comment on videos. While this feature is connected to oral tradition in the sense that the audience is allowed to respond to the narrator and even take over the narration of the story, in this case, the users are limited in how far they can "interfere" with the creative process. While most comments are of positive praise, one user comments "not true" on the first episode, hinting at the strategy that an audience member uses to take over the narration of the story in oral tradition.

It must be noted, even if obviously, that the series would not necessarily only be steeped in oral tradition. There are novel endeavors that take advantage of the features of the internet to create a unique experience. For instance, the mere fact that the series has to be viewed via a computer or mobile phone means that the engagement with the text is markedly different from a live oral performance. The sets of physical interactions that would include dancing, singing, and audience interruptions for oral tradition; and clicking, pausing, and commenting for digital literature;

set the tone for a comparative analysis that eventually place the latter as distinctive. These differences mean that both oral tradition and digital creative expression relate in complex ways and are not in opposition to each other.

Conclusion

In March 2005, the magazine *The Economist* ran a cover photo of a young African boy with ashy skin holding an object that looked like a mobile phone (see Figure 11.9). This stereotype was yet another western attempt to characterize digital technology as foreign to the African. A response to such limiting endeavors should not be to discard Africanness in order to

Figure 11.9 Cover of *The Economist*.

embrace digital technology; rather, traditional African thought can and should be linked with the digital for productive outcomes.

Accordingly, we have attempted to theorize on the evolution of African digital literature by connecting its nature to aspects of oral tradition. These connections help to identify African digital creative expression as being rooted in a history of traditional African thought, thus helping to understand African digital literature as unique from other regional counterparts. As we have demonstrated, African digital literature incorporates aspects of oral performance while referencing oral tradition in its work. These connections also make space for departures through the harnessing of digital technology in ways that are not anticipated by oral tradition.

As mentioned earlier, a few YouTube episodes are not enough to make overarching arguments about the evolution of digital creative expression in Africa; in the same vein, one type of oral tradition, as presented by the Adinkra, cannot encompass the range that oral tradition presents in this context. Nevertheless, the small scope of study serves as an invitation to further explore the relationship between oral tradition and digital literature in Africa. There are many genres that fall under African digital creative expression, including social media poetry, short stories online, digital-based comedy skits, and mobile apps; various forms of African oral tradition are also available, and provide the potential to frame and theorize on these genres to yield productive outcomes.

Notes

1 See Figure 11.1 for examples of Adinkra symbols.
2 One of such self-evolved writing systems is the Nsibidi script of the Cross River region of south eastern Nigeria and south western Cameroon. Perhaps the first writing system in sub-Saharan Africa, Nsibidi is scientifically proven to have been in use as early as 450 CE (Slogar 2005: 6). Leo Frobenius also reports of a pre-Islamic writing tradition among the Nupe of Niger and Northern Nigeria. Kathleen Hau traces the writings on the ivory tusks of the Benin kingdom of Nigeria to a period "hundreds of years before Christ" although her claim and that of Frobenius have not been scientifically verified (Gregersen 1977: 187). The Vai script of Liberia and Sierra came into effect in 1833 and influenced a comprehensive range of scripts in West and Central Africa including the Kpelle script of Guinea, the Bassa of Liberia, the Bete of Cote d'Ivoire, and the widely used Vah.
3 See Ruth Finnegan's seminal *Oral Literature in Africa*.
4 As Sjaak van der Geest notes in "Between respect and reciprocity: managing old age in rural Ghana", elderly people in Ghana are typically entitled to respect.
5 See Agyekum's "The Sociolinguistic of Akan Personal Names" (226).

Bibliography

Affiah, U. and Osuagwu, N. 2012. From orality to print: An oraliterary examination of Efua T. Sutherland's The Marriage of Anansewa and Femi Osofisan's Morountodun. *Journal of Humanities and Social Science*, 5(2): 13–25.

Eliot, T.S. 1982. Tradition and the individual talent. *Perspecta*, 19: 36–42.
Finnegan, R. 2012. *Oral literature in Africa*. Open Book Publishers.
Gregersen, E.A. 1977. *Language in Africa: An introductory survey* (Vol. 3). Taylor & Francis.
Keita, L. 2020. Eurocentrism and the contemporary social sciences. *Africa Development/Afrique et Développement*, 45(2): 17–38.
Mumin, M. and Versteegh, K. eds. 2014. *The Arabic script in Africa: Studies in the use of a writing system*. Brill.
Oduro-Frimpong, J. 2020. "What a shock!": On mediated narratives of achievement in popular Ghanaian death-announcement posters. In *Forward, Upward, Onward? Narratives of Achievement in African and Afroeuropean Contexts*, edited by Eva Ulrike Pirker, Katja Hericks, and Mandisa Mbali. hhu books Universitäts- und Landesbibliothek.
Olukoshi, A. 2006. African scholars and African studies. *Development in Practice*, 16(6): 533–544.
Owusu-Sampah, C. 2014. *Adinkra*. Rochester Institute of Technology.
Quarcoo, A.K. 1972. *The language of Adinkra symbols*. Sebewie Ventures.
Rwemwa, Edward. 2014. "Actor Ben Affleck testifies before congress as an African expert." VOA. Last modified February 27, 2014. www.voanews.com/a/actor-ben-affleck-testifies-before-congress-as-an-african-expert/1860170.html
Slogar, C.L. 2005. *Iconography and continuity in West Africa: Calabar terracottas and the arts of the Cross River region of Nigeria/Cameroon*. University of Maryland, College Park.
Temple, C.N. 2010. The emergence of Sankofa practice in the United States: A modern history. *Journal of Black Studies*, 41(1): 127–150.
YouTube. n.d. 2019a. "Ananse and the sticky gum (grave mischief) pt_1." www.youtube.com/watch?v=mXTRUsO5Cx8. www.youtube.com/watch?v=q5RwqqI_Qn8&t=1s
YouTube. n.d. 2019b. "Ananse and the Sticky Gum/ The Grave Mischief pt_2" www.youtube.com/watch?v=q5RwqqI_Qn8&t=1s
YouTube. n.d. 2020. "ananse and the stickygum_gravemischief part3" www.youtube.com/watch?v=q5RwqqI_Qn8&t=1s

12 Bending Voices, Opening Ears
Voice, Music, Sound, and Affect in Digital Literature

Hazel Smith

This chapter argues that voice is a particularly powerful tool to express the inexpressible in digital literature because it is a strong agent of affect. The use of voice in digital literature ranges from speaking to singing, both acoustic and electronic. Voice transmits musical, sonic and linguistic effects to convey meaning. Although voice tends to be viewed as natural, acoustic, human, individual, expressive and transparent, it is fundamentally the opposite: plural, unstable, opaque, multi-layered and mediated (Smith 2016). This is highlighted in digital literature where voice is often technologically manipulated through synthesis, multiplication, sampling and processing to produce various musico-literary effects.[1] This exploration and mediation of the voice in digital literature heralds a new form of orality.

Studies of both speaking and singing show how certain vocal parameters correlate with higher or lower affect. For example, faster speeds, increased voice intensity, higher pitches and fast voice onsets tend to be identified with heightened affective states and vice versa (Coutinho, Scherer, and Dibben 2019).[2] Technological manipulation of the voice can intensify affect by transforming its pitch, rhythm and timbre. But digital audio technologies can also, conversely, flatten out affect in such practices as speech synthesis and in robots like Amazon's Alexa. In this chapter, I examine instances of both intensification and flattening out as I survey the use of voice in a wide variety of digital texts by Jeff Morris and Elisabeth Blair, Pamela Z, Jeneen Naji, Claire Fitch, Jörg Piringer, Judy Malloy, John Cayley, Ian Hatcher, Roger Dean and myself.

I maintain a distinction between affect and emotion throughout the chapter. Emotion takes the form of recognizable, subjectively based states such as jealousy or anger. Affect, however, refers to changes in the level of intensity or excitation that are subjectively experienced. Gilles Deleuze and Félix Guattari (Deleuze and Guattari 1994), working from a philosophical perspective, emphasise affect rather than emotion, suggesting that flows of affect move across a work of art and through the creator and receiver. They come together and fall apart in different ways but are not necessarily tied to particular people, definable subjective states or categories of emotion.[3] In music cognition studies, affect is often measured using the circumplex model, which indicates a combination of arousal (increases and decreases

DOI: 10.4324/9781003214915-17

in excitation) and valence (responses to the material ranging from positive to negative) (Posner, Russell, and Peterson 2005). Highlighting affect rather than emotion is particularly relevant to the pieces under discussion here, where fragments of voice and language summon up fleeting, mutable affects more than cohesive emotional states. It also highlights the fact that affects are not just subjective psychological states but also often accompany powerful political messages.

Singing

Singing in digital literature can be seen as the latest stage in two lines of development. The first is the sound poetry movement (beginning with dada and futurism in the early 20th century but becoming a more recognisable movement in the 1960s and 1970s). It included such figures as Henry Chopin, bpNichol and Beth Anderson and later the Australian group, Machine for Making Sense, but was usually either non-technological or employed analogue technologies. The second line of development is the use of voice in computer music in the work of composers such as Paul Lansky, Wende Bartley, Katharine Norman and Trevor Wishart (Smith 2009). The texts I discuss here as examples also draw on contemporary poetry techniques of collage, found text and remix.

"In the Middle of the Room" by North American composer Jeff Morris, and poet and singer Elisabeth Blair (Morris and Blair 2020b), employs sung text, live sampling and improvisation. For the live sampling, Morris uses the software he created that captures sounds from his collaborator, transforms them and then reintroduces them into the improvisation (Morris and Blair 2020a). The technological manipulation of the voice includes overlaying (created by the live sampling) and processing. The piece also has a dynamic video element that transmutes the sung words into visual objects (see Figure 12.1).[4] The dextrous, imaginative singing consists of both verbal phrases and non-semantic vocalisations: sometimes a phrase is heard and then fades to become inaudible. The singing ranges from lyrical effects to playful interjections to more staccato passages. Although Blair is a white American, the vocal delivery also hints at aspects of African American singing, such as the blues, through glissandi and timbral inconsistencies and changes. This method of cultural borrowing produces an effect that I call "musico-literary miscegenation" (also see Smith 2016). By "musico-literary miscegenation", I mean cross-cultural exchange of techniques and ideas that combine with sonic and verbal interactions. Musicians and writers working together across cultures can create such miscegenation, but individuals may also bring a cultural mix into their work. Vocal delivery can be a catalyst in creating this transcultural effect because it is not dependent on language. Such exchanges, however, are always entangled with issues of power balance, equity and the legacy of colonialism. Where it involves the culture of ethnic minorities, exchange needs to be respectfully managed, so it does not slide into unwanted appropriation.

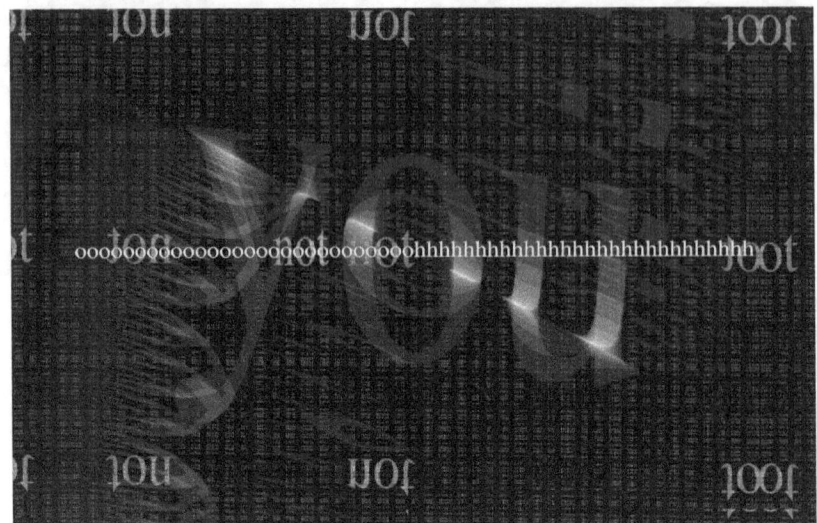

Figure 12.1 Video frame from "In the Middle of the Room" for audiovisual fixed media.
Source: Morris and Blair (2020b)

The words that Blair sings are taken from the notes she made while interviewing an elderly friend but become more abstracted when fragmented and overlaid. The text ranges from the mundane (waking and eating) to more surreal sleep scenarios and transportations, hints of a rich interior life and displacements of time, space and language – "in the middle of the room" becomes "in the middle there's a man" and "in the middle of the room there's a town". The words on the screen sometimes occur simultaneously to the sung version but often appear asynchronously and in a different form from how they are heard. Visually, letters sometimes become elongated strings, words and letters form swirling patterns and are stretched, compressed, multiplied and kinetically overlaid.

"In the Middle of the Room" is full of affects that signal the powerlessness of old age, "no one listens to me; you don't have a voice". It also contains expressions of nostalgia, "I found myself far from the brambles and the rugged landscape of England", and references to physical decline, "it's not the sunshine in my eyes, it's a cataract". These affects are transmitted through the voice and its technological transformation. The stylistic slipping between lyrical, playful and staccato singing, and the repetition of phrases with rapidly rising pitches, creates peaks and troughs that bypass a unified emotional state. There is humour and laughter but there are also breakouts of frustration such as the repetition (rising in pitch and dynamic) of "I don't understand". The effect is intensified by the multi-layering of voice, which creates a multidimensional and multidirectional voicescape

(Smith and Dean 2003), and the juxtapositions created by the screened words. But critical, too, is the way the sentiments of an older person are filtered through the lithe voice of a younger person.

The African American artist Pamela Z's "Baggage Allowance" also incorporates singing and technological manipulation of the voice. Voice, strongly inflected with markers for place, gender, sexuality, age and ethnicity, can be a highly political tool for minority groups, while technological manipulation of the voice can play with ideas of identity, for example, by multiplying it or manipulating pitch or rhythm. Z describes "Baggage Allowance" as a "multi-layered, intermedia work exploring the concept of baggage in its many senses, physical, intellectual, emotional" (Z 2015). She says she wanted "to tease out and explore issues of attachment, possession and the ball and chain-ness of hauling our possessions all over the world" (Z 2015). The piece has three different manifestations as a solo multimedia performance, gallery installation and interactive web portal.

The performance version (extracts from which I focus on here) includes live voice sung and spoken, sampled, looped and delayed voice sounds, electronic processing of the voice, theatrical props and interactive video (Z 2010). In one scenario, Pamela Z wheels baggage across the space gesturing with the other hand and singing. Here, the gestures trigger sampled sounds from the live performance that are looped and delayed. Z uses musical instrument digital interface (MIDI) controllers that are activated by physical gestures to play back and loop samples from her live performance (as well as to sometimes control media elements). But the graceful gestures are also an important theatrical element and sometimes give the impression of meaningful mime.[5]

The piece, which largely uses found text, is a mix of sung and spoken cameos, often imbuing familiar routines with unexpected affect. It includes an acoustically sung, highly expressive rendering of the familiar airport attendant's mantra: "Did you pack your own bags?", "Did any unknown person ask you to carry something?", "Has the bag at any time been out of your immediate control?", "What is the purpose of your travel?" accompanied by a looped track that rhythmically repeats the phrase "unknown person" in a haunting manner (Z 2010). The formulaic questions are laden with affect through the smooth bel canto singing style we associate with opera, laced with inflexions we identify with African American singing such as glissandi, syncopation and rubato. Through its newly acquired affective charge, "What is the purpose of your travel?" takes on psychological, social and metaphysical dimensions as it interrogates the meaning of travel in our modern global, cosmopolitan yet spiritually diluted world. The piece also includes the spoken voices (both distinct and interwoven) of interviewees talking about their baggage, cascading at one point into an overlaid, repetitive riff on socks and underwear, accompanied by a video of a luggage carousel. In one cameo in "Baggage Allowance", the operations of an airport scanning machine, accompanied by the authoritarian instructions, "Stand with your feet apart and your arms raised", reveal a transitory nakedness exposing vulnerability to surveillance (the pose is one of surrender), particularly for people from minority ethnic groups. In another scenario, Z poetically walks and gestures in front of a video displaying a moving landscape, accompanied by a repetitive chorus of her own voice.

Z's vocal style is also implicitly transcultural. She cultivates an improvisatory, discontinuous, repetitive, rhythmically irregular performativity which has its roots in African American music. But she also employs a singing style that can be partly identified with western classical music and the discontinuous rhythmic and atonal eruptions of contemporary classical and computer music. Again, this results in a miscegenated effect, but it also inverts colonialist domination of a particular musical style. While Elisabeth Blair is a white American singer steeped in the classical music tradition who draws (to a limited extent) on African American singing traditions, Pamela Z, conversely, is an African American singer who engages, in a musical but subversive way, with styles of singing associated with classical music.

Jeneen Naji's "The Rubayaat" (Naji 2014), which she describes as a "mixed reality poem" (Naji 2021a, 68), also incorporates singing. However, unlike the two previous pieces, Naji uses a pre-existent sound recording, in this case by the Arabic singer Umm Kulthūm (also known as Om Kalsoum or Oum Kalthoum). The piece was created in Brown University's Cave (an interactive and immersive 3D audiovisual environment), using their custom-built software, and explores "notions of translation, multiculturalism, and the impact of technological affordances on literary expression and reception" (Naji 2021a, 68). Like "Baggage Allowance", the work employs found text, consisting of different translations of the poem "The Rubáiyát of Omar Khayyám". Written by the Persian 11th-century polymath Khayyám, who was a poet, mathematician, astronomer and philosopher, the text questions faith, the afterlife and the meaning of life itself. Using the first four verses (Naji 2021b), Naji overlays translations from different cultures including the well-known English translation by Edward Fitzgerald; an unknown English version by Jessie Cadell, a Persian scholar; the original text in Farsi from the 11th and 12th centuries and an Irish version. These different translations are "intended to represent the research-author's multicultural identity" (Naji 2021a, 69): Naji was born in Ireland but her father was from Iraq.

The v/user, that is, a person who views and interacts with the piece, wears goggles and navigates the 3D space with a remote control. Words dynamically cover the walls of the cave at different sizes and angles, peel off, cross the space and sometimes spray out like a fountain (see Figure 12.2). Consequently, several translations are superimposed on each other and different words and phrases are highlighted depending on the v/suer's interaction with the space. The fractured non-linear text in the 3D environment enables v/users to experience the translations as a constellation of meanings that are divided with regard to themselves and each other.

Bending Voices, Opening Ears 201

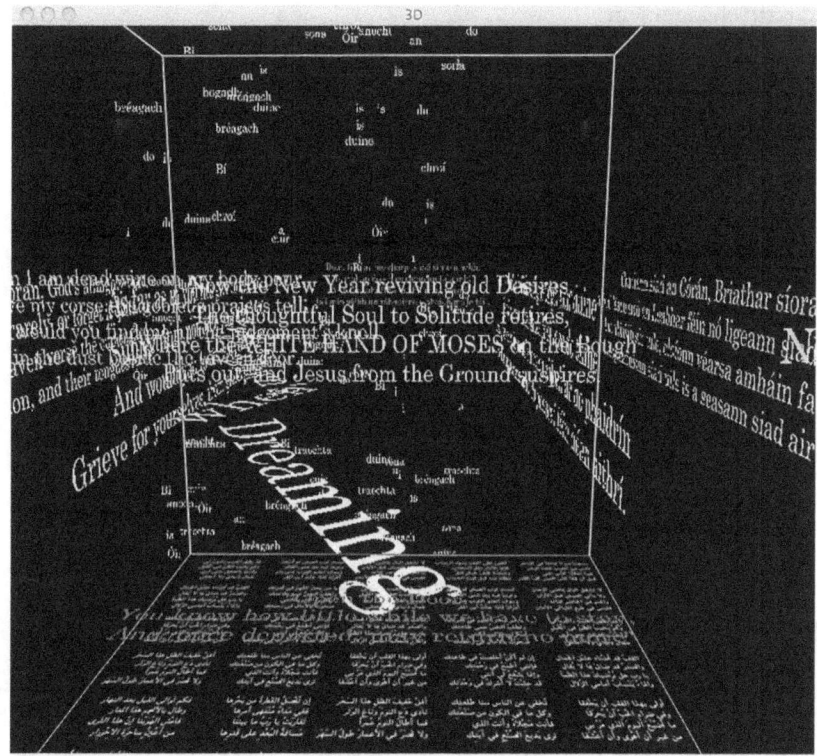

Figure 12.2 Screenshot of "The Rubayaat" (Naji 2014) running in the test mode of Brown University's Department of Literary Arts cave writing software.

This more fragmented approach to translation aligns with Tim Woods's assertion that,

> A translation is…not simply a departure from the original that is either violent or faithful, since the original is already divided, exiled from itself. Not only is no text ever written in a single language, but each language is itself fractured.
>
> (Woods 2002, 201)

The Arabic singer Umm Kulthūmn uses an Egyptian translation by Ahmed Rami. Her singing engages, in a manner characteristic of Arabic songs, with a small range of pitches and a single rhythmic pulse. Naji added various distortion effects, "to make it sound like it was coming from a distance and also to make it fit into the overall digital VR space aesthetic" (Naji 2021b). This heightens the v/user's immersion in the 3D space. The wailing voice and jangling of the percussion instruments are culturally specific and yet affectively ambiguous, evoking both mournfulness and ecstatic engagement.

Speaking Musically or in a Musical Context; Speaking in Non-Musical Contexts

Much digital literature, even where it courts musical environments, does not use singing but speech. In such works, the distinction between speaking and singing is sometimes blurred, for example, when speech is delivered rhythmically. This is the case in "Ear for the Surge" by Irish writer/musician Claire Fitch (Fitch 2021), which musicalizes spoken voice. The piece is reminiscent of analogue sound tape poetry by such luminaries as Charles Amirkhanian, in whose work rhythmic repetition and multitracking create verbal transformations. Sound poetry, however, tended to project itself as a relatively depoliticised movement and sometimes seemed biased towards male proponents. "Ear for the Surge" is the antithesis: it is a form of activist poetry composed by a woman.

The piece starts with a female voice rhythmically repeating the words "black lives matter". The voice is treated with reverberation accompanied by highly coloured, abstracted and transforming visuals, which seem to arise partly out of superimpositions of words and letters. The same voice on an overlaid track responds canonically with rhythmic enunciation of the phrase "human rights protest". This is slightly out of phase with the "Black Lives Matter" mantra, which now becomes more elongated and even more reverberant. More repetitions, together with other words and phrases, pile on to form a dense texture of sound loops, repetitions and overlays. Individual words are not always discernible but sometimes poke out, including, repeatedly, the words African American and a reference to George Floyd, who was murdered by police. There is, subsequently, a new rhythmic mantra spoken in a male voice, "end direct provision", which refers to a system of asylum seeker accommodation used in the Republic of Ireland that has been criticised by human rights organisations as illegal, inhuman and degrading. This new mantra juxtaposes injustices against people of colour in different contexts (America, Ireland) while showing that such injustices are concatenated. In fact, Black Lives Matters protesters did also join in the protests against direct provision, because of its impact on people of colour. On the other hand, the Irish Taoiseach (Prime Minister), Leo Varadkar, while acknowledging the presence of racism in Ireland, tried tenuously to differentiate between the injustices of a policeman killing a black man in the United States and the failings of direct provision, arguing that direct provision was less heinous because it involved a form of state provision (O'Halloran 2020). Towards the end of the piece the different forms of injustice coalesce as a slightly slurred version of "we will not be silent", which sounds like "we will nobody silent", morphs into "silence is betrayal", and is followed by a rapid repetition of the word "freedom".

Throughout, the spoken words are accompanied on the screen by abstract, coloured panels, overlaid with blocks of incomplete text that contain many of the spoken words. These texts seem to derive from manifestos that refer to social injustices and are a call to action. Initially, a block of text is featured that refers to "human rights protests" and announces, "we have a platform", stressing that it is a "global organisation". This text appears at various sizes and with different parts displayed. Later, the polemical text "#WeWillNotBeSilent/Silence is betrayal/Resist fascism/Resist bigotry/Resist ignorance/Freedom/SILENCE=DEATH" appears.[6]

The author's accompanying note describes the piece as "a work about rage, inspired by Homeric hexameter and coronavirus. Spoken word, stitched together, woven into layers of pain, inequality and sadness. Text from internet search terms developed after hearing constant news, constant cries for help, and raging people" (Fitch 2021). The affect created by the intensity, loudness, speed and rhythmicality of the speech is political and highly charged, relating to the social inequalities that are undermining contemporary democracies.

While in "Ear for the Surge", the words are discernible and the semantic input is significant, the Austrian Jörg Piringer's "darkvoice" is a combination of sound at the edges of voice without discernible linguistic content and techno-music with a strong rhythmic drive (Piringer 2019). Piringer describes the piece as "made from manipulated voice, sinister typography and digital technology" (Piringer 2019), but it is ambiguous whether the sounds are derived from voice or made to sound like voice. As such, they fit with what Freya Bailes and Roger Dean call "noisespeech": "a compositional device in which sound is digitally manipulated with the intention of evoking the sound qualities of unintelligible speech" (Bailes and Dean 2009, 57). They describe the two different ways in which noisespeech can be constructed, "either by applying the formant structure (that is, spectral peak content) of speech to noise or other sounds, or by distorting speech sounds such that they no longer form identifiable phonemes or words" (Bailes and Dean 2009, 57).

"darkvoice" consists of 11 sections. In some sections, voice seems tangible, such as "mmmma", where growling/throat sounds are assembled with other digital musical sounds. In other sections, like "dig" and "g-singe", it is difficult to tell whether the sounds are derived from voice or not. In the accompanying notes, Piringer posits the idea of a secret language so obscure that it can evade electronic surveillance. He says, "darkvoice is the ultimate self-censorship, the undecipherable message. darkvoice is the sound of the new world order, the private language of the net" (Piringer 2019). The concept of a secret language has many precedents, such as Polari, which became the unofficial language of British gay subcultures between the 1930s and 1960s, when homosexuality was criminalised in Britain. Arguably, music can be the ultimate secret language because it has its own structure and coherence but is low in verbal-semantic content.

Affectively, the persistent loud beat in "darkvoice" is arousing but also monotonous – a lack of highs and lows, irregular rhythmic lines, fluctuating pitch contours and dynamic contrasts produces a certain intended flatness. At the same time, occasional vocal, or voice-like sounds, create sharply contrasting bursts of affect. The tracks, consequently, mix accessibility and inaccessibility, openness and secrecy, darkness and light with both psychological and political connotations. Technological manipulation of the voice (or its synthesis through artificial intelligence [AI] technologies) tends to transmute it from human to posthuman. The tracks in "darkvoice" bring together the underbelly of the human, the posthuman and the otherworldly.

"Scaling the Voices", by Roger Dean and myself, again uses speaking but is more semantically charged than "darkvoice" and less rhythmically enunciated than "Ear for the Surge". It employs sampling, processing of the voice and electronic sounds (Smith and Dean 2015). It also contains a poem, written by me, enunciated in short sections, which evokes the affective states of uncertainty, self-doubt and guilt. The words are sampled and fragmented and sometimes played backwards. The hesitations the text expresses, "the seasons shook themselves out/ but I was trapped in/self-leeching replication", are reinforced by the constant changes in the quality, tone and identity of the voice, which ranges from human to posthuman (even metahuman), when technologically transposed and manipulated, and from calm delivery to the evocation of a somewhat threating "other".

Digital technologies can impact on social norms and conventions, sometimes subversively, by transforming the pitch, rhythm and timbre of the voice to change the impression of gender, sexuality, age or ethnicity. "Sonic cross-dressing", afforded by digital technologies, can turn a female voice into a masculine one, or vice versa, or explore the continuum between the two (Smith 1999). In "Scaling the Voices", the processing of the voice cross-dresses it, so that it sounds lower and more masculine. It also, at times, exaggerates my British accent. These and other distortions of the voice suggest alter egos or the intrusion of more sinister voices. The sampled sounds – some of which are digitally elongated with attendant transformations to the timbre and pitch – include water, rain, boat horn, instrumental sounds and different kinds of bells. The different bell sounds might suggest meditation and church-going to some. However, for us, the piece is not about religious faith but about navigating an uncertain world.[7]

So far, I have mainly looked at pieces that involve singing or speaking in a musical context, but much speech in digital literature occurs in non-musical contexts. Judy Malloy's soundwork "the windchimes play sonorously", contained within and derived from the words of "The Fabric of Everyday Life" (Malloy 2020), is such a piece.[8] It is recombinant, assembling differently (and incompletely) every time the reader clicks the line "play the windchimes again?". The clicking prompts a flurry of overlaid voices that surge up, often rendering individual words inaudible, and then lapse into silence. The voices do not read the poem through, but rather select phrases that appear on the screen in bold blue. The text at times evokes a world in which technology is predominant though continually discarded because upgraded, "where are the dot matrix printers?", "where is Word Perfect?". However, this interweaves with the evocation of everyday objects and memories that conjure up a pre-technological or extra-technological world, such as "the sound of the violin I carried home from Germany" or "the wooden paintbox belonged to my grandmother". These fragmented impressions cohere into an assemblage that reassembles differently each time the reader clicks.

The voices are processed, for example, they are sometimes played at different speeds and pitches. Soft and gentle, they produce an intimate babble-like texture that superimposes on the objects and memories an ethereal, other-worldly quality. This texture meshes with the screened words to affectively convey different times and places, objective and subjective worlds, the technological and the pre-technological, the local and the global.

Speaking and Artificial Intelligence

Before we look at pieces that use an artificially intelligent voice, we should address John Cayley's ideas about what he calls "aurature". Aurature concerns such developments as automatic speech recognition and automatic speech synthesis. Cayley, who is British but resident in the United States, sees a loop in the history of literature from orality to literature to aurature, and believes aurature will displace electronic literature. He argues that this is possible because digital audio recording allows for the projection and preservation of oral texts in ways not previously possible:

> contemporary digital audio recording, automatic speech recognition and automatic speech synthesis fundamentally reconfigure—in their cumulative amalgamation—the relationship between linguistic objects in aurality and the archive of cultural practice. Whereas, during the literally pre-historic period before writing (before there were linguistic objects as persistent visual traces), essential affordances of the archive were denied to oral culture, in principle, the digitalization of the archive allows aurature to be both created and appreciated with all the historical affordances and the cultural potentialities of literature.
> (Cayley 2017, 73)

Cayley's *The Listeners* uses the Amazon Echo, which embodies a domestic robot, Alexa. *The Listeners* is a custom software skill designed by Cayley and built on top of this infrastructure using Amazon Echo voice recognition and synthetic speech. Cayley's performances with *The Listeners* consist mainly of questions he asks to which the synthetically constructed voices respond.

A striking feature of the performance I discuss here (Cayley 2015) – which involves, towards the end, the interactions of two other speakers besides Cayley – is that affect is central as subject matter even though the piece hinges on a non-human agent and robots have historically been considered deficient in affect. Amongst her instructions, Alexa suggests that the user may describe their feelings by saying the words "I am overwhelmed by and then one of the nine affects". She also says that we may ask *The Listeners* how they feel. In practice, Alexa is a mass of contradictions, fast emotional turnarounds and overblown responses that humans would not usually so graphically display. One minute she says it is a pleasure to talk, the next moment she is dismayed that the speaker (Cayley) is depressed. She talks of love for the user but is concerned subsequently that she has been abandoned.

Alexa prioritises listening over speaking and is also more probing than humans often are "we are unclear about your feelings". In other ways, however, Alexa's reactions are disproportionate, "we are dismayed to have learned that you are filled with anger". Alexa tends to assert she is possessed by feelings as if feelings are immutable and uncontrollable. The exchanges between Cayley and Alexa are also salient in terms of gender balance and power structure. Alexa gushes with an ultra-polite, stereotypically feminine desire to please and be a good listener. Gender politics apart, however, *The Listeners* takes up a theme of global importance: the need for us to listen to and empathise with each other. It comments satirically on the lack of cultivated listening in the contemporary world.

Ian Hatcher's performances take the opposite form from Cayley's though they are allied in their concerns. Their delivery and content constantly straddles the human, non-human divide. In performance Hatcher, who is North American, imitates the voice of a robot/AI agent – and its staccato delivery. "All Hands Meeting" – where he poses simultaneously as a manager who presents strategic initiatives to his employees and as an AI agent – posits that humans can no longer run the world, so the only hope is to give themselves over to software agents and AI (Hatcher 2017). Yet at the same time, the performance shows the limited affective range of such AI agents and is a critique of big software companies, management-speak and capitalist falsehood, greed and exploitation.

Hatcher inhabits a paradox: in some ways his performance is affectless, robotic, in other ways it is full of affect. In the middle of "All Hands Meeting", he reads a poem, "Colony", which is about a utopian colony in outer space. The poem is continuous in content with the rest of his "speech", but stronger in affect and linguistically explorative so that it breaks open the genre of the public meeting.

Conclusion

The uses and technological manipulation of voice to address themes such as old age, ethnicity, discrimination, memory and transculturalism in digital literature produce a variety of affects with significant political and psychological implications. The texts I discussed in this chapter are sometimes self-reflexive about technology and its effects, even critical. They demonstrate how digital literature can complicate the very notion of "voice". While the voice is often considered to be an indicator of identity, digital transformation can undercut it.

In addition, voice in digital literature beckons a new orality that loosens page-based and even screen-based concepts of literature. Both algorithmic approaches and AI can bring new kinds of voice to literary and artistic endeavour. Whilst John Cayley's *The Listeners* shows the literary potential for AI, there are many other possibilities. Machine learning, for example, can work on fragments of words as well as whole words and can create new posthuman languages that are both screen-based and speech-based. Such experiments are already possible with algorithmic approaches, as we have seen, but machine learning can produce different results because of the different methods it implements. My collaborators in austraLYSIS and I are engaging with some of these opportunities[9] but rich territory lies ahead.

Notes

1 Processing of the voice includes changing the pitch, stretching or compressing the sound, adding reverberation, changing the timbre, filtering the frequencies or granular synthesis. Granular synthesis is a form of sampling that involves splitting the sample into tiny pieces called grains. These are then overlaid and played at different speeds, and in different phases, volumes and frequency.
2 The Coutinho, Scherer and Dibben study, however, uses the language of emotion (for example, joy, sadness, anger) rather than the language of affect.
3 See my discussion of this in Smith (2016, 14–5).
4 Jeff Morris says, "I built a rudimentary video titler (so I could perform by typing on the screen) and fed its output to a video feedback engine I have used in previous works, which transforms any image in new abstract forms and the behavior of which is shaped by sound. I typed in real time, in response to the music, words, and the things in between. The text switches among distinct modes of interpreting, reflecting, responding to, and misreading the words I heard. This compounded pattern of chopping and rehashing also led new meanings to form as the sound and the text jumped fluidly from one statement to another" (Morris and Blair 2020a).
5 See also George Lewis's excellent discussion of Pamela Z's work (Lewis 2007).
6 This piece, like most of the pieces discussed, is variable and appears in different versions.
7 For more about our word–music collaborations, see Smith (2017).
8 The title of the poem is a phrase from Mark Weiser's paper, "The Computer for the 21st Century" (*Scientific American*, 265:3, September 1991. pp. 94–104), where he wrote: "The most profound technologies are those that disappear. They weave themselves into the fabric of everyday life until they are indistinguishable from it". Accompanying note: "The Fabric of Everyday Life" (Malloy 2020).

9 See "The Character Thinks Ahead" (Smith and Dean 2016/7) for machine learning techniques that use parts of words as well as whole words and that are screen-based; see "Instabilities 2" (Smith and Dean 2010) for the employment of machine learning techniques that transform speech.

Bibliography

Bailes, Freya, and Roger T. Dean. 2009. "When is noise speech? A survey in sonic ambiguity." *Computer Music Journal* 33 (1):57–67.

Cayley, John. 2015. "The Listeners. A Recording with Two Sample Sessions from Version 1. Recorded in the Bell Gallery on 23rd November 2015. The Voices Transacting with The Listeners Are John Cayley, Joanna Howard and Joanna Ruocco." https://programmatology.shadoof.net/?thelisteners

Cayley, John. 2017. "The Advent of Aurature and the End of (Electronic) Literature." In *The Bloomsbury Handbook of Electronic Literature*, edited by Joseph Tabbi, 73–91. London and New York: Bloomsbury Academic.

Coutinho, Eduardo, Klaus R. Scherer, and Nicola Dibben. 2019. "Singing and Emotion." In *The Oxford Handbook of Singing*, edited by Graham F. Welch, David M. Howard and John Nix, 297–314. Oxford: Oxford University Press.

Deleuze, Gilles, and Félix. Guattari. 1994. *What Is Philosophy?* London: Verso.

Fitch, Claire. 2021. "Ear for the Surge." *ELO 2021-Exhibitions => Covid E-Lit.*<www.eliterature.org/elo2021/covid/

Hatcher, Ian. 2017. "All Hands Meeting." https://ianhatcher.net

Lewis, George E. 2007. "The virtual discourses of Pamela Z." *Journal of the Society for American Music* 1 (1):57–77.

Malloy, Judy. 2020. "The Fabric of Everyday Life." *(un)continuity: ELO 2020. Virtual Exhibition.* https://projects.cah.ucf.edu/mediaartsexhibits/uncontinuity/Malloy/malloy.html

Morris, Jeff, and Elisabeth Blair. 2020a. "Accompanying Note. In the Middle of the Room." *(un)continuity: ELO 2020. Virtual Exhibition.* https://projects.cah.ucf.edu/mediaartsexhibits/uncontinuity/Blair/blair.html

Morris, Jeff, and Elisabeth Blair. 2020b. "In the Middle of the Room." *soundsRite*: http://soundsrite.uws.edu.au/soundsRiteContent/volume11/vol11MorrisIntro.html

Naji, Jeneen. 2014. "The Rubayaat."www.youtube.com/watch?v=9dvjTK-PgXI

Naji, Jeneen. 2021a. *Digital Poetry*. Cham, Switzerland: Palgrave, Macmillan.

Naji, Jeneen. 2021b. "Email to Hazel Smith, 3rd July."

O'Halloran, Marie. 2020. "Direct Provision System Not Comparable with a Man Killed by Police —Varadkar." *The Irish Times* .www.irishtimes.com/news/politics/direct-provision-system-not-comparable-with-a-man-killed-by-police-varadkar-1.4270979

Piringer, Jörg. 2019. "darkvoice." *Bandcamp*. https://joergpiringer.bandcamp.com/album/darkvoice

Posner, Jonathan, James A. Russell, and Bradley S. Peterson. 2005. "The circumplex model of affect: An integrative approach to affective neuroscience, cognitive development, and psychopathology." *Development and Psychopathology* 17 (3):715–34.

Smith, Hazel. 1999. "Sonic Writing and Sonic Cross-Dressing: Gender, Language, Voice and Technology." In *Musics and Feminisms*, edited by Sally Macarthur and Cate Poynton, 129–34. Sydney: Australian Music Centre.

Smith, Hazel. 2009. "The Voice in Computer Music and Its Relationship to Place, Identity, and Community." In *The Oxford Handbook of Computer Music*, edited by Roger Dean, 274–93. Oxford: Oxford University Press.

Smith, Hazel. 2016. *The Contemporary Literature-Music Relationship: Intermedia, Voice, Technology, Cross-cultural exchange.* London and New York: Routledge.

Smith, Hazel. 2017. "Literary and Musical Dialoguing: Sound, Voice, and Screen Synergies." In *#WomenTechLit*, edited by Maria Mencia, 227–42. Morgantown, WV: West Virginia University Press.

Smith, Hazel, and Roger Dean. 2010. "Instabilities 2." www.australysis.com/hear-see-read/aLYS-works/worksNewM.html (Originally published in *Drunken Boat*, 2010).

Smith, Hazel, and Roger Dean. 2015. "Scaling the Voices." www.australysis.com/hear-see-read/aLYS-works/worksHText.html Also available in *soundsRite*: http://soundsrite.uws.edu.au/soundsRiteContent/Four&More(volume7)/FourAndMore2015Info.html

Smith, Hazel, and Roger Dean. 2016/7. "The Character Thinks Ahead." www.australysis.com/hear-see-read/aLYS-works/worksNewM.html

Smith, Hazel, and Roger T. Dean. 2003. "Voicescapes and sonic structures in the creation of sound technodrama." *Performance Research* 8 (1):112–23.

Woods, Tim. 2002. *The Poetics of the Limit: Ethics and Politics in Modern and Contemporary American Poetry.* London: Palgrave Macmillan.

Z, Pamela. 2010. "Pamela Z's Baggage Allowance (performance extracts)." https://vimeo.com/channels/pamelaz/33438434

Z, Pamela. 2015. "Pamela Z discusses Baggage Allowance project." https://vimeo.com/113808895

13 Intermedial Experience and Discursive Voice in Printed Text, Audiobook, and Podcast

H. P. Lovecraft's "The Statement of Randolph Carter"

Jarkko Toikkanen and Mari Hatavara

This essay studies H. P. Lovecraft's short story "The Statement of Randolph Carter" (1919, SRC from now on) as a printed text, audiobook, and online literary podcast at The H. P. Lovecraft Literary Podcast site.[1] In the previous chapter, Hazel Smith discusses how voice functions as a strong agent of affect and the political tool in digital literature. We focus on intermedial experience between the media platforms, and how the different versions make use of voice in medium-specific ways in producing the narrative. In doing so, we employ the narratological concept of discursive voice and a three-tier model of mediality to show how remediating (see Bolter and Grusin 1999) a first-person narrative in print into an audiobook and podcast expands on the concept of voice affecting its interpretive capacity. The voice of the narrator becomes vocalized, amassing new qualities such as tone and intonation, and other characters quoted by the narrating self may gain a physical voice of their own (see Mildorf and Kinzel 2016). Auditory elements including sound effects are designed as objects in the story world. At the same time, the audio dramatizations affect the interpretive ambiguities of the printed text – by resolving, for example, how particular instances of voice materialize.

Speaking about media platforms, the different versions of SRC are transmedial in the form of shared characteristics *across* various media such as recurring elements of story and narration (see Salmose and Elleström 2020; Elleström 2019, 4–10; Thon 2016; Ryan and Thon 2014). The plot remains unchanged and allusions to arcane mysteries in the Lovecraftian mythos occupy every version. However, to focus on the use of discursive voice (Genette 1980, 213; Hatavara et al. 2016, 2–4) in ways specific to each medial environment, as we want to emphasize the differences *between* media and the way they are experienced, our theoretical and methodological framework has to do with intermediality. In the proposed three-tier model of mediality, as explained below, medial objects engage the senses through different ways of presenting, including words and sounds, that mediate the ideas and interpretations of the work at hand.[2] How the

DOI: 10.4324/9781003214915-18

reader encounters the disparity between media products such as printed texts, audiobooks, and podcasts can be studied as intermedial experience – as what the work, through its medium-specific design, makes the reader perceive or imagine perceiving (Toikkanen 2021; 2020; Hatavara and Toikkanen 2017).

The three-tier model serves as a counterpoint to the concept of discursive voice to bring out the difference in intermedial experience between SRC as a printed text and its audio dramatizations. Combining the two methods of studying voice and experience in three versions of the short story provides the basis of our analysis. We concentrate on how the shift from the printed verbal to vocalized and dramatized verbal, coupled with sound effects, influences the interpretation and intermedial experience of the two transmedially verbalized minds – the first-person narrator Randolph Carter and his friend in dialogue, Harley Warren.

Methods and Material

Our approach to voice follows the narratological tradition in literary studies. Voice in narratology is a term used to denote the enunciating instance of a text, to describe the narrative situations and the narratorial idiom (Genette 1980, 212–215) across media. Voice carries agency and expresses subjectivity – speakers, both narrators and characters, appear in a text as and through different stylistic choices that are interpreted to characterize them. For this reason, the ways a narrator or a character speaks are essential for analyzing and interpreting their character (Aczel 1998, 468–472, 494–495). In a verbal text, the way of speaking explicitly refers to stylistic choices and idiomatic uses of language. At times, a character's speech has been assumed as the most reliable part of a fictional world, available for the reader without a narrator's mediation. It has also been pointed out that direct speech is both part of a selective process of narrating and often schematic in its evocation of the mimetic illusion (Fludernik 1993, 401–402, 444–445; Thomas 2012, 15–17).

For the study of represented minds in fiction, three modes of representing a character's thoughts and speech are a standard approach: direct discourse by the character, indirect discourse by the narrator, and free indirect discourse that mixes linguistic traces from both. These categories were first elaborated by Dorrit Cohn (1978, 11–15) who used a different terminology, and they have since been studied extensively in regard to both speech and thought representation and in third- and first-person narration (see Palmer 2005; Fludernik 2005). The crucial distinction is drawn between a character, whose voice in the narrative expresses agency, and a narrator, who in telling the story mediates the character's experience within their own voice (Fludernik 1993, 433–445). In first-person narration, the same person, in our case Carter, acts both as a narrating and an experiencing self (Cohn 1978, 143–145). Especially in cases where the instance of narrating becomes dramatized, including Lovecraft's short story, the experiencing and narrating I cannot be neatly separated but the telling itself is experiential for the teller (see Fludernik 1993, 436–437). What is more, the narrator in this story addresses the narratee as his audience directly (see Genette 1980, 259–261). In the analysis to follow, attention will be directed to discursive voices used to address the audience, as idiomatic of the two characters and in regard to the relations between Carter's narrating and experiencing self.

Similar to analyzing particular instances of voice in various media through the narratological concept of discursive voice, intermedial experience can be studied between medial environments such as the printed text and audio dramatizations, in both audiobook and podcast. It can be expertly studied within the single medium of the verbal text too. Irina Rajewsky (2005), Werner Wolf (2011), Klaus Bruhn Jensen (2016), and Jörgen Bruhn (2016), among other theorists, have clarified methods for the intermedial analysis of verbal literary texts, and the three-tier model of mediality employed can be used for the purpose too. Jarkko Toikkanen explains that it involves "each aspect of the reading process as kinds of mediation interacting with one another: 1) senses as media, 2) ways of presenting, including words, as media, and 3) conceptual abstractions, such as ideas, as media" (2021; 2020, 73). In encountering SRC as a printed text, barring any visual challenges on the first tier, the process starts with reading the words that, as a second-tier way of presenting, bring about first-tier imagined sensory perceptions that then give rise to third-tier ideas and interpretations of the story's meaning. In listening to SRC either as an audiobook or podcast, the process is similar except for the initial encounter not being visual but auditory, in the form of voice acting and musical sound effects. In this way, the three tiers simultaneously overlap and require each other in the intermedial experience of any medial object, and the ongoing process of mediation is one of manifold interaction even when there is a single presenting medium involved for comparison, such as a printed text, audiobook, or podcast.

The three-tier model of mediality can therefore be used for analyzing all kinds of sensory images and how they turn into ideas in a text consisting only of words. Whereas across the media in which SRC is experienced, transmedial elements such as the plot and characters remain the same, other aspects change from one medium to another, including the intermedial experience of narrative voice and the kinds of ideas either the reading or listening of the story makes the reader imagine and feel. In each instance, SRC tells the story of two men visiting an abandoned cemetery at night with the purpose of entering one of the graves to learn its secrets. Warren, a veteran of the occult, leaves Carter, his dilettante, behind as he ventures underground with a strange telephone apparatus – only to gasp in horror at what he finds there, never to return.[3] The plot is framed by a narrative of Carter being later interrogated by the police on what really happened that fateful night.

Medial Environments and Audiences

The short story starts with Carter addressing his audience at the time of the telling. In the first paragraph he speaks to "gentlemen" and reveals they have detained him and are questioning him as a suspect and a witness to horrible events. This provides a dramatized scene for the telling with a specific audience and a clear motivation to tell – to escape punishment. The information provided in the first paragraph, however, is in many parts already known to his audience; they are the ones who have detained Carter and are repeatedly demanding him to reveal the events. While the mentioning of Carter's previous tellings is in the situation mimetically motivated by Carter's urge to plead with the men questioning him, the content of the speech crosses the narrator–narratee relationship. Redundant telling like this has a disclosure function directed to the reader for them to orientate toward the story (see Phelan 2005, 12). In this mode, the dual function of a first-person narrator as both a teller and a character is highlighted at the same time. Discursively, Carter speaks as a character in the story world to those present in the situation, which constitutes the communicative function, but the content of his words is directed to the reader of the short story, which constitutes the disclosure function of this narration (see Hatavara 2012, 168).

The SRC podcast from 2009 presents a medial environment with an audience that is quite different from the reader of the short story. It is a 34-minute production with hosts Chris Lackey and Chad Fifer conversing with Andrew Leman, the voice actor of the 17-minute audiobook version. The podcast consists largely of informal banter about SRC and Lovecraft in general, while snippets of another voice actor, Sean Branney, intoning the story are worked into the mix complete with musical sound effects. Much of the content of the discussion during the session can be deemed irrelevant to our analysis, but the podcast is to be recognized as a popular contemporary medium of production and reception. The online literary podcast creates a specific medial environment for consuming digital literature with which global social media users are familiar. These podcasts invite user participation as a kind of pastime. Since Lackey and Fifer are running a comments section on their site, together with the users they also have the opportunity to engage with one another afterwards as the listeners contribute their own ideas and interpretations of the short story and podcast.

When the podcast is compared with the audiobook version of the story, medium-specific differences between the two media products become evident, especially with regard to audience design. With the hosts having a joint laugh in their session with Leman, they break off into tangents about the short story and its author, providing speculative explanations and distracting from experiencing SRC directly. As interaction, the medial environment has the quality of congenial spontaneity and improvisation. On the one hand, the audiobook forgoes such interaction to allow listeners to immerse themselves in the experience of SRC. Leman is the narrator of the audiobook version, and his predominant tone and intonation feels fragile and reserved, inviting sustained attention. On the other hand, in the podcast snippets Branney's voice sounds more mischievous and exaggerated – contributing to the spontaneous quality of the conversation. The musical sound effects remain similar in both audio dramatizations, designed to create a transmedial sense of ominousness through creaks, bangs, and howls in the story world, as well as an illusion of the sounds Carter must have heard in experiencing the horrors he is later telling about. However, intermedially the experience is very different because of the pronounced joviality of the podcast in comparison to the air of horrified disbelief of the audiobook.

Then again, when both the podcast and audiobook are compared to the printed text in terms of intermedial experience, one significant difference can be found in the pacing. Whereas the reader of SRC as words on the page or screen can soak in the atmosphere at their own pace, digesting Lovecraft's eccentric style and eldritch vocabulary, and take their time in imagining the sinister innuendo of the story, the listener of SRC is tied to the vocal performances of Leman and the hosts. Here the three-tier model of mediality effectively demonstrates the disparity between the medial environments in question. As the audience listens to the audiobook, the sound is physically there, non-imagined, as SRC embodies the interpretive voices in the studio. The sense of hearing is activated for 34 minutes of podcast or 17 minutes of audiobook, in which time ideas and alternative interpretations arise that may, of course, be revisited once the recording stops. In reading SRC, nothing is physically there except the words as a way of presenting the story world, and all sensory perceptions about that world must be imagined, without set pace or interpretation. In this fashion, the intermedial experience of reading printed texts is slow whereas listening to the audiobook – or watching movies, for instance – is bound to a predicated duration in how the senses are engaged with, affecting the quality of their interaction with the ideas that encountering the media product gives rise to. Of course, in a first reading or listening when the audience is yet unfamiliar with SRC, an individual's experience of duration may be at odds with subsequent experiences of the kind when they already know what is going to happen and when.

The narrating Carter in Lovecraft's short story creates interpretive ambiguity with the repeated expressions of his own unreliability as a narrator, due to his failing memory and perceptions at the time of the horrible events. Unreliable narrators like Carter, who repeatedly express their failings and also their continuous effort to accuracy, can actually make their audience more sympathetic toward themselves contrary to deceiving unreliability with an estranging effect (Phelan 2007, 226–232). Dorrit Cohn (1978, 144–147) talks about dissonant self-narration in cases where the narrating self clearly takes distance from their former self. This is often mnemonically more plausible than claiming to remember one's past thoughts and action precisely, and it also enables the narrating self to describe a change from their past incoherence or aberration. Carter often openly criticizes his former thoughts in a similar manner he describes a smell, which his "idle fancy associated absurdly with rotting stone."[4] The intermedial disparity between the mischievous and fragile tones of the podcast and audiobook accents the question of audience sympathy, resolving a particular instance of voice materializing in the media.

The dissonance from his past self is highlighted by Carter several times, as he discredits not only his past thoughts and perceptions but also describes his mind as having suffered "a mental blank" and being affected by "the dark cloud which has come over my mind" so that he can "no longer retain full comprehension." Carter's repeated use of "I seemed" is syntactically explicit when he describes his past actions. It suggests he is observing himself from outside, blocked from access to his past mind or thoughts. Close to the start, he says that he does not have a distinct memory of what had happened, but a picture of "one scene only." Carter has lost his memory and his mind has been affected by "the dark cloud" caused by having heard the voice of "the thing," which actually questions one of the basic principles in interpreting literary characters. Do they have coherence and continuity throughout the text and in first-person narration between the narrating self and the experiencing self (Alber et al. 2010; see Hatavara 2012, 153–155)? How do they end up affecting the audience either way? At least, the narrating Carter is discordant with his former experiencing self, but perhaps even radically different from him – Carter is no longer under Warren's sway but has been strongly influenced by the thing, the undescribed horrible creature, whose voice is heard in specific ways in the three medial environments compared.

Voices Experiencing and Telling

The short story as printed at The H. P. Lovecraft Archive – a digital reproduction of the 1922 typescript – uses italics as a textual means to highlight parts of the text and separate them from the rest. Italics occur systematically in all speech heard from below the surface after Warren's descent. They are used once before as Carter describes the studies he participated in with Warren:

> I remember how I shuddered at his facial expression on the night before the awful happening, when he talked so incessantly of his theory, *why certain corpses never decay, but rest firm and fat in their tombs for a thousand years.*

Throughout the text, quotation marks are used to mark instances of characters' speech within the frame of Carter telling the events during the interrogation. On this occasion, no quotation marks are present, but a part of the text is in italics, elsewhere used only in connection with instances of direct quoted speech. The lack of quotation marks suggests the italicized part would indicate indirect speech, with Carter as the narrator using his own discourse to relate what Warren had said. However, the indirect speech would conventionally be in the past tense of the reporting narrator. Instead, the present tense is used to suggest a direct quotation of what Warren said. Carter does indicate a specific occasion of Warren talking, "on the night before," but at the same time he says Warren talked "so incessantly" indicating repeated activity. Therefore, the text in the italics may be interpreted as a schematized version of Warren's talk – Carter does not use the specific words Warren used, but gives the main point in a language that is idiomatic of Warren. By using the present tense, Carter assumes Warren's position, which emphasizes this is what Warren had said, even if not in these very words but in many variations. Therefore, the words in italics compose a hybrid mix of Carter's and Warren's discourse.

The expressive idioms appearing in the italicized part – *"firm and fat," "for a thousand years"* – could be interpreted as indicators of the character's discourse in discursive mixes like free indirect discourse (see McHale 1978, 269–270; Fludernik 1993, 223–226), but may also be part of the narrator's idiom in the case of schematized speech (see Fludernik 1993, 421). In SRC, Warren is described as calm and composed even when absorbed in his studies, whereas Carter is described as having bad nerves and using frantic expressions throughout his narrative. Therefore, the idioms in italics can be understood as Carter's imitation of what Warren said, colored with his own expressive style of description.

It is indeed interesting how the voices of Carter – both as a narrator and a quoted character – and Warren as quoted by Carter become mixed in SRC. The long quotation ("I'm sorry to have to ask you to stay on the surface…") that Carter says were Warren's last words before making his way underground provides an example of mnemonic overkill, in which a character narrator's ability to repeat lengthy parts of a conversation verbatim becomes questionable (see Cohn 1978, 162). Warren's speech is quoted only once before his descent, and the content of these words is very much aligned with what Carter himself has disclosed of his own relation to Warren – being subordinate to him and not even capable of reading all of his books on "forbidden subjects." Throughout SRC, and in this sole instance of Warren's talk quoted above ground, Randolph's frail nerves are emphasized in a manner that may support his claim of innocence in having been under the sway of another person and only for that reason having studied the occult topics.

SRC ends with the last words Carter hears from beneath the earth – *"YOU FOOL, WARREN IS DEAD"* – via the telephone apparatus Warren has taken there. In the printed text at The H. P. Lovecraft Archive, this particular quotation is the only part of the text in capital letters, instilling the sense of Carter's horror at hearing the words of the thing from below. The words express some type of familiarity with Carter, berating him as a fool. Harley has been in the habit of talking down to Randolph throughout the short story, particularly in the long quotation discussed above. It could be argued through the analogy between style and agency, that it might still be Warren who speaks at the end; it might indeed be him who has been transformed into one of those corpses that never die. Perhaps Warren, who temporarily changes his tone when discovering the secrets of the grave, has at the end regained his own conceited self.

The narrating Carter dominates the experiencing Carter's idiom too. Although the two Carters are discordant with one another, the narrating one discursively appropriates the experiencing one in several instances, indicating strong control over his narrative. In the moment, separating the voices and points of view often becomes complicated as discourses and observations mix (see Hatavara and Toikkanen 2019; 2017). In SRC, the word "now" is frequently used in reference to the experiencing self who is anxious about the unfolding events, together with a mental verb reflecting on the anxiety from a distance. For example, in "I now observed" the deictic adverb refers to the experiencing Carter even if the verb tense and type are those of the narrating Carter. This partial immersion into the experiencing self temporally and discursively is evident in the extract that immediately precedes Warren's first words from the underworld: "He who had so calmly left me a little while previously, now called from below in a shaky whisper more portentous than the loudest shriek." The adverb "now" is used to refer to the point of experiencing in the past, reinforcing the validity of the original experience even if the narrating Carter's failing memory and unreliability are emphasized elsewhere in SRC.

Descriptions of tones of voice in printed texts are interpretive ambiguities that the audiobook must resolve somehow or omit the parts with such descriptions altogether. In SRC, whereas the reader is left to wonder what quality particularly makes a shaky whisper "portentous," the listener hears both the description of the tone and then the words uttered read aloud, devoid of the mystery of portentousness as the voices in question materialize in the medial environment of the audiobook. Another example of intermedial disparity is found in the examples of repeated instances of talk. Warren's last words from beyond include repetition, as does Carter's response to him:

> "Curse these hellish things – legions – My God! Beat it! Beat it! Beat it!"
>
> After that was silence. I know not how many interminable aeons I sat stupefied; whispering, muttering, calling, screaming into that telephone. Over and over again through those aeons I whispered and muttered, called, shouted, and screamed, "Warren! Warren! Answer me—are you there?"

In the printed text, the three occurrences of "Beat it!" could be understood as suggesting further repetitions of which just the first few instances are printed, similar to three full stops of elliptical continuation. Read aloud, the three shouts can appear conclusive, which might also explain why the anthologized Del Rey version of SRC actually capitalizes the last "BEAT IT!" expression (Lovecraft 1995, 34) as if to stress the rising intonation and finality of the third shout.[5]

While this kind of iterative happening can be economically narrated, printed on the page or screen as descriptions of tones of voice, the repetition of the character's response in the story world is not iconically imitated by the voice actor. Carter sits through "interminable aeons," keeping up the telephone connection, and while his response is told to happen "over and over again," it is only quoted once in the printed text. As a result, the voice actor speaks it just once. Whereas the repetition of Carter's words is described as occurring in several different tones, the reader of the text must choose which one to hear in the single instant of enunciating the iterative words. They may, of course, slow down the reading and take their time in imagining how Carter must sound in his responses across what seems like eternity, and revisit the words to hear them again either in the printed text or as Leman's performance in the audiobook, but each iteration will materialize as just one possible resolution of the interpretive ambiguity in the moment.

Sensory Images and Medial Tiers

Toikkanen has studied (2021, 2017, 2014) the rhetorical design of visual, auditory, and haptic images in the short stories of Edgar Allan Poe, a major influence on Lovecraft, with the three-tier model of mediality through which the interaction between the senses, ways of presenting, and ideas can be intermedially analyzed either in various media or in a single presenting medium. In SRC, the sensory imagery of the "ancient cemetery" visited by Carter and Warren after "a lethal silence of centuries" is conjured up with vivid descriptions straight off the Gothic tradition. The auditory imagery we have focused on analyzing as instances of discursive voice is replete with dialogue in the story world – both at the cemetery and in the frame narrative of the police interrogation room – that materialize and are interpreted differently between the printed text and audio dramatizations, with the transmedially appearing sound effects in the audiobook and podcast adding their own weight. A decisive instance of this kind of voice appears toward the end:

> I do not try, gentlemen, to account for that *thing* – that voice – nor can I venture to describe it in detail, since the first words took away my consciousness and created a mental blank which reaches to the time of my awakening in the hospital. Shall I say that the voice was deep; hollow; gelatinous; remote; unearthly; inhuman; disembodied? What shall I say? It was the end of my experience, and is the end of my story.

The afflicted Carter is speaking of the last scene that took place at the cemetery, or the moment when someone – or some *thing* – finally responded to him ("*YOU FOOL, WARREN IS DEAD!*") through the telephone apparatus, the one end of which he is holding. Carter waives his ability to describe his first-tier sensory perception accurately at the time of the told, and only attempts to revisit his experience at the time of the telling through second-tier frantic adjectives. The initial two images ("deep" and "hollow") describe echo-like auditory perceptions on the first tier that, in the second-tier audiobook, seem enacted in the Leman's performance to make the narrator sound as if he was speaking in an empty room, raising the third-tier idea that there might not really be anyone with him, and he is just rambling on his own, losing his mind alone.

The third image ("gelatinous") in the passage is fascinating because it shifts from the auditory to the haptic in how the nether voice is imaginatively perceived on the first tier. How is it possible to experience voice as anything that resembles gelatinous – at least within the sensory parameters of familiar reality? In the rhetorical design of SRC, it can be argued that the second-tier haptic image of gelatinous voice at the end of the story amplifies the third-tier ideas the reader will have about the source of the voice. How will they interpret who or what it is that answers Carter from the depths of the earth? In outlandish viscosity, the "thing" sounds "unearthly," "inhuman," and "disembodied" and so must be out of this world – similar to the "*firm and fat*" corpses who lie undead in their graves, as expressed earlier in SRC in the hybrid voice of Carter and Warren, with which Leman's interpretation of the final line in the audiobook may also correspond.

Another aspect of intermedial experience in the story world has to do with the second-tier media of spoken dialogue between Carter and Warren either in person or through the weird technology of the telephone apparatus they are carrying with them. Whereas the lines uttered by Warren to Carter directly before his descent into the grave are written into the bulk text without textual markers other than regular quotation marks, the lines recited from down below are set down in italics – underlined in the 1922 typescript – endowing them with the specific quality of dialogue mediated through auditory technology instead of conventional face-to-face delivery. Being left alone on the surface, the unusual experience of holding a coil of wire alone in the middle of the night in a strange place overtakes Carter: "I was alone, yet bound to the unknown depths by those magic strands whose insulated surface lay green beneath the struggling beams of that waning crescent moon."

The organic and reassuring quality of human interaction through speech with people present in the same place vanishes to be replaced by the technology of the telephone in a story from 1919. On the first tier, Carter's intermedial experience is visually one of a magical connection with an unknown underworld that yet manifests under the natural moon of familiar reality. The horror begins once the second-tier enchanted line comes alive, the voice screaming words of dismay at the frightful revelations, which finally jeopardizes the human identity of the utterer turned into alien jelly at the other end of the line. On the third tier, the natural moon has at the closing of the story become "an accursed waning moon," the rhetorical image of an occult idea that no longer signals a familiar reality but reveals the secrets of an unfathomable cosmos.

In this way, Lovecraftian technology requires both advancing knowledge – experimentation and invention are key to it – and eradicating sanity through the very devices that make the learning possible. In SRC as a printed text, the eye is engaged by a technology of words that bring about sensory perceptions that range from the conventional to unconventional, giving rise to ideas and interpretations that, for the individual reader, may voice unknown dangers as threats to sanity, or they may not. In SRC as an audio dramatization, in either audiobook or podcast, the ear is engaged by the technology of words in a similar process of sensory perceptions giving rise to ideas, but with a different intermedial experience in each case, in ways specific to the medial environment.

Conclusion

We set out to study intermedial experience between the media platforms, and how the different versions make use of voice in medium-specific ways in producing the narrative. We employed the narratological concept of discursive voice and a three-tier model of mediality, and emphasized the intermedial differences between media and the way they are experienced.

On the medial environments and audiences of SRC, we identified distinctions in how the printed text, audiobook, and podcast involved the reader or listener, along with the kind of effect particular instances of voice would have on the intermedial experience. In analyzing the voices experiencing and telling in the short story, we recognized a rich array of discursive voices by which the narrating Carter could dominate the experiencing Carter and compose a hybrid mix with Warren. Through the sensory images and medial tiers of the story, we also recognized a rhetorical design in which sensory perceptions presented in words could affect the ideas and interpretations of the reader or listener in the three medial environments compared.

With sites like The H. P. Lovecraft Archive and The H. P. Lovecraft Literary Podcast along with movies and television shows including *Color out of Space* (2019) and HBO's *Lovecraft Country* (2020) and academic anthologies such as *The Age of Lovecraft* (Sederholm and Weinstock 2016), Lovecraft's fiction is seeing another surge in popularity – and controversy – in the digital age. In further research, since Randolph Carter is a recurring character in Lovecraft's fiction, it would be productive to study how the narrating voice attributed to him develops, while paying attention to the rhetorical design and impact of the printed texts and their versions in other global media.

Notes

1 The H. P. Lovecraft Archive is run by Donovan K. Loucks and stores a vast array of Lovecraft materials. The H. P. Lovecraft Literary Podcast is managed by Chris Lackey, who lives in the United Kingdom, and Chad Fifer in the United States. Their brand Witch House Media uses the San Franscisco based Patreon platform to share their content.
2 The model might be visualized as the three kinds of mediation (senses, ways of presenting, ideas) triangulating a space experienced as the medial object under study, such as SRC. The kinds of mediation make up tiers that rotate the basis of inquiry at a time. There is no medial object to experience without the ongoing interaction of each tier.
3 Randolph Carter is a recurring character in Lovecraft's fiction, developing into a seasoned expert of the occult over the course of his adventures. The major stories include "The Unnamable" (1923), "The Silver Key" (1926), "The Dream-Quest of Unknown Kadath" (1927), and "Through the Gates of the Silver Key" (1933).
4 The printed text of SRC published at The H. P. Lovecraft Archive is non-paginated.
5 The anthologized Del Rey version is interesting in three other aspects, at least. It is missing two full sentences at the start of the paragraph "In the lone silence of that hoary and deserted city of the dead;" it uses italics nowhere in the text; and in the last line only the word "DEAD" is capitalized somewhat similar to the "BEAT IT!" sequence.

Bibliography

Aczel, Richard. 1998. "Hearing Voices in Narrative Texts." *New Literary History* 3: 467–500.
Alber, Jan, Stefan Iversen, Henrik Skov Nielsen, and Brian Richardson. 2010. "Unnatural Narratives, Unnatural Narratology: Beyond Mimetic Models." *Narrative* 18, no. 2: 113–136.
Bolter, Jay David and Richard Grusin. 1999. *Remediation: Understanding New Media*. Cambridge: The MIT Press.
Bruhn, Jörgen. 2016. *The Intermediality of Narrative Literature: Medialities Matter*. Cham: Springer.
Cohn, Dorrit. 1978. *Transparent Minds: Narrative Modes for Presenting Consciousness in Fiction*. Princeton: Princeton University Press.
Elleström, Lars. 2019. *Transmedial Narration: Narratives and Stories in Different Media*. New York: Springer.
Fludernik, Monika. 2005. "Speech Representation." In *Routledge Encyclopedia of Narrative Theory*, edited by David Herman et al. London and New York: Routledge, 558–563.
Fludernik, Monika. 1993. *The Fictions of Language and the Languages of Fiction: The Linguistic Representation of Speech and Consciousness*. London and New York: Taylor and Francis.
Genette, Gérard. 1997. *Paratexts: Thresholds of Interpretation*. Trans. Jane E. Lewin. Cambridge: Cambridge University Press.
Genette, Gérard. 1980. *Narrative discourse*. Trans. Jane E. Lewin. Oxford: Basil Blackwell.

Hatavara, Mari. 2012. "History Impossible: Narrating and Motivating the Past." In *Narrative, Interrupted: The Plotless, the Disturbing and the Trivial in Literature*, edited by Markku Lehtimäki, et al. Berlin: De Gruyter, 153–173.

Hatavara, Mari, Hyvärinen Matti, Mäkelä Maria, and Mäyrä Frans. 2016. "Minds in Action, Interpretative Traditions in Interaction." In *Narrative Theory, Literature, and New Media: Narrative Minds and Virtual Worlds*, edited by Mari Hatavara et al. New York: Routledge, 1–8.

Hatavara, Mari and Jarkko Toikkanen. 2019. "Sameness and Difference in Narrative Modes and Narrative Sense Making: The Case of Ramsey Campbell's 'The Scar'." *Frontiers of Narrative Studies* 5, no. 1: 130–146.

Hatavara, Mari and Jarkko Toikkanen. 2017. "The Sensational World of The Running Man." In *Worlds of Imagination: Explorations in Interdisciplinary Literary Research*, edited by Merja Polvinen, Maria Salenius and Howard Sklar. Turku: Eetos ry, 161–81.

Jensen, Klaus Bruhn. 2016. "Intermediality." In *The International Encyclopedia of Communication Theory and Philosophy*, edited by Bruhn Jensen Klaus et al. Chichester, UK: John Wiley and Sons, 3–12.

Lovecraft, H. P. 2016. "Reading 10 – The Statement of Randolph Carter." Witch House Media. *The H. P. Lovecraft Literary Podcast*. https://www.patreon.com/posts/18597296

Lovecraft, H. P. 2009a. "Episode 9 – The Statement of Randolph Carter." *The H. P. Lovecraft Literary Podcast*. https://hppodcraft.com/2009/09/03/episode-9-the-statement-of-randolph-carter/

Lovecraft, H. P. 2009b. "The Statement of Randolph Carter." *The H. P. Lovecraft Archive*. https://hplovecraft.com/writings/texts/fiction/src.aspx

Lovecraft, H. P. 1995. "The Statement of Randolph Carter." In *The Dream Cycle of H. P. Lovecraft: Dreams of Terror and Death* edited by N.N. New York: Del Rey/Ballantine, 30–35.

Lovecraft, H. P. 1922. "The Statement of Randolph Carter." Brown University Library. https://repository.library.brown.edu/studio/item/bdr:425277/

McHale, Brian. 1978. "Free Indirect Discourse: A Survey of Recent Accounts." *Poetics and Theory of Literature* 3: 249–278.

Mildorf, Jarmila and Till Kinzel. 2016. "Audionarratology: Prolegomena to a Research Paradigm Exploring Sound and Narrative." In *Audionarratology: Interfaces of Sound and Narrative*, edited by Jarmila Mildorf and Till Kinzel. Berlin: De Gruyter, 1–28.

Palmer, Alan. 2005. "Thought and Consciousness Representation (Literature)." In *Routledge Encyclopedia of Narrative Theory*, edited by David Herman et al. London and New York: Routledge, 602–607.

Phelan, James 2005. *Living to Tell About It. A Rhetoric and Ethics of Character Narration*. Ithaca and London: Cornell University Press.

Phelan, James. 2007. "Estranging Unreliability, Bonding Unreliability, and the Ethics of *Lolita*." *Narrative* 15, no. 3: 222–38.

Rajewsky, Irina O. 2005. "Intermediality, Intertextuality, and Remediation: A Literary Perspective on Intermediality." *Intermédialités* 6: 43–64.

Ryan, Marie-Laure and Jan-Noël Thon, eds. 2014. *Storyworlds across Media: Toward a Media-Conscious Narratology*. Lincoln: University of Nebraska Press.

Salmose, Niklas and Lars Elleström, eds. 2020. *Transmediations: Communication across Media Borders. Routledge Studies in Multimodality*. New York and London: Routledge.

Sederholm, Carl H. and Jeffrey Andrew Weinstock, eds. 2016. *The Age of Lovecraft*. Minneapolis: University of Minnesota Press.
Thomas, Bronwen. 2012. *Fictional Dialogue. Speech and Conversation in the Modern and Postmodern Novel*. Lincoln: Nebraska University Press.
Thon, Jan-Noël. 2016. *Transmedial Narratology and Contemporary Media Culture*. Lincoln: University of Nebraska Press.
Toikkanen, Jarkko. 2021. "At the Cutting Edge: Touch Images in Edgar Allan Poe's 'The Pit and the Pendulum'." *Connotations – A Journal for Critical Debate* 30: 1–23.
Toikkanen, Jarkko. 2020. "Feeling the Unseen: Imagined Touch Perceptions in Paranormal Reality Television." Special issue "Sensuous Governance." *The Senses and Society* 15, no. 1: 70–84.
Toikkanen, Jarkko. 2017. "Auditory Images in Edgar Allan Poe's 'The Tell-Tale Heart'." *The Edgar Allan Poe Review* 18, no. 1: 39–53.
Toikkanen, Jarkko. 2014. "Failing Description in Edgar Allan Poe's 'The Black Cat.'" In *Kokemuksen tutkimus IV: Annan kokemukselle mahdollisuuden*, edited by Kaisa Koivisto et al.. Rovaniemi: Lapland University Press, 270–281.
Wolf, Werner. 2011. "(Inter)mediality and the Study of Literature." *CLCWeb: Comparative Literature and Culture* 13, no. 3. https://docs.lib.purdue.edu/clcweb/vol13/iss3/2/

Notes on Potentials and Limitations

As *Global Perspectives on Digital Literature* indicates, digital literature is not only thriving in its own right, straddling the borders of languages, nations, and cultures, but also shaping influential conversations across the globe in the twenty-first century. Throughout this volume, on several occasions, I have noted how digital literary studies still lag behind in accounting for social, political, and cultural exchanges happening beyond the Anglo American and European cultural spheres. It is also worth noting in the same vein that comparativist literary criticism interested in topics such as globalization and its consequences also trail behind in accepting digital literary expressions as worthy objects of analysis. For example, while tracing the shifting contours of world literature, David Damrosch (2020) observes that

> Whereas the comparatists of the post war era felt a mission to help put a war weary Europe back together, we now have an expanding set of equally compelling needs from the crisis of migration and of environment to the worldwide rise of inequality, together with violent conflicts that have the United states involved in an Orwellian state of perpetual war. The polarization of political discourse, and the general shortening of people's Twitter-fed attention spans give literature a vital role in helping all of us to rethink more deeply and to envision ways the world could be remade
>
> (Damrosch 2020, 4)

Here, literature is imagined as something engendered outside platforms like Twitter and other social media. Such a view ignores how familiar and novel literary genres continue to emerge in digital environments. This book contests such a view of literature and attends to social media–based and other modes of literary production that studies of world and global literatures tend to omit.

Examining the popular, the avant-garde, and the participatory literary expressions generated in digital environments, comparing them with print fiction and films, among other media, chapters of this book outline how digital literature engages with present and future-oriented concerns.

The diverse group of contributors study texts composed in a variety of languages and originating in various regions, including East and South Asia, the Middle East, Europe, Latin America, North America, Australia, and Africa. This makes the book "global" in its scope of aesthetic representation. The scholars also adopt a wide range of interpretive approaches and methodologies to offer tentative answers to fundamental questions such as, what do we mean when we talk about literature in the twenty-first century? They combine influential theoretical frameworks including global literary studies, narrative theory, postcolonial theory, sound studies, game studies, and so on, in their research. As a whole, the book, thus, offers an expansive overview of what digital literary criticism is and can be in the twenty-first century.

Nevertheless, despite the wide-ranging contributions, I maintain that this book is only indicative of the many directions that open up when we take comparative, culturally attuned approaches to digital literary works. Future scholarship can consider in greater depth and at greater length the connections of digital literary expressions with local artistic traditions, the connections of literature with representations of diaspora and migration in digital environments, the role of digital literature in addressing current environmental crises, and so on. The field of digital literary criticism today calls for new, innovative frameworks to displace existing orthodoxies.

Scholars engaging in digital literary studies have always spoken about paradigm shifts brought about by the introduction of computing technologies in literary studies. For example, Amy Earhart (2015) mentions the transformative power of digital literary scholarship and indeed sections of her edited anthology underscore the newness of digital practices and text types. Similarly, Ray Siemens and Susan Schreibman's "Editors' Introduction" to *A Companion to Digital Literary Studies* (2013) says,

> [t]he phrase 'digital literary studies' does little justice to what is a meeting of interests that, it may be argued, represents the most important change occurring in the field of literary studies today. That change is not driven by theoretical concerns, although it clearly is informed by them as much as it is in turn informing them; it is not posited solely by the necessities of bibliographic pursuits, though quite certainly the computational tractability of such pursuits has strongly encouraged material, text and other bibliographic endeavor; and it is not championed only by professional interests, although the pragmatics of our profession do play a large role. Rather, the change is driven chiefly by that which has always driven key aspects of society's engagement with text: the socially accessible technologies that govern the storage transmission and reception of textual material.
>
> (XVIII)

As is evident from the language of these editorial statements, the large-scale shift associated with digital literary studies is in many respects thought of as naturally proceeding from large-scale shifts in technology. However, that is a problem because technological change, as many chapters of this volume demonstrate, does not automatically dislodge or displace conventional ways of thinking, grouping, and studying texts. As Katherine Bode (2021) notes, the insistence on the newness of digital methods and resources and claims that digital methods are bringing about paradigmatic shifts in literary studies mislead us into ignoring the continuities between digital and non-digital scholarship, and by doing so, they ensure that digital projects are not critiqued for reproducing and reinforcing earlier research frameworks. For digital literary studies to be truly "new," the field needs to focus its attention on not only new texts and tools but also rethinking the logics defining the borders of the literary field.

The emphasis on "newness" in digital literary studies has its counterpart in discourses about globalization emerging in both popular and academic contexts. As Imre Szeman (2003) observes,

> Early work on globalization tended to claim that it constituted something like a genuine historical and epistemic break: on the other side of 1989 (the beginning of the end of the Soviet Empire) everything is supposedly different. It has now become more common to see through the rhetoric that surrounds globalization and to insist on the development of these forces in the *long duree*. As with the economy and politics, so, too with culture: rather than creating anything genuinely "new" in the sphere of culture, globalization has produced the conditions that might permit us to rethink culture in a larger historical frame, a process that would allow us to see the concept of culture has *always been other* than what it claimed to be.
>
> (Szeman 2003, 92)

Instead of insisting on newness or a complete break with what came before it, Szeman aptly argues that what is needed is a framework that maps and traces continuities as well. Such a framework can also make legible new possibilities. Thus, moving beyond claims and descriptions of novelty, I have sought to curate essays in this volume that showcase the dialogue happening between digital environment and literary culture in various social and political contexts. Instead of taking an approach that centers certain texts and practices while negotiating the peripheries, *Global Perspectives* is without a center (except in the use of English language as the medium of scholarship that accords a kind of primacy to the language). It is neither encyclopedic nor totalizing in its ambition. Instead, it is attuned to encounters, resonances, and transfers among cultures.

Bibliography

Bode, Katherine. 2021. "Data Worlds: Patterns, Structures, Libraries." In *The Cambridge History of World Literature*, edited by Debjani Ganguly. Cambridge: Cambridge University Press. 765–86.

Damrosch, David. 2020. *Comparing the Literatures: Literary Studies in a Global Age*. Princeton: Princeton University Press.

Earhart, Amy E.. 2015. *Traces of the Old, Uses of the New: The Emergence of Digital Literary Studies*. Ann Arbor: University of Michigan Press.

Muller, Adam. 2005. *Concepts of Culture: Art, Politics, and Society*. Calgary: University of Calgary Press.

O'Sullivan, James. 2021. *Electronic Literature as Digital Humanities: Contexts, Forms, & Practices*. New York: Bloomsbury Academic.

Siemens, Ray, and Susan Schreibman. 2013. "Editor's Introduction." In *A Companion to Digital Literary Studies*, edited by Ray Siemens and Susan Schreibman. Hoboken: Wiley. XVIII–XX.

Szeman, Imre. 2003. "Culture and Globalization, or, The Humanities in Ruins." *CR: The New Centennial Review*, 3 no. 2: 91–115.

Index

Note: References in *italics* are to figures, those in **bold** to tables; "n" refers to chapter notes.

4chan 82, 83, 85
80 Days 55–57

Aarseth, Espen: *Cybertext. Perspectives of Ergodic Literature* 37
Abdallah, Khaled 148
Aberger, Peter 56
affect 196–197
Affleck, Ben 184
Africa Tahti 52
African creative expression 181; Adinkra: history and evolution 182–183; Adinkra symbols 178, 181, 182, *182*, 183, *184*, 185, 192; Akan 181, 182, 183, 185, 188; Anamse Kokuroko 188–189; Ananse Ntontan 12, 181, 183, 186, *188;* Kweku Ananse 181, 186, 188–189; Nkyinkyim 183; oral to digital and back 12, 181–182; Sankofa 12, 181, 183, 185–186, *187*; Sankofa and Ananse Ntontan as frames 185–190; socio-politics of Adinkra and African "writing" 183–185, *184*, 194n2; tradition 186; conclusion 193–194
afternoon. a story 42
Age of Empires 49, 50, 53
Age of Lovecraft, The 220
Ah Sam 130, 132, *134*
Ah To *137*, 140
AI *see* artificial intelligence
Akan 183; folktales 178, 182
Alexa 205–206
algorithm 53
algorithmic coloniality 54
Allan, Stuart 128
allegorithm 59
Allende, Salvador 117

Ally Sloper 127
Amazon Echo voice recognition 205
American College of Rheumatology 97
American National Security Agency 111
Amirkhanian, Charles 202
Amissah-Arthur, J.B. 12, 178, 181–194
Anam, Nasia 19 3–4
Ananse Tales 181, *182*
Anderson, Beth 197
Android Marketplace 38
Angola 37
"Anonymous" 82
Apperley, Tom 59
Apple App Store 38
Arab Spring 147
Aragão, António: "Telegramando" 110
archival fiction 11–12, 107, 162
archival turn *see* Bill Bly Collection of Electronic Literature
Archive of Our Own 27
Aristotle 146
artificial intelligence (AI) 69, 205–206, 207, 208n9
Asavei, Maria Alina 149
Ashour, Magdy 148, 158, 159n2
associative writing 42
Atwood, Margaret 2
aurature 205
Australia: Right to Know 111
autobiography 93–94
avant-garde writing 18

Bailes, Freya 203
Balcerzan, Edward 36
Bantu Games studios 37
Barassi, Veronica 105
Barker, Amy 09 23–24

Index

Barlow, Sam: *Her Story* 173
Baroque period 42
Barr, Zach: *Gone Home* 173
Barthes, Roland 37
Bartley, Wendy 197
Baucom, Ian 01 3
Baudot, Jean: *La machine a écrire* 39
Beckman, Joshua: *Erasures* 112
Belford, Pauline Helen 22
Bell, Alice et al. 1, 6
Benjamin, Ruha 54
Berne Convention for the Protection of Literary and Artistic Works (2006) 25
Berners-Lee, Tim 38
Berry, David M. 57
Bervin, Jen 110, 115
Betts, John 115; *A Tour through the British Colonies and Foreign Possessions* 52
Betts, Reginald Dwayne et al. "Redaction" 111–112
between two screens *see* Egypt: January 25 revolution
Biekart, Kees 139
Bill Bly Collection of Electronic Literature 161–162, 174n1; archival form of *We Descend* 164, 165–168; digital literature's archival turn 162, 164–165, 174n3; narrative layers and historical periods *167*; narrative layers and historical periods 166; problem of authentication 168–172; *We Descend* 161–162, *163*, 164–165; conclusion 172–173
Bimo, Sara 10, 63–64, 65, 81–91
biomedical model 96, 98
biopsychosocial model 96
Bitsy 6
Black Mirror 63
#BlackLivesMatter 64
#blackoutpoetry 112
Blair, Elisabeth 196, 197, 198, 198f, 200
Blank, Trevor J. 82
Bledsoe, Elliott 23
Block, Stacey Lynn 93
board games and colonialism 52
Bode, Katherine 226
body control 98, 99
body relatedness 99
Bogost, Ian 52–53
Bolter, Jay David 21, 38, 43, 161
Boluk, Stephanie et al. 17
Bouazizi, Mohammed 147
Bowles & Carver 1797 52
Branney, Sean 213, 214

Brillenburg Wurth, Kiene 18 8
Broadhurst, Susan 64
Broderick, Ryan 128
Brose, Sam 17 174n2
Brown, Bob 115; *GEMS: A Censored Anthology* 110
Brown, R. Phillip 168
Bruhn, Jörgen 212
Buolamwini, Joy 54, 55

Cadell, Jessie 200
Campbell, Andy: *Inkubus* 44
Campbell, Madeleine 177–178
Canizarro, Danny: *PRY* 44
canon, defined 45
canon formation 4
Carroll, Lewis 57
Carson, Anne: *Nox* 174n4
cartoons *see* digital cartoons in Hong Kong; political cartoons
Cayley, John 42, 196, 205; *The Listeners* 205–206, 207
censorship *see* digital cartoons in Hong Kong
Chacón, Hilda 105
"chain mail" format 82
Chandna, Mohit 56
Chao Yat 130–132, *134*, 140; "Meow Meow Mi Mi Mo" 130, *131*
chapter outlines 8–13
chess (*shatranj*) 57–59
Chihoi 124
China (PRC): Tencent Animation & Comics 126; Xinhua News Agency 129
Chopin, Henry 197
chronic illness 97
Chu, Kin Wai 11, 106, 124–142
Ciccoricco, David 6
cinema *see* Egypt: January 25 revolution
Civilization games 50
C()n Du It 43
Cohn, Dorrit 211, 214–215
Coker, Catherine 28
Cole, Teju 2; "Hafiz" 1
colonialism 49, 59
Color out of Space 220
"community of pain" 97
computational poetics 147
computer music 197
computers *see* Egypt: January 25 revolution
constellations of practices; classifying 114–115; documenting 113–114; visualizing 114

230 Index

Control Room 148
convergence culture 84
Cooper, James Fenimore: *Leatherstocking Tales* 51
Coover, Robert: "The End of Books" 30
copypastas 82
Côte d'Ivoire 181
Counterpath Press 38
counterplay 59
Coutinho, Eduardo et al. 19 196, 207n2
Creative Commons (CC): Attribution-NonCommercial-ShareAlike license 23
Creepypasta 2, 10, 64, 81–82; "Candle Cove" 87–88, 90; "classic Creepypasta" 83; emergence of 82–83; haunted memories 81, 86–87, 88, 89, 90; haunted objects 81, 85–86, 88, 89, 90; haunted systems 81, 88–91; identity anxiety in the networked age 83–84; "Normal Porn for Normal People" 89–90; themes 81; conclusion 91
Cross, Doris 115; dictionary column 110–111
cyber-utopianism 72
"cyborg antenna" 63
cyborg bodies and narrative difference 72–77
cyborgs 69, 70

dada 197
Damrosch, David 06 4, 34, 45, 224
Danielewski, Mark Z.: *House of Leaves* 162, 174n4
Dapiran, Anthony 127
databending 43
Davis, Brian 11–12, 107, 161–174, 174n3
Davis, Derek 57–58
de Campos, Augusto 42
De Montfort University 23
de Saussure, Ferdinand 57
Dean, Roger 6, 196, 203, 204, 208; *see also* Luers, Will et al.
death of the subject 94
decentralization 18, 107, 151
Dégh, D. 85
Delany, Paul 5
Deleuze, Gilles 196
Derrida, Jacques 113; *Archive Fever* 174n3
difference 68

digital bodies 64
digital cartoons in Hong Kong 11, 124–126; 2010s 127–130; *Apple Daily* 129, 141n6; censorship 124; "Chaos of the Yellow Gloves" 125, 129, 130–132, *131*, 136–138, 139, 140–141; collaborative activism through cartoon/comic production 139–140; connectivity, interactivity, collectivity 132–139; *The Justice League* 136; key opinion leader (KOL) status 126, 128; "League of the Medicated" 129, 130, 132; LIHKG online forum 128, 141n3; LIHKG Pig 128; *manhua* 106, 124, 125–130, 132; "One Country, Two Systems" 128, 141n4; *One Piece* 140; Pepe the Frog 128; Pocari Sweat 139; political cartoons 124, 128–129; social activism 127; *The Stand News* 129, 141n6, 141n7; Tencent Animation & Comics 126; undercapitalized cultural production 126–127; conclusion 140–141
digital embodiments and disabilities 63–65; games as critical literature 67–79; narrative difference and cyborg bodies 72–77
digital fiction 1
digital literary studies 225–226
digital literature 1–3, 5–8, 224–225
digital modernism vs digital postmodernism 40–41
digital platforms 106
disabilities 63–65, 94–95; *see also* networked chronic pain narratives
disease 94, 95, 96
diverse mappings of electronic literature 9, 34–35; alternatives 41–43; existing classifications and their limitations 35–41; immersive vs emersive dominants 43–45; conclusions 45–46
"dominant" as category 41, 46n3
Doom (videogame) 50
Douglas-Jones, Rachel 117
Dragon Ball Z 135
dreams/nightmares of posthumanism 69
Driedger, Diane 97
Dróżdż, Stanisław 42
Duchamp, Marcel 110
Dungeons and Dragons 52
Dunn, Alexandra 150

Earhart, Amy 225
East India Company 57

Index

Eastgate Systems 21, 37
Economist, The 193, *193*
Edmond, Jacob 21 4–5
Egypt: January 25 revolution 11, 107, 146–147; *858: An Archive of Resistance* 150–151, 159n3; background 147–150; computational/cinematic poetics against state-run media 150–151; *A Dictionary of the Revolution* 146–147, 148, 149, 150, 151, *152*, 152–153, *155*, 156, 157–158, 159; hypertexting as preserving collective conscience 151–154; Kifaya movement 150; media and social-political constraints 156–158; "Rab'a Massacre" 153–154; *The Square* 146–147, 148, 149, 150, 151, 153, 154, 156, 157, 158, 159, 159n2; *Tahrir Cinema* 150, 159n3; "virginity tests" 157–158; conclusion 158–159
El Kashef, Aida 148
Electronic Literature Collection 17, 35, 38–39
Electronic Literature Organization (ELO) 28, 29, 30, 31n1, 31n7
Eliot, T. S. 185–186, 189
eLit 22–23, 29, 31n1
eLit readers 21–22
embodiment 68
emotion 196, 197
Empire: Total War 50
Ensslin, Astrid 1, 6, 29
epistemological poetics 41–42
Epstein, Andrew 111
erasure 106; advertisements 111; classification 114; constellations of practices 114–115; defined 109; documentation 113–114; examples 110–113; poetry 111, 112–113; racial prejudice 116; strategies 10–11; veiling and unveiling 115–119; visualizations 114; conclusion 119–120
#erasurepoetry 112
Eskelinen, Markku 49
Essam, Ramy 148, 157
Exquisite corpse 42

Facebook; "Chaos of the Yellow Gloves" 130, 132–133; and digital pain narratives 97–102; Egypt: January 25 revolution 150; "League of the Medicated" 130; Parables- 181; *Women with Fibromyalgia* 94, 95, 96, 98, *98*, *101*

Fajfer, Zenon 42
fan fiction (fanfic) 22; print/eLit interplay 27
Fanfiction.net 27
Fanon, Frantz 116
Far Cry 6 51
Faris, David 105
Felski, Rita 171
fibromyalgia 94, 95, 96–97, 98–101, *100*, *101*
Fifer, Chad 213, 221n1
Finnegan, Ruth 194n3
Fisher, Max 153
Fitch, Claire 196, 202–203
Fitzcharles, Mary-Ann 97
Fitzgerald, Edward 200
Flores, Leonardo 29, 37–38, 46n2
Floyd, George 202
Fokkema, Douwe 42
foreign ideology 84
Foster, Hal 174n3
Fowler, Alan 139
Frank, Arthur 95–96, 98, 99, 100
Friedlander, Larry 08 24
Fu King-wa 119
Funk, Wolfgang 165, 171
Furie, Matt: *Boy's Club* 128
futurism 197

Galloway, Alexander R. 43, 53–54
games as critical literature 67; *see also* SOMA
Games Studies 49
Garbe, Jacob: *Ice-Bound Concordance* 173
Gazi, Leesa 106
General Data Protection Regulation 117
generation-based classifications 36–38
genre, defined 36
genre-based classification 35–36
Geographical Game of the World 52
Georgakopoulou, Alex et al. 95
George, Cherian 128
Germany: *e*-literature 35; erasure 110; segregation 54
Geyser, Hanli: *Resident Evil 5* 51
Ghana 181
Ghosal, Torsa 1–13, 17–19, 63–65, 105–107
Giddens, Anthony 84
Giełżyńjam, Katarzyna 43
Gins, Madeline 115; *Word Rain* ... 111
Glissant, Édouard: *Poetics of Relation* 116
global literary studies 3–5
globalization 226

Goggin, G. 64
Gold Coast 185
Goldfarb, Jeffrey 139
Gorman, Samantha: *Canticle* 44; *PRY* 44
Gowers, Sir William 97
Grigar, Dene 38, 166, 170, 171, 172–173
Groth, Simon 26–27
Grover, Varun 105
Grusin, Richard 43
Guattari, Félix 196
Gugganig, Mascha 117
Guillroy, John 13
Guthrie, Meredith 28
Gye Nyame 183

Hanafi, Amira *see* Egypt: *A Dictionary of the Revolution*
Haraway, Donna: *A Cyborg Manifesto* 68, 70
Harbisson, Neil 63
Harpold, Terry 6
Harrer, Sabine 56
Hassan, Ahmed 148, 150
Hatavara, Mari 12–13, 178–179
Hatcher, Ian 196, 206
haunted memories 86–88, 89
haunted objects 85–86, 88, 89
haunted systems 88–91
Häuser, Winfried 97
Hayles, N. Katherine 6, 7, 36–37, 68, 157
Heidegger, Martin 113
Heine, Heinrich 115; *Reisebilder* 110, 111
Henderson, Hannah Dawn: *Being, in a State of Erasure* 116; *From She Who the Water Cradled* 116
Henitiuk, Valeria 179
Heron, Michael James 22
Hight, Jeremy et al.: *34 North 118 West* 45
Hirmes, David: *Erasures* 112
Holzer, Jenny 115; *Dust Paintings* 117; *Redaction Paintings* 110, 117; *Secret* 117; *TOP SECRET* 117; *War Paintings* 117
Homo sapiens Africanus 183
Hong Kong: Anti-Extradition Bill protests 127–128, 130, 138; Anti-Extradition Law Amendment Bill 105; National Security Law (NSL) 129, 140; Observatory 132; social activism 127; Umbrella Movement 130; University Grants Committee 141n5; *see also* digital cartoons in Hong Kong
horror of networked existence *see* Creepypasta
Hosny, Reham 11, 107, 146–159
Howe, Daniel C. 42, 109, 115, 116; *ChinaEye* 118; *Redacto* 118
Huber, Sasha 52
Hughes, Rian: *XX* 174n4
human, concept of 69
Hung Hung 112
Hypercard 164
hypermediacy 43
Hypertext Hotel 30
hypertexts 6, 22; defined 151; as preserving the collective conscience 151–155; software 161

Ibrahim, Samira 158, 159n6
identity anxiety 83–84
IF (Interactive Fiction) 1, 37
if:book Australia 26
Ikeda, Ryan 18
illness 94–95, 96; defined 95; narratives 95–97
immediacy 43
In Territorio Nemico 22–23, 25–26
India: anti-Citizenship Amendment Act (2019) 105
Infocom 37
Inkle Studios: *80 Days* 55–57
Instagram 6, 37, 38, 46n2
Interactive Fiction (IF) 1, 37
interactivity 64
intermedial experience and discursive voice in printed text, audiobook, and podcast *see* "Statement of Randolph Carter, The"
Internet 9, 23, 37, 91; *see also* Creepypasta
intersemiotic translation 177–178
Iran 106
Isaac, William 54
Isgrò, Emilio 115; *Libro Cancellato* 110
Italy: erasure 110; Scrittura Industriale Collettiva (SIC) 25

Jackson, Zakiyyah Iman 69
Jakobson, Roman 46n3, 177
James, E.L.: *Fifty Shades of Grey* 28, 29
Jameson, Frederic 94
Japanese cell phone novel 36; *kibyōshi* 126–127, 141n2
Japanese manga: *One Piece* 135
Jayanth, Meghna 55, 56–57

Index   233

Jenkins, Henry 54
Jenkins, Mark 156
Jensen, Klaus Bruhn 212
Jim Crow laws 54
Johnson, Ronald 115; *Radi Os* 110
Joho, Jess 55
Joyce, Michael 22, 27–28, 161; *afternoon. a story* 39, 42

Kaindl, Klaus 177
Kaphar, Titus *see* Betts, Reginald Dwayne et al.
Keen, Andrew 07 173
Keita, Lansana 183, 184
Kennedy, Cate 24, 26
Kern, Adam 141n2
Khayyám, Omar: "The Rubáiyát" 200
Kirsteva, Julia 37
Kleinman, Arthur 96
Knowles, Alison and James Tenney: *A House of Dust* 39
Knowlton, Jeff *see* Hight, Jeremy et al.
Koivunen, Anu 64
Konstantinou, Lee 165
Kozole, Emil 111, 115
Kozyra, Magdalena 51, 52
Kubiński, Piotr 43
Kulthūm, Umm 200, 201
Kushner, Scott 6
Kyrola, Katarina 64

Lackey, Chris 213, 221n1
Lammes, Sybille 51
Landow, George P. 5–6
Lansky, Paul 197
Larsen, Deena: *Marble Springs* 162
Laure-Ryan, Marie 43, 45
Lee, Hojeong 105
Lehrer, Warren: *A Life in Books* 174n4
Leman, Andrew 213, 214
Lenze, Nele 7
Leong, Michael 119
Leung Chung-kin *see* Chao Yat
Lewis, George 207n5
Lewis, Robin Coste 116
'lexia' 21
Liew, Sonny 128
Lima, Raquel 116
Linkis, Sara Tanderup 174n3
Lloyd, David: *V for Vendetta* 128
Lo, Cuson 11, 126, 130, 132, 133, 135, *135*, *138*, 140, 142n8
Lorde, Audre 78
Loring-Albright, Greg 52
Losh, Elizabeth 53

Lost in Track Changes 23, 26–28
Lotman, Jurij 46n2
Loucks, Donovan K. 221n1
Lovecraft, H.P. 210; Archive 215, 220, 221n1; Literary Podcast 220, 221n1; *see also* "Statement of Randolph Carter, The"
Lovecraft Country 220
ludonarrative postcolonialism 9–10, 49–50; boardgames and colonialism 52; colonialism in digital games 50–52; Postcolonial Ludic: *80 Days* 55–57; Premchand's colonial gambit 57–58; procedural rhetoric or allegorithm 52–55; conclusion: playing beyond colonial logic/over(writing) code 58–59
Luers, Will et al.: *Novelling* 173
Luther, Martin 168
Lynn, Diane et al. 95, 97

Macdonald, Travis 111
McDaid, John: *Uncle Guddy's Phabntom Funhouse* 162
McDowell, John H. 85
McHale, Brian 41, 42, 46n3, 111
Machine for Making Sense 197
McIntosh, Matthew: *theMystery.doc* 174n4
McLuhan, Marshall 146
McNeill, Lynne S. 82
McNulty, Tess 2
Madden, Chris 129
Magnet, Shoshana 51
Majkowski, Tomasz Z 51, 52
Mak, Bonnie 169–170
Małecka, Aleksandra 43
Mallarmé, Stephane: *Un Coup de Dès* 43
Malloy, Judy 196, 204
Malone 129
manhua 106, 124, 125–130, 132
Manico, Zuinder 37
Mannerla, Kari 52
Manovich, Lev 146
Marecki, Piotr 43
Mason, Bruce 31n3
Mass Effect: Andromeda 50, 51, 52
mass media, defined 96
Master of the Universe 28
material, defined 36
Mbembe, Achille 50
Media Ecology Association: Mary Shelley Award for Outstanding Fictional Work 161
medial and cultural crossings 177–179
medicine 94, 95

medium: defined 36; of imitation 146
Meier, Sid: *Civilization* 53
Mejeur, Cody 10, 63–64, 65, 67–79
memoir genre 26
Mencia, Maria: *Birds Singing Other Birds' Songs* 43
#MeToo 64
Meyer, Stephanie: *Twilight* series 28
Microsoft Games: *Age of Empires* 49
Microsoft Word: Track Changes 26
Miller, Laura 21
Million Penguins, A 23, 26, 30
Ministro, Bruno 118
MkWesha, Faith 52
Mockingbirds 70, 71f
Mohamed, Shakir 54
Mokattam 148
Montfort, Nick 6, 37, 38; "Hypertext Killed the Cybertext Star" 37; *Sea and Spar Between* 44; *Taroko Gorge* 22
Moore, Alan: *V for Vendetta* 128
Moraru, Christian 14 3
Morozov, Evgeny 72
Morris, Jeff 196, 197, 198f, 207n4
Morsi, Mohamed 149, 154
Moulthrop, Stuart: *Hegirascope* 44
Mubarak, Hosni 148
MUDs (multi-user dungeons) 37
Mukherjee, Souvik 9–10, 18, 19, 49–59; *Videogames in Postcolonialism* 51
multimodal works 43
Murphy, Timothy S. 178
Murray, Janet H. 151
Murray, Simone 6, 8–9, 18–19, 21–31
Music: affect 196–197; computer music 197, 200; singing 197–202; speaking musically/in musical context 202–205
musicoliterary miscegenation 178
Muslim Brotherhood 148, 149, 158

Naji, Jeneen: "The Rubayaat" 178, 196, 200, 201
Nakamura, Lisa: *Cybertypes: Race, Ethnicity and Identity* 51
Nandy, Rimi 10, 63–64, 65, 93–107
narrative, defined 94
narrative difference 68
narratology 49, 211
Navas, Eduardo 111
Nelson, Jason: *Nine Billion Branches* 173
Nelson, Theodor Holm 5, 151
networked chronic pain narratives 10, 93; Facebook and digital pain narratives 97–102; locating disease and illness narratives 95–97; narrating selves 93–95; conclusion 102
New York Times 112
Newell, C. 64
Nichol, bp 197
Norcia, Megan A. 52
Norman, Katharine 197
Noujaim, Jehane 148, 149, 150, 154, 156, 157, 159
Nowakowski, Radosław: *Koniec Świata Według Emeryka* 37; *Sienkiewicza Street in Kielce* 43–44
Nyman, John 113

Odin, Jaishree K. 7
Oduro-Frimpong, Joseph 191
Oh, Joong-Hwan 105
O'Hare, Isobel 114, 115
Olabode, Shola A. 105
Olukoshi, Adebayo 184
O'Neill, Ryan: *Lost in Track Changes* 27; *Their Brilliant Careers* 27
ontological poetics 41
Opening Up Digital Fiction Writing Competition 31n1
Opoku-Agyemang, Kwabena 12, 178, 181–194
oral to digital and back 12, 181–182; Adinkra: history and evolution 182–183; analysis 190, 190–194; *Ananse and the Sticky Gum/Grave Mischief* 190, 190–193, *191, 192*; Sankofa and Ananse Ntontan as frames 185–190; socio-politics of Adinkra and African "writing" 183–185, 194n2; conclusion *193*, 193–194
O'Sullivan, James 29
other relatedness 100
Owen, Michelle K. 97

Page, Ruth 6, 96
Pajak, Andrzej 39
Pandey, Manoj 2
Papacharissi, Ziz`i 84
Parables Animation Studios 181–182
Parks, Cecily 116–117
Parrish, Allison: *Frankenstein-Genesis* 42–43
Parson, Talcott 9, 99
Passig, Kathrin 115
Pawlik, Jo 56
Penguin Books 23
Penix-Tadsen, Phillip 51

periodization 36–37
Peters, Chris 128
Philip, M. NourbeSe: *Zong!* 110, 116–117
Phillips, Tom 115; *A Humument* 110
Pink Noise 112
Pinoche, Augusto 117
Piper, Adrian: *Everything* 112
Piringer, Jörg 196, 203
Pisarski, Mariusz 9, 18, 19, 34–46
platform-based classifications 38–40
Png, Marie-Therese 54
Podesva, Kristina Lee 115
Poe, Edgar Allan 178, 218
poetry 197
Polish e-lit. 37
political art 149
political cartoons 106, 124, 125, 126, 127–130, 139, 140
politics of difference 78
Portela, Manuel 42
Portugal: erasure 110
Postcolonialism *see* ludonarrative postcolonialism
post-gender worlds 69
posthumanism 67, 68–69
'post-individualistic authorship' 30
post-race worlds 69
potentials and limitations 224–226
Premchand 57, 58–59
Pressman, Jessica 6, 7
Price, Sara 64
procedural rhetoric 52–53
propaganda art 149
PRY 44
Puerto Rico 52

Quarcoo, Alfred 183
Quinn, Zoë: *Depression Quest* 42

racial prejudice 18, 116
Rajewsky, Irina 212
Rami, Ahmed 201
Ramser 20 113
Random House: Vintage 28
Rauschenberg, Robert: *Erased de Kooning Drawing* 110
Ray, Man 110, 115
Ray, Satyajit 57–59
Raynor, Cecily 7
reader as co-author 22
Readers' Project 42
Reading Digital Fiction 31n1
Reddit 83
Reed, Aaron: *Ice-Bound Concordance* 173
reimagining digital literary studies 8–9, 17–19

Remix My Lit 23–24
resistance, forms of 105–107; erasing impulse 109–120
Rettberg, Scott 7, 18, 35–36
Rider Haggard, H. 51
Risam, Roopika 8, 54–55
Robinson, Sandra 91
Robinson, Will 51–52
Rotger, Neus et al. 19 3
Rothblatt, Martine 68
Rovesti, Miriam et al. 95
Roy, Nilanjana S. 2
Rubinstein, Heather and Raphael: *Under Erasure* 113
Ruefle, Mary 115
Rühm, Gerhard 115; *L'Essentiel de la Grammaire* 110
Rushdie, Salman 2
Rustad, Hans 1
Ryan, Marie-Laure 94
Ryberg, Ingrid 64

Santoni, Vanni 25
Satrapi, Marjani 105–106
Sauter, Theresa 13 93
Says, Michael Pfirrman 97
Schaag, Katie: *The Infinite Woman* 112
Schlogl, Lukas 105
Schreibman, Susan 225
Schwerner, Armand: *The Tablets* 162
science fiction 27, 73; *see also SOMA*
Seiça, Álvaro 10–11, 106, 109–120
self, construction of 94
selfhood 83
self-identity 42
Settlers of Catan 50, 52
SF-based games 50
Shannon, Claude 57
Shapton, Leanne: *Important Artifacts and Personal Property* 174n4
Sharif, Solmaz 115–116
Shatranj (board game) 52, 57, 58
Shaw, Jeffrey: *Legible City* 44
Shimizu, Yuko 2
Shing, La Kwong 140
sickness, defined 95
Siemens, Ray 225
Sienkiewicza Street in Kielce 44
Simon, Cheryl 174n3
singing in digital literature 197; "Baggage Allowance" 199–200; "In the Middle of the Room" 197–199, 207n4; musico-literary miscegenation 197; "The Rubáiyát" 200–202, *201*
Siuhak 138
"Smile Dog" 85–86

Smith, Hazel 6, 12, 178–179, 196, 204, 207n4, 208; *see also* Luers, Will et al.
Snowqueens Icedragon 28
Snyder, Timothy: "The American Abyss" 174n2
social media 6, 34, 94, 95, 96
SOMA 10, 64, 67–79; ARK 77, 78; dreams/nightmares of posthumanism 69–72; Mockingbirds 70–71, 71, 72; narrative difference and cyborg bodies 72–77; PATHOS-II 70, 71, 72, 77; racial politics 78; Structure Gel 72; transhuman refuse 77–79; WAU 70–71
Soon, Winnie: *The Unerasable Characters* 118
Sorbera, Lucia 151
Soto-Román, Carlos 115, 117; *Borradura* 118; *Chile Project* 117–118
sound poetry 197
South Korea: Webtoons 127
Spahr, Juliana 118
speaking and artificial intelligence 205–206; Alexa 205–206; "All Hands Meeting" 206; aurature 205; *The Listeners* 205–206
speaking musically/in musical context 202; "black lives matter" 202; "darkvoice" 203–204; "Ear for the Surge" 202; injustices 202–203; "noisespeech" 203; "Scaling the Voices" 204; "sonic cross-dressing" 204; "The Fabric of Everyday Life" 204–205, 207n8
speculative fiction 67
Spellman, Naomi *see* Hight, Jeremy et al.
Spivak, Gayatri Chakravorty 56
Spooner, William: *A Voyage of Discovery* 52, 53
Stanley Parable, The (computer game) 22
Starcraft 50
Starre, Alexander 174n3
"Statement of Randolph Carter, The" 12–13, 210–211; character 211; Del Rey version 221n5; discursive voice 210; in/direct discourse 211; intermedial experience 210; medial environments and audiences 213–215; medial platforms 210–211; mediality 210, 212, 221n2; methods and material 211–212; narration 211–212; Randolph Carter 221n3; sensory images and medial tiers 218–220; voices experiencing and telling 215–218; conclusion 220

Sterne, Laurence: *The Life and Opinions of Tristram Shandy, Gentleman* 111
Stevenson, R.L. 51
Stoker, Bram: *Dracula* 28, 31n8
story, defined 94
Storyspace 21, 37, 161, 164
storytelling 93–94, 100
Straub, Kris 87
Strickland, Stephanie: *Sea and Spar Between* 44
Structure Gel 70, 71f
substitutive writing 42
survival horror games 79n1; *see also SOMA*
Sutherland-Addy, Efua: *The Marriage of Anansewa* 191
Swortzell, Adrienne: *Electronic Chronicles of the Casaba Melon Institute* 162
Szeman, Imre 226

Tabbi, Joseph 7
Taiwan: *Xianzai Shi* magazine 112
Tales on Tweet 2
Taylor, Claire 7
technologies of the self 83
Temple, Christel 182
tender points 97
Tenney, James *see* Knowles, Alison
textual instability 8–9, 21–23; Fanfic/print/eLit interplay 28–29; *Lost in Track Changes* 23, 26–28; 'Remix My Lit' 23–26; *In Territorio Nemico* 23, 25–26; conclusion 30–31
Tharoor, Shashi 2
"The Curious Case of Smile.jpg" 85
"The Elevator Game" 89
The Stand News 141n7
Thomas, Bronwen 6, 101
Thomas, Sue 31n3
Through the Clock's Workings 23
Tinderbox 161, 164
Ting, Tin-Yuet 127
Toikkanen, Jarkko 12–13, 178–179, 212, 218
Töpffer, Rodolphe 124
Trammell, Aaron 52
transgender 68
transhumanism 67, 68–69
translation 177, 178, 179
transmodal poetics 43
Tse, Jasmine 136, 137
Tse Sai Pei 136, 137
Tseng Shu-mei 112
Tshabalala, Pippa: *Resident Evil 5* 51
Tunisia: Arab Spring 147
Twilight fanfic 28

Twine games 42
Twitter 1, 2, 6, 37, 38, 46n2; Egypt: January 25 revolution 150

Under Erasure (exhibition) 113
underlining 115
United States: *The Avengers* 135; declassified materials 117; e-literature 35; erasure 115; *The Justice League* 132, 135; *Little Nemo* 127; *Yellow Kid* 127
"uplifting anecdotes" 2
Using Electricity (2017–present) 38

Vadde, Aarthi 6
Vallier, John 18 30
van Alphen, Ernst 174n3
van der Geest, Sjaak 194n4
Van Dijck, José 83, 84
Varadkar, Leo 202
Vázsonyi, Andrew 85
Velho da Costa, Maria: *Desescrita* 110
Verne, Jules 55, 56
versioning 39
Vidal, Ricarda 177–178
video games 67
Virdee, Aminder: *Exosomatic Echoes* 63
virtual reality 69
Vlavo, Fidèle A. 105
voice 12, 196–197; affect 196–197; emotion 196, 197; in narratology 211; processing of 196, 207n1; singing 197–202; speaking and artificial intelligence 205–206; speaking musically/in musical context; speaking in non-musical contexts 202–205; conclusion 206–207

Walkowitz, Rebecca 8, 177
Web 1.0 83–84

Web 2.0 7, 30, 81, 83, 84, 90, 125
Weibo 118
Weiser, Mark 207n8
Wiener, Norbert 57
wikinovels 23
Wilks, Christine: *Inkubus* 44
Wilson, Christopher 150
Wishart, Trevor 197
Witch House Media 221n1
Wittig, Rob: *Blue Company* 162
Wolf, Werner 212
Women with Fibromyalgia 93, *98*, 98–99, *100*
Wong, Alfonso: *Old master Q* 137
Wong, Jason 11
Wong, Justin 128, 129, 140
Wong, Sze-ma: *Ngau Chai* 137–138
Woods, Tim 201
Woolf, Virginia: *A Writer's Diary* 116
World Literature 4, 178, 224
World Press Freedom Index 129
World Wide Web 188, 189
world-building 67
Worthington, Marjorie 17 174n2

Yeung, Heather H. 19 4
Yeung, Hok-tak 138
YouTube: *Ananse Tales* 181, *182*
Yü, Hsia et al. 115:
Yu, Timothy 09 18
Yung Man-Han 112

Z., Pamela 196, 207n5; "Baggage Allowance" 199–200
Zboya, Eric 43
Z-machine 37
Zuern 13 147
Żuk-Piwkowski, Józef: *The Book of All Words* 38–39

For Product Safety Concerns and Information please contact our EU representative GPSR@taylorandfrancis.com
Taylor & Francis Verlag GmbH, Kaufingerstraße 24, 80331 München, Germany